ADHD GROWN UP

A Norton Professional Book

ADHD GROWN UP

A Guide to Adolescent
and Adult ADHD

Joel L. Young, M.D.

W. W. Norton & Company
New York • London

ADHD Grown Up discusses diagnostic procedures, medications, dosing, and clinical correlations in a manner designed to assist clinicians providing care. Much of the work is rooted in evidence-based research, although other sections rely on clinical consensus or the author's experience. The book is not intended to be encyclopedic or offer recommendations for individual patients. Dosing strategies reflect common practice and may not conform to FDA guidelines. In addition, sometimes off-label medications can be effective at treating ADHD symptoms, and these medications are also discussed. Relationships between ADHD and comorbid conditions may not be widely accepted. The clinician is advised to consult the package insert for definitive guidelines on indications for dosing, drug-drug interactions, and contraindications. The medical literature, as always, remains the authoritative source.

For information about permission to reproduce
selections from this book, write to
Permissions, W. W. Norton & Company, Inc.,
500 Fifth Avenue, New York, NY 10110

Production Manager: LeeAnn Graham
Manufacturing by R.R. Donnelley, Harrisonburg

Library of Congress Cataloging-in-Publication Data

Young, Joel L.
ADHD grown up: a guide to adolescent and adult ADHD / Joel L. Young.
p.   cm.
"A Norton professional book."
Includes bibliographical references and index.
ISBN-13: 978-0-393-70468-6
ISBN-10: 0-393-70468-8
1. Attention-deficit disorder in adolescence. 2. Attention-deficit disorder in adults. I.
Title.

RJ506.H9Y66   2006
616.85′89—dc22   2006048647

W. W. Norton & Company, Inc., 500 Fifth Avenue, New York, N.Y. 10110
www.wwnorton.com

W. W. Norton & Company Ltd., Castle House, 75/76 Wells St., London W1T 3QT

1   3   5   7   9   0   8   6   4   2

I am not convinced that my book is worthy of the person to whom it is dedicated: David J. Young, M.D. My father graduated from the University of Michigan Medical School as the youngest but highest-ranked student in the class of 1952. Throughout his career as a young military officer serving in Korea, and later as a seasoned internist at Providence Hospital in Southfield, Michigan, he transmitted to his children the great privilege and awesome responsibility of being a doctor. Parkinson's disease ended his medical career 20 years too soon, but not before he demonstrated in totality the virtues of tenacity, curiosity, and gentleness. His courageous daily struggle with his illness inspires me.

Contents

Acknowledgments   ix

Introduction   xiii

PART I: DIAGNOSING ADHD IN ADOLESCENTS AND ADULTS

Chapter 1:   The Diagnostic Screening Process   3

Chapter 2:   Coping With Comorbidities in Diagnosis and Treatment   44

Chapter 3:   Patients Most Likely to Be Diagnosed: Those With ADHD Hyperactive-Impulsive Type   67

Chapter 4:   Patients Least Likely to Be Diagnosed: Those With ADHD Inattentive Type and ADHD Combined Type   83

Chapter 5:   Reasons for Misdiagnosis   99

PART II: ADHD PATIENT POPULATIONS

Chapter 6:   Adolescents and Young Adults   113

Chapter 7:   Gender Issues: Considering Girls and Women   155

Chapter 8:   Challenging Patients, Difficult Treatment Choices   179

PART III: MEDICAL AND PSYCHOLOGICAL ASPECTS OF ADHD TREATMENT

Chapter 9:   ADHD Medications   211

Chapter 10:   Psychotherapy, Coaching, and Other Techniques   252

Chapter 11:   ADHD, Fibromyalgia, Chronic Pain,
and Associated Syndromes   274

APPENDICES

Appendix A: Self-Evaluation for ADHD   295
Appendix B: Adult ADHD Self-Report Scale—
V1.1 (ASRS-V1.1) Screener   297
Appendix C: Adult ADHD Self-Report Scale (ASRS)
Symptom Checklist and Instructions   299

References   303
Index   313

Acknowledgments

Writing a book is a deeply personal experience—in my case a project I have been hoping to complete for some time. I am grateful to the many people who have generously helped me. Meg Ataman and Brenda Berris manage my practice with great dedication. Staci Kinney, my administrative assistant, organizes my professional life. Didi Nuculaj, Lilli Schuetz, and Katie Brundage see to it that the needs of my patients are met daily.

Karen Lenhardt, M.S.W., and Melissa Falb, M.A., run our clinical research studies. Debra Luria, Ph.D., Lisa Michaux A.P.R.N., Melissa Oleshansky, Ph.D., Marie McMahon, M.S.W., Marie Moren, M.S.W., Lynn Florek, M.A., Carol Rembor, M.S.N., and Molly Schwartz, M.A., are superb colleagues. Jaime Saal, M.A., has become an irreplaceable part of many of my endeavors. I am thankful to spend every working day with these capable women.

I trace my interest in ADHD back to my training at the University of Michigan's Department of Psychiatry. Since that time, I have enjoyed advancing the conversation with thoughtful practitioners like William Dodson, M.D., Howard Schubiner, M.D., Steven Spector, Ph.D., and Paul Jacobs, Ph.D. I marvel at the commitment of David Giwerc, who as president of the Attention Deficit Disorders Association, energizes all around him. Eric Young, M.D., inspires me to read more, write better, and make judicious conclusions from my observations.

Birgit Amann M.D. has been a joy to partner with since 1999. We drive each other hard, sometimes at a crazy pace, but I cannot imagine sharing the experience with anyone else.

Christine Adamec, a veteran writer, helped me immeasurably with the organization and research of this book. Every author should have a collaborator of this caliber. My editor at Norton, Deborah Malamud, has guided me with great patience and wise oversight. Her associate, Michael J. McGandy, steadied my shaky hand and kept me on deadline (more or less). Casey Ruble's copyediting and suggestions were incredibly perceptive. Kristen Holt-Browning efficiently assembled the final pieces of the project. Sara Stillman added detailed background to many of the case histories and Judy Redmond, M.A. and Rebecca Young helped research the chapter concerning ADHD and chronic pain.

My life revolves around my family. A sentence here could never fully acknowledge the role of my wonderful mother and sister, so I will not try. I am blessed for my children, Benjamin, Katie, and Emily, and thank them for sharing me with this project. My wife, colleague, and soulmate, Mindy Layne Young, J.D., M.S.W., allows me to engage her with ideas while not letting the demands of my work overtake the reality of the day. Thank you for supporting me through this book.

Doctors have no better teachers than those who entrust them with their care, and I gratefully acknowledge my patients. The following pages contain sketches of some of their lives. I have taken care to tell their stories but protect all confidences.

Joel L. Young, M.D.
March 2006
Rochester Hills, Michigan

ADHD GROWN UP

Introduction

Working in psychiatric hospitals and outpatient clinics over the past 15 years, I have had the opportunity to evaluate a wide array of different psychiatric disorders, including attention-deficit/hyperactivity disorder (ADHD). Ironically, early in my career I harbored great skepticism about the entire condition. My psychiatric training program did not emphasize ADHD beyond childhood. Impulsivity, inattention, and distractibility were not specifically identified among adolescents and adults, or were explained away by other psychiatric diagnoses.

Even if a group of adolescents and adults had these symptoms in excess of others, I questioned whether such characteristics could cause distress. Was it so unusual to lose one's possessions, forget appointments, or blurt out unfiltered comments? Was not ADHD primarily a problem of prepubescent boys, who invariably would outgrow the disorder with the onset of puberty? Was it merely an excuse for unacceptable behavior — simply a rationalization for an individual's chronic underperformance or a medically sanctioned way of saying, "I simply cannot help myself"? These questions and suspicions dominated the psychiatric landscape of the early 1990s.

When I was a young psychiatrist, two psychologist colleagues began referring me perplexing patients whom, frankly, I was not eager to treat. I was prepared to treat psychoses or depression, and I was well-versed in behavioral and pharmacological treatments of anxiety, but these patients were different. Certain characteristics emerged among them. They were impulsive — not occasionally, but on a daily basis. They were poorly organized; they did not lose items occasionally like the rest of us, but routinely forgot where they placed their driver's licenses, keys, wallets, and watches.

Unlike the bulk of severely ill, hospitalized patients I had spent the previous several years treating, most of these patients were functioning, usually marginally, at work or school. They were even raising families, but they were not doing well. On the job, they were underperforming; the demands of school were incredibly frustrating. Confusion and disorganization permeated their entire lives, at work, school, and home. They urgently sought my assistance, but I did not know what to do for them. Sheepishly, and with the encouragement of some senior clinicians, I diagnosed these patients with adult ADHD and started them on stimulant medications.

My personal epiphany occurred when I saw how dramatically the treatment transformed so many of their lives. Adolescents who previously could not concentrate in their classes and were failing school were, with medication and either therapy or coaching, now receiving good grades. Suddenly they began discussing their applications to good colleges, an entirely unrealistic goal before treatment. I started to consider the diagnosis of ADHD in adults who had been fired from their jobs or were constantly late to work. When treated for ADHD, they no longer blurted their uncensored thoughts to others; they got to work on time and no longer behaved in ways that jeopardized their jobs. Individuals whose lives were chaotic started putting the pieces back together again. As their outlook brightened, I became increasingly intrigued and confident in my approach.

Since these initial experiences, I have seen hundreds, and probably thousands, of adolescents and adults with ADHD. Many have benefited from knowing that they have a valid condition and that their symptoms have a name and a treatment. Their symptoms were not due to some inner inexplicable fault of their own; their chronic distractibility, procrastination, forgetfulness, and impulsivity constituted a treatable condition.

Some patients respond dramatically to medication, virtually turning their lives around. However, even with the most robust response, some problems remain. Medication treatment does not remove all obstacles, but it moors patients so they can benefit from suggestions made in therapy or coaching. Combining the various modalities of treatment allows ADHD patients to become more adeptly equipped to handle their day-to-day life.

An accurate diagnosis is essential to a patient's successful treatment. Performing an accurate ADHD diagnosis requires a combination of discipline, knowledge, and experience. Discovering the patient's intention in seeking treatment is the essential first step. Listening to and observing the patient are also crucial aspects of the diagnosis. I discuss these issues in Chapter 1.

The basic diagnostic process includes: obtaining a careful medical history to rule out medical problems that may mimic the symptoms of ADHD; taking a psychiatric history; and carefully considering any family or genetic history of medical and psychiatric problems. Some helpful tools to quickly and comprehensively evaluate distressed patients are also discussed in Chapter 1.

Comorbidities are extremely common among patients with ADHD. It is more likely than not that at some point in their lives, patients with ADHD will be comorbid for another disorder. Chapter 2 explores adult comorbidities and provides information about the known comorbid prevalence rates and a method to assess severity. Emphasis is placed on the most common ADHD comorbidities, including mood and anxiety disorders. In addition, because the symptoms of ADHD and bipolar disorder can be difficult to differentiate, a chart detailing the differences between the two conditions is offered. Finally, the chapter covers ADHD and comorbid oppositional defiant disorders, eating disorders, and learning disabilities.

The diagnosis of ADHD seems obvious to the clinician. Many of them have had behavioral difficulties since childhood. They are hyperactive and experience serious problems at work and at home. They are fidgety and impatient, they receive numerous traffic violations, and they experience seemingly endless relationship problems. Both they and the people around them know that they need help, but many times psychiatric help comes only after it is mandated by court order. Chapter 3 explores these types of patients.

ADHD comes in several different flavors. Although hyperactivity is often thought to be an essential feature of the diagnosis, some patients with ADHD (predominately inattentive subtype) have no such symptom. These patients are typically female. As children, they were inattentive and distractible; they underperformed but did not demonstrate overt behaviors typical of their hyperactive brethren. Most clinicians overlook their symptoms. But their impairments persist into adulthood and become complicated by factors like anxiety, depression, and fatigue. These patients report feeling overwhelmed at work and at home. They do not break any laws, nor do they draw attention to themselves. Most try hard, and with great effort they can marshall their resources sufficiently to bring themselves up to an acceptable daily performance. Yet the psychic energy needed to keep pace is ultimately exhausting. They present for evaluation because they feel alienated and unfulfilled and because they suspect they have ADHD. These issues are explored in Chapter 4.

Many clinicians, as well as the general public, continue to underappreciate the significance of ADHD. Individuals with procrastination, inattentiveness, and distractibility are considered lazy or malingering by the general public. Mental health professionals often overlook ADHD symptoms and persist in diagnosing these patients with anxiety, depression, or personality disorders. This is a serious and continuing problem among mental health professionals, and I discuss this in Chapter 5.

Chapter 6 explores diagnostic and treatment issues in adolescents. Adolescents with untreated ADHD have high rates of substance abuse and serious accidents. Treatment significantly decreases their risks, but the challenge is to identify them and convince them of the need for compliance. Adolescents tender their thoughts sparingly, and the clinician needs to employ interviewing techniques that elicit maximum clinical information; for example, rather than ask the teenager *if* he has received any traffic tickets, which may be easy to deny, directly ask him *how many* traffic tickets he has received. Often the adolescent is startled into blurting out a number of tickets that is greater than one.

Chapter 6 also outlines common adolescent mindsets. Some teenagers believe that the privilege of youth is maximum enjoyment, right now. Others believe that considering the consequences of behavior is generally a waste of time, or that their parents have little to do except hassle them. Their psychological insight is inversely proportional to the length of time they can play XBox. These mindsets need to be addressed through therapy, which, when combined with medications (and the passage of time), can add ballast to a struggling ADHD teenager.

Chapter 7 is devoted to women with ADHD. This population remained entirely unexplored for years; only since the 1990s has the treatment community begun to consider the depth and prevalence of the problem. Women with ADHD have lifelong struggles, and their symptoms affect all aspects of their lives—mood, health, and sexuality. Women with ADHD often raise children with ADHD, a difficult undertaking in the best of circumstances. They have special challenges balancing work, family, and intimacy.

Patients with ADHD are at increased risk for substance use disorders. Therapists must grapple with how best to serve this population, and they may need to confront the myths surrounding ADHD patients with current or past substance use disorders to provide the best treatment. Chapter 8 tackles whether previously addicted patients should be prescribed stimulants, whether stimulant exposure can lead to re-addiction, and whether there are relative levels of dependency associated with each stimulant.

Chapter 8 also covers specific issues related to male adolescents with ADHD. These patients exhibit problem behavior, substance-related and otherwise, in far greater proportions than do female adolescents with ADHD. The chapter offers suggestions about working through therapeutic resistance and treatment noncompliance.

The chapter speaks to physicians who responsibly prescribe scheduled drugs but worry about patients who overuse or divert their medications. Abuse risk factors (family history, age, etc.) and diversion behaviors like "doctor shopping," forging prescriptions, stealing drugs from others, and buying from Internet pharmacies are detailed. This chapter offers a template to assess these clinical occurrences and insight into causes of medication noncompliance. The chapter ends with a discussion of self-injury, abuse, and sexual issues as they relate to the ADHD patient.

Medications are of paramount importance in ADHD treatment and are discussed in Chapter 9. To obtain the best outcome, most patients need medications; however, there is great variation in needs between patients, even within the same subtype. Stimulant medications have long been the

mainstay of ADHD treatment. Some patients do well with a basic psychostimulant, whereas others require stimulants delivered through more sophisticated systems, such as long-acting medications, and still others benefit from an entirely different class of medication. Nonstimulant ADHD
medications are newer offerings, but they serve a large number of patients.
Among their unique properties is a complete lack of abuse potential. This
chapter also reviews the use of antidepressants and mood stabilizing medications taken in concert with stimulants or nonstimulants, as well as other
medication combinations needed for conditions comorbid with ADHD.

In Chapter 9 I also discuss concerns about possible cardiovascular risks
associated with stimulants, based on articles in 2006 in the *New England
Journal of Medicine* about emergency visits caused by stimulants as well as
one physician's insistence that stimulants be given a "black box" warning. The Food and Drug Administration has rejected this recommendation (Cohen, Jhung, & Budnitz, 2006; Nissen, 2006).

This issue of a potentially serious health risk is of concern, not only as
an issue that must be considered, but also because of alarmist media stories that trumpet the risk of stimulants, while often failing to discuss or
explain that a major part of the risk lies with those few adolescents and
young adults who sell or abuse their stimulant medications. It is important
to note that a study in the *Journal of the American Academy of Child &
Adolescent Psychiatry* (Wilens, Gignac, Swezey, Monuteaux, & Biederman, 2006) has found that there are certain risk groups of individuals
who are the most likely to divert or misuse stimulant medications, a subject covered in Chapter 8 on challenging patients.

Chapter 9 also addresses common fears that patients experience regarding taking medications for ADHD. These include the fear that the
medication will be addictive and blunt their personality. Patients may
also be concerned that the medications will cause them to lose control or
produce extreme side effects. These fears interfere with treatment compliance, and strategies to counteract them are included.

Chapter 10 discusses psychotherapy for patients with ADHD. Traditional psychoanalysis and most other forms of long-term psychotherapy
are impractical for patients who have ADHD, not because past life experiences are irrelevant, but because their current behavior is causing their
primary difficulties in life. Cognitive behavioral therapy (CBT) focuses on

the here and now and is currently the dominant psychotherapy used in patients with ADHD. Key CBT concepts are covered in this chapter.

Many ADHD patients benefit from coaching, a highly practical approach in which the coach helps the "client" develop goals and work in partnership to create prioritized action plans. Coaches concentrate their efforts on functional improvements: getting to work on time, streamlining paperwork, and decreasing the tendency to procrastinate. Chapter 10 also explores the primary principles of coaching and helps differentiate coaching from psychotherapy.

Chapter 11 examines ADHD as a pervasive condition that drives unpleasant somatic symptoms. Subgroups of adults with ADHD develop gnawing physical symptoms, fatigue, and sometimes pain syndromes that greatly interfere with life quality. Despite considerable efforts by medical doctors, patients with fibromyalgia, chronic fatigue syndrome, irritable bowel syndrome, atypical migraine headaches, and other nebulous medical problems are mired in the medical system.

Chapter 11 also presents my findings that self-referred patients with fibromyalgia and chronic fatigue syndrome have high rates of ADHD. Stimulant medications have proved useful in improving these patients' levels of attention and concentration. My serendipitous finding was that the pain, fatigue, and other distressing symptoms remitted as well. I propose that extreme distractibility may intensify the patient's pain perception. Treatment with stimulants allows these patients to filter extraneous stimuli and more accurately report objective pain. This chapter offers a working foundation for further study.

My goal in writing this book was to provide the clinician dealing with ADHD, as well as the patient suffering from it, a concise overview of the many issues associated with this disorder through adolescence and adulthood. ADHD is a highly researched area, and every year brings new developments. My hope and expectation is that new findings will soon replace the words that are written here. Toward that end, I encourage readers to use the book as a starting guide. My hope is that it will give greater perspective into a condition that affects so many and quietly causes so much human suffering.

I

Diagnosing ADHD in Adolescents and Adults

Chapter 1

The Diagnostic
Screening Process

ATTENTION-DEFICIT/HYPERACTIVITY DISORDER (ADHD) is a pervasive neu-robehavioral disorder that affects an estimated 9 million adolescents and adults in the United States. It has been suggested that 2.9–4.7% of the adult population has the condition (Faraone & Biederman, 2004). The majority — at least 7 million individuals — in this group is undiagnosed and untreated. Consequently, they continue to suffer from the disorganization, distracti-bility, impulsivity, and lack of focus that define the illness. Without proper diagnosis, the individual with ADHD continues to experience mood swings, missed appointments, and self-defeating behaviors. Some patients with untreated ADHD, particularly adolescents, are prone to receiving multiple traffic tickets and exhibiting risky behavior such as eschewing "safe sex," using illegal drugs, or engaging in daredevil activities like rac-ing with others on the highway. The repercussions on the individual with untreated ADHD take a major toll and also have a profound impact on family members.

Unlike some illnesses that wax and wane in severity, ADHD symptoms are continuous throughout the day, year in and year out, affecting the home, school, and work life of individuals. ADHD can lead or contribute to substance abuse, depression, and, as discussed in Chapter 11, even chronic physical pain. Individuals with ADHD have higher rates of marital problems, driving accidents, and sexually transmitted diseases, and lower levels of educational achievement. Clearly, it is extremely important to make a correct diagnosis of the patient with ADHD, not only for the patient him- or herself, but also for family members, coworkers, and society at large.

This chapter describes the basic diagnostic process used in screening patients for ADHD. An accurate diagnosis is essential to create a thorough treatment plan, which usually involves medications and psychotherapy. Because there are no laboratory or other tests that can definitively detect ADHD (although brain imaging techniques may be developed in the future), the interview and supporting screening tools play the central role. Diligent clinicians need to develop a *differential diagnosis*, essentially a list of possible explanations of the patient's complaints. This process can be laborious: It involves listening to patients and their families, observing patients' behavior; recording their childhood, medical, and family history; and ordering and interpreting labs and psychological testing.

The clinician must understand and apply criteria from the *Diagnostic and Statistical Manual of Mental Disorders* (DSM), and, perhaps most importantly, be able to recognize the many inherently contradictory and paradoxical patterns of adolescent and adult presentations of ADHD. Of course, many of these tasks often must take place within the 50-minute period (or less) that is available for an initial interview. The plan provided in this chapter for making the diagnosis of ADHD and related conditions involves an interactive and dynamic process. The plan requires the clinician to consider all relevant diagnostic conditions that mimic or cooccur with ADHD — not just the conditions with which the clinician is most knowledgeable or familiar.

Using this formal procedure is important in the ADHD field, as physicians inevitably will encounter individuals who insist that they have tried stimulant medication and have noticed some positive effects — ergo, their diagnosis of ADHD must be valid. This premise is incorrect. Some individuals who do *not* have the condition *have* reported that after taking a few doses of stimulants they experienced improved attention, but in general these individuals do not tolerate stimulants over the long haul. Clinicians should not shortchange the diagnostic process, but they should not be paralyzed by fear that ADHD medications will be misused.

There are very wide variations between how clinicians conduct the diagnostic process and the more detailed parameters are desirable. This chapter outlines a preferred method using techniques that are deeply rooted in the traditional psychiatric interview. Key "chief complaints" and prototypical clinical presentations are compiled. Reliance on the *DSM-IV-TR* (American Psychiatric Association, 2000) and the use of screening tools is emphasized.

CONSIDERING *DSM-IV-TR* SYMPTOMS

The *DSM-IV-TR*, the bible of psychiatric diagnoses, provides the fundamental criteria of ADHD. Clinicians need to be familiar with all aspects of these criteria and precise with terminology. For example, it is important to distinguish between *hearing* problems (associated with the ear or associated neurological pathways) and *listening* problems (where the client *can* hear but may not process information clearly or may be too distracted to pay attention). Listening problems are associated with ADHD, whereas hearing problems are not. The clinician should also differentiate the ADHD symptom of *restlessness* from the nonspecific excessive energy. Using accurate, consistent nomenclature for all psychiatric presentations improves the clinician's ability to communicate effectively with patients and other professionals.

Currently there are no biological markers that allow clinicians to make the diagnosis of ADHD with absolute certainty. For this reason, clinicians must perform a thorough examination of the patient, obtain collateral input from the patient's family, teachers, or primary care doctor, and remain familiar with the diagnostic criteria spelled out in the *DSM*. The core symptoms of ADHD include: inattention, hyperactivity, and impulsivity.

Essentially, ADHD comes in three basic variants: ADHD predominately hyperactive-impulsive type, ADHD predominately inattentive type, and ADHD (combined type). The last variant is the most common. A fourth designation, ADHD not otherwise specified, or ADHD (NOS), is designated for patients who did not have noticeable impairments due to ADHD until after age 7, as well as for those who had some but not all of the specified symptoms. *DSM-V*, not due out until 2013, may eliminate the minimum age standard necessary for the diagnosis. Undoubtedly it will also update the descriptive wordings to reflect the adolescent and adult experience.

Table 1.1 details the *DSM* diagnostic criteria for the primary forms of ADHD.

The *DSM* identifies criteria for ADHD not otherwise specified as follows:

314.9 Attention-Deficit/Hyperactivity Disorder Not Otherwise Specified
1. Individuals whose symptoms and impairments meet the criteria for Attention-Deficit/Hyperactivity Disorder, Predominantly Inattentive Type but whose age at onset is 7 years or after
2. Individuals with clinically significant impairment who present with inattention and whose symptom pattern does not meet the full criteria for the disorder but have a behavioral pattern marked by sluggishness, daydreaming, and hypoactivity

Hyperactivity: Not Essential for the Diagnosis

As hyperactivity is considered the core symptom of childhood ADHD, a common misconception about ADHD in adolescents and adults is that if hyperactivity is not demonstrated, ADHD can be ruled out. This belief is flawed on two levels. First, even hyperactive adolescents can remain quiet if they are particularly interested in the task at hand or if they are in a novel situation. For this reason, evaluating hyperactivity in the exam room is of limited benefit. Secondly, adults tend to outgrow their motor hyperactivity as they age.

In a study of 149 adults with ADHD, it was inattention, rather than hyperactivity, that was the primary presenting symptom and was noted to be present in more than 90% of the subjects. In this group (using older *DSM-III* criteria), 56% of the adults were diagnosed with the combined ADHD subtype and 37% were diagnosed with the inattentive subtype.

TABLE 1.1
DSM Criteria for ADHD

A. Either (1) or (2)

  (1) six (or more) of the following symptoms of **inattention** have persisted for at least 6 months to a degree that is maladaptive and inconsistent with developmental level:

Inattention

  (a) often fails to give close attention to details or makes careless mistakes in schoolwork, work, or other activities
  (b) often has difficulty sustaining attention in tasks or play activities
  (c) often does not seem to listen when spoken to directly
  (d) often does not follow through on instructions and fails to finish school-work, chores, or duties in the workplace (not due to oppositional behavior or failure to understand instructions)
  (e) often has difficulty organizing tasks and activities
  (f) often avoids, dislikes, or is reluctant to engage in tasks that require sustained mental effort (such as schoolwork or homework)
  (g) often loses things necessary for tasks or activities (e.g., toys, school assignments, pencils, books, or tools)
  (h) is often easily distracted by extraneous stimuli
  (i) is often forgetful in daily activities

  (2) six (or more) of the following symptoms of **hyperactivity-impulsivity** have persisted for at least 6 months to a degree that is maladaptive and inconsistent with developmental level:

Hyperactivity

  (a) often fidgets with hands or feet or squirms in seat
  (b) often leaves seat in classroom or in other situations in which remaining seated is expected
  (c) often runs about or climbs excessively in situations in which it is inappropriate (in adolescents or adults, may be limited to subjective feelings of restlessness)
  (d) often has difficulty playing or engaging in leisure activities quietly
  (e) is often "on the go" or often acts as if "driven by a motor"
  (f) often talks excessively

(*continued*)

TABLE 1.1
(Continued)

Impulsivity

(g) often blurts out answers before questions have been completed
(h) often has difficulty awaiting turn
(i) often interrupts or intrudes on others (e.g., butts into conversations or games)

B. Some hyperactive-impulsive or inattentive symptoms that caused impairment were present before age 7 years.
C. Some impairment from the symptoms is present in two or more settings (e.g., at school [or work] and at home).
D. There must be clear evidence of clinically significant impairment in social, academic, or occupational functioning.
E. The symptoms do not occur exclusively during the course of a Pervasive Developmental Disorder, Schizophrenia, or other Psychotic Disorder and are not better accounted for by another mental disorder (e.g., Mood Disorder, Anxiety Disorder, Dissociative Disorder, or a Personality Disorder).

Code based on type:

314.01 Attention-Deficit/Hyperactivity Disorder, Combined Type: If both Criteria A1 and A2 are met for the past 6 months

314.00 Attention-Deficit/Hyperactivity Disorder, Predominantly Inattentive Type: If Criterion A1 is met but Criterion A2 is not met for the past 6 months

314.01 Attention-Deficit/Hyperactivity Disorder, Predominantly Hyperactive-Impulsive Type: If Criterion A2 is met but Criterion A1 is not met for the past 6 months

This text was reprinted with permission from the American Psychiatric Association from *Diagnostic and Statistical Manual of Mental Disorders Text Revision* (*DSM-IV-TR*, 2000).

Only 2% were diagnosed with the hyperactive-impulsive subtype of ADHD (Millstein, Wilens, Biederman, & Spencer, 1997).

Hyperactive behavior is demonstrated by fidgetiness, overtalking, and a need to always be on the go. Hyperactive behaviors can change as the patient ages. Because they have learned to inhibit their impulses, adolescents may no longer dart about the classroom. Instead, they may flit from one thought to the next. Some adults with ADHD complain that they cannot settle at the appropriate times and that their "brain won't shut off." *Cerebral hyperactivity*, the constant flow of ideas and worries, interferes with sleep.

Patients with cerebral hyperactivity may have persistent, nonrestorative, fitful sleep. Complete physical exhaustion may be the only prelude to sleep. These hyperactive symptoms are frequently misinterpreted as racing thoughts: a symptom of mania. Although it is counterintuitive, this type of insomnia may improve with administration of late-night ADHD medications.

WHY IS THE PATIENT IN YOUR OFFICE?

The most important instrument that the clinician can bring into the evaluation room is an open mind. The ADHD clinician should stay focused on the key issue of *why* patients have come in for evaluation. The goal of the diagnostic process is to formulate a differential diagnosis. In other words, what are these patients concerned about? Are they describing something normal or abnormal? What has helped them in the past? If the symptoms are abnormal, how can they be defined, described, and treated?

It is important to establish these primary concerns from the perspective of the patient, whether an adolescent or adult, as well as the patient's family and friends. By solidifying the patient's key concerns, the physician can identify "target symptoms." This affords the clinician clear-cut treatment objectives and the opportunity to engage even an ambivalent patient. Significant symptoms and behaviors should be identified so that measurable markers of progress can be developed from the onset.

Approaching the ADHD Interview

Medical students are taught that diagnosing a patient begins in the waiting room, and this is especially true with psychiatric conditions. ADHD patients are a heterogeneous lot; they come in all shape and sizes, both sexes, all ages, mentally challenged and gifted, pierced and straight-laced. Some are happy to be seen, whereas others present with great reservations.

Once inside the office, some patients with ADHD are very anxious and nervous. They may have difficulty staying in their seat or sit very still and rigidly. Highly inattentive individuals may be distracted by the sounds they hear outside the office, the feel of the chair fabric, or the activity of the computer's screen saver. In conversation, some are stoic and unreachable. Others bemoan that nothing in their life is working out and express doubt that the doctor can do much to change things. They assert that the underlying fault must be theirs, and they are frustrated that they cannot learn how to stop being late, forgetting their belongings, and upsetting those around them. Some are angry and insist they do not deserve this suffering. Still others come into the interview fully prepared with cross-referenced research and a certainty that they have ADHD.

Directing the Interview

It is important to discover what patients define as their key problem. Regardless of how accurate the diagnosis is, if the therapist focuses on issues that are not troublesome to patients or their family, then patients will feel that they are not understood and the clinician may never get a chance to describe the benefits of treatment.

When asked what concerned him, Andy, a high school junior who was later diagnosed with ADHD combined type, said he was extremely frustrated that he lost everything in sight. "I forget my books in school, and I can't even find my password to get onto the web page that lists our homework." Andy's parents had different concerns about their impulsive, disorganized son. "He says everything that he thinks," Andy's mother reported. "If he thinks you need to lose weight, he will tell you, whether you asked or not. He insults everyone but really doesn't mean to be cruel."

Upon hearing his mother's complaint, Andy scoffed and reiterated that he wanted help for his memory and poor organizational skills. When pressed, Andy acknowledged that he knew that his parents thought blurting out comments was his major problem, but he was not persuaded that they were right. He turned on his mother and stated dramatically, "Ever since you started this affair with your boss, you have been on me all the time." Both parents appeared shocked and embarrassed at Andy's statement.

Convinced through this interview that the parents' concern about Andy's inappropriate and impulsive behavior was accurate, yet understanding that Andy's agenda was very different from that of his parents, the therapist had to decide how to formulate the chief complaint. In some ways, it mattered little: Both disorganization and impulsive speech are core ADHD symptoms that usually respond to medications and therapy. In this case an effective interviewer must acknowledge both parties' legitimate concerns to ensure that they feel they are being heard and taken seriously. But with Andy, a mercurial teenager with little psychological insight, the premium was on building rapport by emphasizing his concerns; immediately adopting his parents' chief complaint would probably alienate him. Andy's hurtful blurting practices could be addressed once the therapist established credibility with him by helping him combat his disorganization.

So how does one discover what is bothering the patient? Intently listening to what is said is necessary, as is observing behavior and asking questions.

LISTENING STRATEGIES

The Roman emperor Hadrian once said: "The techniques which I was obliged to develop in those unimportant early posts have served me in later years for my imperial audiences: to give oneself totally to each person throughout the brief duration of a hearing; to reduce the world for a moment to this banker, that veteran, or that widow; to accord to these individuals, each so different though each confined naturally within the narrow limits of a type, all the polite attention which at the best moments one gives to oneself." This quotation is helpful for the therapist to keep in mind, as an ideal toward which to strive.

Effective listening is the secret cache of the successful therapist, although it can be difficult to refrain from comment and simply to listen until a comment is indicated. Lives and reputations have been lost or ruined because of miscommunication. A stock broker's hearing "sell" when his client has commanded him to buy, or a doctor's recording medications differently than his patient is taking them, can have disastrous effects. Preventing this communication breakdown should be of the highest concern to clinicians working with ADHD patients.

Clinicians negotiate a tightrope in listening to their patients. When to listen and when to advise during the initial relationship is a function of experience. Collecting data during the evaluation should not be done at the expense of joining with the patient to convey an atmosphere of understanding and guidance. Experts on the diagnostic process encourage physicians to "assume the role of listener when the patient complains, or shows ambivalence and confusion about her goals. Assume the role of expert when she lacks knowledge about her condition and needs information about her disorder. Assume the role of adviser when she has made reasonable decisions, but hesitates to act on them" (Othmer & Othmer, 2002, p. 41).

Some basic listening tips for clinicians follow:

- Use reflective listening. Give patients your version of their story and allow them to revise it.
- Consider whether what is said matches the patients' body language.
- Work with patients to prioritize problems.
- Ask patients if any important information has not been covered—then wait.

Use reflective listening. Reflective listening demands that the therapist establish good eye contact, block out other distractions, and intently listen. At the end of the interview the therapist should summarize the information but forewarn patients that should they *not* agree with the summary, they should feel free to say so. When the therapist gives permission to disagree, patients will feel more comfortable investing trust in the nascent relationship.

Amanda's interaction with her psychologist offers an example of the benefits of reflective listening. Based on her initial interview and the use of rating scales, Amanda was diagnosed with ADHD combined type and panic disorder. Following is a portion of the dialogue from the initial interview.

Therapist: After listening to you, I'm hearing that you are concerned about not finishing projects and the criticism you receive about your tendency to cut people off. You seem to be down about how this is affecting your relationship with your husband. Am I getting this right? Let me know if I'm not getting it.

Amanda: I don't expect anyone to understand. . . . I'm really angry. No one notices at work that I don't mess up on purpose like a jerk. Okay, I do forget to do some of the things I promise to do, but that doesn't mean I'm not trying!

Therapist: So are you saying that you feel like you are perceived as a bad person, for example, by your coworkers? And you don't know how to make her see you as you feel you really are?

Amanda: Yes, that's it! I would be more patient with them if they saw me for what I am . . . a good person.

Therapist: Maybe we could also work together to find some ways to change your behavior too, once a diagnosis has been made. Do you think that might help?

Amanda: Well, I guess. And I guess I can't expect others to do everything. Some of this stuff really is my fault. What should I do?

Therapist: First we need to arrive at a diagnosis of your problem, and then we will work on the treatment. But I am very hopeful that your situation can improve a lot.

Amanda: Thanks for trying to understand.

Consider whether what is said matches the patients' body language. Many times, what a patient is saying does not correspond at all to what the patient's body says. For example, it is natural to say things are "fine" when one is clearly upset; the man who reports to be "doing well" through gritted teeth and clenched jaw is clearly *not* doing well. Thus, clinicians also need to "listen" for anomalous behavior. It can be tricky to differentiate common ADHD behavior from symptoms that might indicate a problem with a person who does not have ADHD. For example, shifting in one's seat and fidgeting is abnormal behavior for most adults and might connote other problems to some clinicians (anxiety, depression, or just being angry at the doctor). However, when the adult has the primarily hyperactive type of ADHD, it is classic and typical behavior.

Sometimes patients' attire belies what they are actually feeling. Wade, a tall and stocky 15-year-old, was brought in by his parents because he was smoking marijuana and doing poorly in school. He entered the office dressed in a long trench coat, bandana, and silver rings on all his fingers. The office staff was intimidated and expressed their apprehension to the doctor. Wade's bravado was evident throughout the interview—most of his responses were grunts. After 30 minutes, the interview changed tone.

> **Doctor:** (*feigning control and hoping not to transmit his own discomfort*) Wade, I get the sense that you aren't interested in talking. I think that you don't want to be here. You aren't answering any of my questions.
> **Wade:** I'm pretty sure no one is listening. Why try?
> **Doctor:** You look scary—like one of the Columbine kids.
> **Wade:** That's the point. Since I started dressing this way a couple of kids thought it was cool, but none of the teachers is even coming up to me.
> **Doctor:** Sounds like you want to have contact. Your clothes are pushing people away. That maybe was not your goal.
> **Wade:** No, that wasn't the plan. I want to be cool but I'm still me.
> **Doctor:** Well, in here, I will listen to you. It's safe. Be yourself—I take what you say seriously and I promise I always will.

Work with patients to prioritize problems and clarify confusion. During some initial evaluations, patients will describe a litany of problems that they want help in resolving. Faced with this stream of consciousness, therapists should not concede that they are overwhelmed, but rather help the patients identify the most important two or three problems. Do not accept statements that they are all equally important. Instead, tell patients that it is necessary to determine which ones are the most troublesome. It may help if the clinician and the patient work through the list together, discussing the prioritization.

Ask patients if any important information has not been covered—then wait. At the end of the initial diagnostic session, it is helpful to summarize to patients what has been discussed and thank them for providing valuable and sensitive information. Then ask if there is anything else they want to add. Wait at least a minute or two and be able to tolerate silence.

Most patients will automatically respond by saying that no, that is all there is. But as the clinician waits, the patient may decide to add more information. This therapeutic technique works not only to establish rapport ("he really cares to ask me to tell him more"), but also offers the patient an opportunity to reveal additional relevant facts.

For example, at the end of an intake, the clinician asked if Jennifer had other thoughts that had not been covered. She initially demurred but after a minute added, "I told you nobody in my family has ADHD. Well, that's as far as I know. But actually, I was adopted. I don't really know if the family I was born to has this problem. They might."

It may be difficult to ascertain whether Jennifer's biological parents have symptoms of ADHD. But setting ADHD aside as a diagnosis merely because no one in her (adoptive) family had the remotest sign of symptoms would, of course, have been a bad idea. In addition, some studies have indicated that adopted children have a greater risk for ADHD than others. This does not mean that Jennifer certainly has ADHD, but considering it as a possibility would be wise.

Some clinicians may resist asking the "is there anything else" question at the end of a session because it can potentially extend the session for too long. If this is a concern, the question could be asked earlier, not as an afterthought, but as a diagnostic tool. Additionally, if the session looks like it is going to run over, the clinician can advise the patient that this issue can be raised in the next session. Note it and discuss it at the next opportunity, after reviewing the key points the patient shared in the previous session.

OBSERVING THE PATIENT'S BEHAVIOR

In addition to carefully listening to what patients say and interjecting questions and remarks, clinicians are advised to look carefully at patients' behaviors and listen intensely to their stories. Taken alone, individual stories may be unpersuasive, but when they are considered as a whole, the astute clinician can gain a full-dimensional appreciation of the struggle of the ADHD patient. The following observations are frequently made during the initial evaluation.

- Patients seem jittery and have trouble sitting still.
- Patients' thoughts quickly swing from one subject to another—many things remind them of something else (and these thoughts are rational and there is no sign of mania).
- Patients express difficulty with being on time.
- Patients complain about losing household items.
- Patients express concern about their disorganized life.
- Patients self-blame or externalize their failures onto others.
- Patients' behavior reveals that they act impulsively.
- Patients' self-descriptions reveal that they have a quick temper and low tolerance for frustration.

Patients seem jittery and have trouble sitting still. Although childhood ADHD is often characterized by hyperactivity, these symptoms tend to diminish with time. But not always. The inability to sit still through the interview is a strong sign of hyperactivity. Many adolescents and adults complain of having "ants in their pants" and may experience an irritating need to pace. Their fidgetiness may be more problematic to those around them than it is to the patients themselves. "I'm exhausted by his energy," said Becka of her husband's perpetual motion. "I wish he could sit and watch a movie with me. He always needs to be busy. He is always on the move, but usually he has nowhere to go."

Although hyperactivity is a lifelong ADHD symptom, it might be more evident at various times of a patient's life. If patients have the ability to sublimate excessive energy through exercise or hard work, hyperactivity can be a nonissue. But if they are temporarily immobilized due to a broken bone or permanently slowed by a stroke, they are suddenly deprived of a natural coping method. Not uncommonly these patients present aggressively—not realizing that by losing this physical release, their energy is negatively diverted into agitation.

Patients' thoughts quickly swing from one subject to another. In the clinical interview, distractible patients shift quickly from one idea to another. All these subjects may seemingly be related, but they result in a mosaic difficult for the clinician to follow. Spencer, a physical therapist undergoing an evaluation, demonstrated this erratic thought process.

Doctor: "Tell me, how are things going at work?"
Spencer: "Not so good. I am always a guy who lets people know what I am thinking."
Doctor: "Okay."
Spencer: "Like I told my in-laws, and this made my wife mad, that the Buick they just leased looked out of date as soon as they brought it home. I think the American designers should learn more from the Germans. They really make great cars. Imagine that! We won the war, but we need them to help us with what we do best. Pretty soon there will be no auto jobs here in the Midwest. All that free trade stuff. The damn unions couldn't do a thing with the Democrats. That's why Clinton should be so ashamed of himself. What do you expect from a guy who has no morals? My supervisor loved him when he was president in the 90s and that's how we clash."
Doctor: "So . . . how are things going at work?"

These types of patients are often fun to interview; they may be smart and have plenty of opinions. But basic questions are barely answered and the dialogue can start in one place and end in an entirely different one. Spencer was not grandiose or manic, but he was profoundly tangential and overly inclusive. Family members and coworkers may have difficulty managing the verbal barrage from people like Spencer. These tangents may also give the evaluator pause—"Why can't I get my questions answered, and why is this interview taking so long?"

Patients express difficulty with being on time. Lateness and procrastination are hallmark features of ADHD and generate many of the patient's presenting complaints. Undiagnosed patients with ADHD who are timely may overcompensate by planning to arrive at a location long before their appointment time. Managing time can be an elusive virtue for many ADHD patients. Some have lost jobs or strained relationships because of it.

Clinicians may see early evidence of this behavior if patients are late to appointments. They may also elicit a lifelong pattern of time-management problems with careful interviewing, including asking questions such as, "Do you sometimes lose track of time and are late? If so, why do you think that is?" Patients without ADHD will dismiss this question; a patient with ADHD may readily affirm it. People with ADHD can be completely baffled about why they are still at Point A when they should have been at Point B hours ago. Patients with inattention and distractibility caused by ADHD may find punctuality and timeliness to be alien concepts.

Patients complain about losing household items. Losing items is another ADHD feature that stems from poor memory and impaired executive skills. The lost items may be minor, such as an unfiled receipt or a cheap watch that is forgotten at the gym. The losses may also be more troublesome, such as losing a passport for the third time or misplacing a cell phone so often that the company will no longer sell the patient replacement insurance.

Some patients compensate for this problem by choosing a specific familiar place to store their cell phone, keys, wallet, and other items. They know that without this routine they will be spending hours in a wasteful, frustrating search.

It is good practice for the clinician to ask, "Do you think that you lose items more than other people?" Or, "Do you spend a lot of time searching for items that you've misplaced?" If the patient responds by saying, "Yes, I always lose things," but then has to think hard to recall losing her watch 2 years ago, this is not notable. However, if she relates that she loses her purse and other key items weekly, this *is* an indication that executive dysfunction is a problem. In assessing the role "losing things" plays in the diagnosis of ADHD, the clinician should consider the chronicity of the symptoms (usually since childhood) and the level of impairment it causes.

Patients express concern about their disorganized life. Individuals with ADHD usually express great distress about their disorganization. Being late or losing possessions are the most evident symptoms, but adults are more likely to express dissatisfaction at their inability to make and execute plans.

Many people with ADHD take on numerous projects, saying "yes" to every request. Their tendency to overpromise inevitably leads to disappointment as they repeatedly fail to deliver, causing distress to themselves and to those who were counting on them. This type of disorganization is not synonymous with sloppiness; rather, it is a miscalculation of how much time and effort it takes to successfully plan and complete a project.

To determine if this is a problem for patients, ask, "How many new projects, at home or work, have you started in the last year?" And then, "Of these, how many did you expect you'd finish when you started?" Often patients with ADHD will report that they started several major home projects and expected to complete them all, ruefully admitting that their spouse did not share their optimism. Sure enough, the spouse was right and all the projects were half-finished, at best.

Patients self-blame or externalize their failures onto others. Self-blame is a common refrain for patients with undiagnosed ADHD. Often they have endured a lifetime of disapproval, having had to accept responsibility for being late, forgetting appointments, or behaving impulsively. (Of course, self-blaming is not exclusive to ADHD patients.) Relentless criticism can force some people into excessive ownership of problems, nearly taking responsibility for the original sin.

The other side of the same coin are patients who reflexively absolve themselves of any responsibility: "My parents never take my side." "I don't care what she says, nobody likes that teacher." "My boss is only in it for himself." Externalization is a primitive psychological defense, and one the ADHD clinician will surely encounter.

Some patients exhibit both self-blaming and externalizing traits. For example, the patient may say that everything that has gone wrong in her life is her own fault because she is stupid, hopeless and so forth, but also adding that if only her mother (husband/sister/brother/others) had been there for her when needed, then she would not be saddled with her current problems. Sometimes patients switch back and forth between self-blame and externalizing blame; this session, no one understands her, and next session, she is entirely at fault for everything gone wrong in her life.

Patients' behavior reveals that they act impulsively. Patients with ADHD may exhibit impulsivity in many different ways. The clinician often can assess this immediately. The patient who comments on everything, asking such trivial questions as, "Is that Oriental rug real?" or the patient who stalks out of the waiting room if she is not greeted quickly enough to suit her, only to call later in the day to reschedule, demonstrates an inability to self-regulate verbal output.

Sometimes impulsive behavior is revealed through history-taking. Impulsive ADHD individuals get themselves into trouble. They may drive 100 miles to a favorite restaurant despite predictions of snow and find themselves stranded. They may blurt out unedited thoughts that are offensive to others. Aunt Amy may have some new stretch marks since her pregnancy, but it is reasonable to expect her 17-year-old niece *not* to publicly declare the obvious at the summer beach party. This lack of self-censoring is a marker of ADHD and a symptom that frequently causes interpersonal problems.

Clinicians must also distinguish the impulsivity associated with ADHD from the mania that is associated with bipolar disorder. In ADHD, impulsivity is chronic; bipolar patients demonstrate this characteristic only when in the manic phase of the illness. Additionally, ADHD impulsivity is usually grounded in reality—people with ADHD may choose to skydive or street race but they are generally aware of the inherent risks associated with such activity. Manic patients, on the other hand, are less rational. They may withdraw every cent from bank accounts and retirement funds and fly to Las Vegas to bet it all on red. This would not be typical behavior of the person with ADHD, who may be impulsive but sees the folly of such an action.

Patients' self-descriptions reveal that they have a quick temper and low tolerance for frustration. Both adolescents and adults with ADHD may exhibit low thresholds for frustration and be quick to anger. The evaluating clinician can assess this trait when exploring marital difficulties, problems with personal relationships, and the causes of frequent job changes. Patients with ADHD, particularly the predominately impulsive subtype, are likely to lose their tempers over events that others would gloss over. Their "short fuses" often cause them trouble at home and at work. Yet they may quickly recover from their anger, like a fire that is readily put out, while others around them still simmer with anger.

Impulsivity manifested in temper outbursts is frequently displayed in the exam room. The impulsive teenager may scream at his mother for getting a small detail wrong. The mother with ADHD may snap at her children for not sitting absolutely quietly while she speaks with her doctor. Impulsive men with ADHD often have little tolerance for slow drivers; road rage is their modus operandi.

COMMON QUESTIONS TO HELP ELICIT NEEDED INFORMATION

Targeted questions can elicit information that is vital to the diagnosis. The patient's responses should be attended to carefully. These questions can be asked in the following order:

1. Begin with a nonthreatening question such as, "How do you hope I can be of help to you?" This gives patients time to think and does not limit their imagination. It differs from the traditional "How may I help you?" which not only may sound like a waiter's opening salvo but also presupposes that the clinician *can* help.
2. "When did you start to notice that you had a problem?" If the problems are new (less than 6 months), consider a diagnosis other than ADHD. ADHD symptoms often persist from childhood, although inattentive symptoms may not be discovered until early adolescence or even adulthood.
3. "Why are you coming in for evaluation now?" By asking this question, clinicians can explore whether patients just learned that they have a treatable condition or have only recently "given themselves permission" to seek help. This question also helps clinicians determine if patients are in crisis and have nowhere else to turn.
4. "Did someone recommend that you seek an evaluation? If so, who and why?" The patient may disclose that a spouse or friend (sometimes another patient of the doctor) has encouraged the evaluation. This information not only helps clinicians assess the impact of the patient's symptoms on others but also provides clues about the patient's support system.

5. "Do you know others who have a similar problem to yours, or someone
   who has been treated for ADHD?" Patients with "mentors" may have
   fewer resistances and will be likely to welcome the clinician's diagnostic and treatment suggestions.

HISTORY-TAKING

In addition to listening, observing, and asking key questions, taking the patient's history is a vital part of the diagnostic process. The clinician needs
information on the patient's medical history, psychosocial history, psychiatric history, family history, and childhood history before a diagnosis can
be made.

Medical History

The careful taking of a medical history is an intrinsically important component of every diagnostic evaluation, because past medical problems, as
well as a family history of medical and psychiatric problems, may have a
direct bearing on the issues that concern the patient today. Like all patients, individuals who may have ADHD should be questioned about their
past medical history at the initial encounter.

ASK ABOUT OTHER MEDICATIONS

It is important to question patients about prescribed medications or dietary
supplements they take. Although it is not common, some of these agents,
like appetite suppressants, antiepileptic medications, excessive caffeine
intake, and the herbal supplement kava kava, can cause agitation or cognitive disturbances that mimic ADHD symptoms. For example, pseudo-
ephedrine, a cold-preparation compound that is increasingly regulated because of its misuse in methamphetamine production, may cause symptoms
such as restlessness and hyperactivity.

The best practice is to ask the patient to bring in all their medications,
herbal supplements, and vitamins during their initial visit. For subsequent
visits patients should be instructed to give the physician an updated list
of current medications. This decreases the likelihood of communication
failures and drug interactions, while excessive doses of medications can be

identified. Maintaining a policy of explicitly requiring this information makes patients less likely to forget, innocently or intentionally, about other medications that have been prescribed. This practice is particularly useful in the medication-seeking dependent personalities.

RULE OUT MEDICAL PROBLEMS

Behavior that appears to be caused by ADHD may instead stem from medical problems, such as thyroid disorder, or iron deficiency anemia. Thyroid disease (either hyperthyroidism or hypothyroidism) is a common illness that may resemble ADHD in its presentation. An estimated 27 million Americans have some form of thyroid disease, and at least half are undiagnosed (Canaris, Manowitz, Mayor, & Ridgway, 2000). Patients with *hyper*thyroidism may exhibit hyperactivity and inattentiveness. They also may behave impulsively, in addition to presenting with clinical signs such as an elevated pulse and blood pressure, moist skin, and bulging eyes. Patients with *hypo*thyroidism may appear to exhibit the inattentive form of ADHD. These patients may seem disorganized and forgetful, in addition to having low pulse and blood pressure, dry skin, and lethargy. Another underlying medical cause of inattention and slowed cognitive processes is iron deficiency anemia. Routine screening tests can rule out these conditions, although the yield in clinical practice is quite low. Of course, a patient may have medical problems in addition to ADHD. A small study of 53 ADHD patients and 27 controls ranging in age from 4 to 14 years revealed abnormally low serum ferritin levels (indicative of iron deficiency anemia) in 84% of the children with ADHD, compared to only 18 percent of the controls (Konofal, Lecendreux, Arnulf, & Mouren, 2004). Although this study was done on children and adolescents and further research is needed, the data may likely be extrapolated to adults. When a preexisting condition is causing or contributing to symptoms that mimic ADHD, that problem should be addressed before a diagnosis of ADHD is made and treatment initiated. The ADHD symptoms can be reevaluated once the medical condition is resolved.

LABORATORY TESTS

In screening patients for ADHD a urine drug screen (UDS) is necessary to assess for illicit drug usage. These screens are usually quite accurate and allow for detection of opiates, marijuana, amphetamines, and cocaine. The routine use of the UDS deters active substance abusers who hope to persuade physicians to supply controlled substances.

Patients, particularly adolescents, should be told of this test before they have urine collected. Informing the patient promotes openness in the therapeutic relationship. Marijuana metabolites can be detectable for 4 weeks, so patients generally cannot "prepare" for their UDS. Cocaine and amphetamines are cleared by the body within hours, making UDSs less telling for these agents.

In addition, the clinician should assess the patient for high blood pressure (hypertension). An electrocardiogram (ECG) should also be considered in order to rule out cardiac disease. Structural imaging such as echocardiography is not routinely needed. All ADHD medications can affect blood pressure and pulse, particularly stimulants, and for this reason, documenting baseline cardiovascular parameters is important.

Laboratory tests of lower priority may include a complete blood count (CBC) to rule out anemia and infection, a thyroid-stimulating hormone (TSH) test to check for thyroid disease, a measurement of vitamin B12 to detect B12 deficiency, and blood tests to screen for heavy metal toxicity. Some researchers believe that a low-level deficiency of magnesium may lead to ADHD symptoms; therefore, it is also a good idea to consider mineral deficiencies. Done routinely, these tests increase the expense of evaluation and consequently the accessibility to treatment for some patients. Thus, the physician needs to balance cost and benefits before routinely adopting these low-yield tests.

WARN PATIENTS THAT NO TESTS RELIABLY DETECT ADHD

Because so many patients are accustomed to receiving a diagnosis that is based on definitive data, such as a positive or negative test on a throat or urine culture, it is critical to emphasize that no laboratory tests can definitively confirm or refute the presence of ADHD. Instead, laboratory tests are useful to rule *out* other diseases. Normal TSH levels infer normal thyroid function. A normal hemoglobin suggests that anemia is not a problem. But no laboratory test can say with certainty, yes, this person has ADHD.

Some argue that brain imaging tests like single photon emission computerized tomography (SPECT) may be used to identify ADHD. Based on thousands of observations, psychiatrist Daniel Amen (2001) asserted that through SPECT technology, specific blood flow patterns could be characterized. He identified six different subtypes of ADHD based on this imaging technique. Amen's work has been enthusiastically received by consumers and some clinicians. His images underscore the neurological basis of the condition and patients ambivalent about the validity of the diagnosis are assuaged when they see them.

Nonetheless, Amen remains controversial in academic circles, and he has been criticized because his work has not been replicated by other researchers. At present few other clinicians use imaging techniques to diagnose or confirm ADHD in their patients and brain imaging is generally used in research studies, rather than for diagnostic purposes. The development of more specific imaging techniques may change this in the near future.

Among the many issues Amen's work has raised is the importance of documenting previous head injury. His brain scans do show this type of injury to be more common than previously thought and he links a history of subtle head trauma to abnormal childhood behavior. Clinicians should note this and routinely inquire about head injury history.

AVOID ATTRIBUTING CLEAR ADHD SYMPTOMS TO MEDICAL CAUSES

Although a medical workup for ADHD should be pursued, clinicians should not cling to the hope that ADHD symptoms can be explained away by traditional medical problems.

I met Doug at a meeting for adults with ADHD and experts who treat the disorder. He had attended to learn more about his son's ADHD diagnosis. My lecture included some information about adult ADHD. Toward the end Doug stood and reported that he personally identified with the description. "After hearing you," he said, "I think I've had ADHD for a long time. But I've been talking to my family doctor and he ordered skin testing. He told me my symptoms were due to food allergies, and he prescribed a restrictive diet."

If it looks like a duck and quacks like one, it usually is one. Chances are low that a medical problem like food allergies will account for a lifetime of ADHD symptoms. Grueling restrictive diets and other nonproductive medical workups may demoralize patients like Doug and deter them from pursuing ADHD medications. I recommended that Doug find an ADHD specialist.

DETERMINING IF MEDICAL SYNDROMES ARE PRESENT

Our clinic has observed that many adults with ADHD have been diagnosed with controversial medical conditions that are resistant to conventional treatment. Fibromyalgia, chronic fatigue syndrome, irritable bowel syndrome, and headaches and infections like Lyme disease and Epstein Barr virus (EBV) are disproportionately reported in this population. Chapter 11 advances the theory that patients with ADHD inattentive type complain of pain and fatigue. They appear to be unable to filter out any unpleasant physical stimuli. Faced with these longstanding complaints, in the absence of physical signs, clinicians diagnose these patients with one or many of the above nebulous medical conditions. It is unclear if this theory will be proven, but clinicians evaluating ADHD should be aware of this possible relationship.

Psychosocial History

Although a person need not have ADHD to have problems with school, work, or home, many patients with ADHD *do* have such problems. In the diagnostic process, it is important to inquire about the history of the following:

- Substance abuse
- Numerous job changes
- School failure
- Many traffic tickets
- Marital problems

SUBSTANCE ABUSE

Numerous studies have shown that patients with ADHD have an increased risk for substance abuse problems, although treatment may mitigate the risk of substance abuse in adolescent boys. Patients who may have

ADHD should be asked about their use of alcohol and drugs, with the reassurance that the information that they provide will be held in confidence. This information is very important, as prescriptions of stimulants may be problematic for patients with substance abuse problems. (This issue is further discussed in Chapter 8.)

NUMEROUS JOB CHANGES

ADHD symptoms often collide with workplace expectations. Because of problems with impulsivity, inattention, and sometimes hyperactivity, many patients with untreated ADHD have encountered problems in holding a job and some regularly bounce from one job to the next. Abby, age 33, had an impressive resume. She had worked on Broadway as a stage hand and in Hollywood as a set designer. She spent 2 years abroad in the Peace Corps and six months in Boston doing art therapy with hospitalized children. Abby sparkled at her next interview for a position as public relations assistant for a Detroit auto firm and beat out four other applicants. Predictably, however, Abby was impressive for the first 6 months, but her restlessness soon surfaced. Her work attendance dropped off and she started complaining of boredom with the job's routines. Within months she was off to another exciting new experience. ADHD medications did improve her patience, but in the end Abby was happy with her erratic journey and decided not to pursue treatment.

Patients should be asked if they currently have a job and if so, how long they have been working in this position or, if they are unemployed, their most recent job. They should also be queried about previous job tenures. Although many ADHD individuals cannot sustain the tedium and discipline of a single job, others with ADHD stay at the same job for years. These individuals may be fearful that they cannot learn the rigors of a new position and this fear motivates them to stay put.

SCHOOL FAILURE

Many patients with ADHD have difficulties in school, starting in grade school and extending through vocational training or college. An estimated 25% of adults with ADHD repeated at least one grade. Adults with ADHD often report numerous problems in school as a child, and they may continue to experience difficulty with training programs at work. If they attend college or vocational school, their inattention may lead instructors to think that they do not care about learning. Chronic failure exacts its toll, and many ADHD sufferers become dejected by the process.

The evaluation for ADHD should explore school history and correlate aptitude with performance. (As with job failures, clinicians should be non-judgmental during the diagnostic process.) ADHD often explains how a patient with a 120 IQ could have received consistent Cs on report cards. At the same time, school failure should not be overweighted during the assessment. Plenty of doctors, lawyers, and CPAs have ADHD. All must have had some proficiency in school to obtain these degrees. Their ADHD symptoms may manifest in areas other than academic underperformance.

MANY TRAFFIC TICKETS

A poor driving record is common among patients with ADHD, especially among males. Treatment often improves the erratic driving patterns. As noted earlier, patients should not be asked *if* they have received a traffic ticket, but rather *how many* tickets they have received in the past year. Several tickets or more may indicate that patients have ADHD if they fit other criteria. Of course, if patients have received no tickets, this does not rule out ADHD. See Chapter 3 for more information on driving problems among people with ADHD.

MARITAL PROBLEMS

Because of their ADHD symptoms, many patients with ADHD struggle with maintaining long-term relationships. Marital problems are common in this population, as are sexual problems (discussed in Chapter 8). Taken alone, marital dysfunction is insufficient to diagnose ADHD, but if other ADHD symptoms are present, marital problems can be considered another indication of ADHD.

Psychiatric History

The majority of patients with ADHD are comorbid with one or more diagnoses in addition to ADHD, and it is important to diagnose the comorbidities as this allows clinicians to prioritize treatment. For example, depression and ADHD often run concurrently. If the patient is exhibiting suicidal thoughts, the depression must be dealt with first. In contrast, if the diagnostic process reveals a low level of chronic depression—a dysthymia superimposed on ADHD—it may be best to treat the ADHD first. (Chapter 2 covers comorbidities more fully.)

That said, past psychiatric diagnoses should be viewed critically, as they could be erroneous. For example, patients previously diagnosed with depression may instead have ADHD, anxiety disorders, or other problems. Bipolar disorder is overdiagnosed in the adult ADHD population, and clinicians should accept this diagnosis only with good substantiation.

Family History

Clinicians must talk to patients about both psychiatric and medical problems in the immediate family. Many psychiatric problems, such as depression, bipolar disorder, and ADHD, have a genetic component. ADHD is among the most heritable of medical conditions, but the presence of ADHD symptoms in other family members does not *confirm* the diagnosis of ADHD (Faraone, 2002). However, a family history of ADHD does increase the probability of the condition in the patient, particularly when other diagnostic steps point in that direction. Similarly, certain medical conditions such as thyroid disease and vitamin deficiencies may also be inherited. A thorough history-taking should include questions about such medical problems to rule out non-ADHD causes of symptoms.

Inquiries into family members' histories should be made with open-ended, nonjudgmental questions. Patients often have strong feelings about family members, and clinicians should avoid making them feel as if they are being cross-examined. Patients placed in defensive postures will yield less accurate information.

In addition, questions should be asked about a family history of hypertension or cardiac disease, since these conditions may also be inherited, and if so, will affect the medication choice if is determined that the patient has ADHD.

Childhood History

Another important aspect of diagnosing ADHD is determining whether symptoms were present in childhood. This can be challenging when your patient is a 40-year-old adult. The first step is to talk to patients about their childhood.

Many patients with ADHD, particularly adults, have received numerous negative comments about their past or current behavior from parents, other family members, teachers, friends, and others they have encountered, and the nature of these comments can help with diagnosis. Patients may have also received valuable feedback in the form of report cards and work evaluations. Obtaining old report cards may be difficult because they are often in the possession of the parents and patients may not wish to discuss why they want them. If this is the case, patients may simply tell parents that they want to show the report cards to their own children or need them for their records.

For balance, it is also helpful for clinicians to ask patients to recall the positive comments that people have made about them in the past. Even positive comments can yield underlying clues of ADHD diagnosis. For example, if a patient recalls that family members said that when she really made up her mind to perform a task, it always was completed, even if she worked 12 hours on it, this may indicate a hyperfocusing tendency that is seen among many patients with ADHD. That is, when patients are very interested in a project, they can devote a great deal of intense time to it, beyond the time that a person without ADHD would expend.

It is also a good idea to (with patients' permission) obtain corroboration for what patients remember about their childhood. Other family members may be willing to discuss the patient's past and current symptoms and may be willing to fill out rating scales designed for collateral contacts. Parents may be particularly adept at recalling the past behavior of the patient, including behaviors that the patient has completely forgotten.

Of course, family members who provide such information about adult patients who may have ADHD should be advised that they will not be provided with information on the diagnosis or treatment of the patient. They can be told that their contribution will help with the diagnosis, but that the patient's confidentiality must be respected.

Considering the Key Elements of ADHD Beyond the DSM-IV

Once basic information has been obtained through diagnostic interviews and collateral contacts, the clinician can proceed to work to understand the patient's unique story. The lives of individuals with ADHD can take many different courses. Many times the symptoms are cloaked in deceptive and paradoxical presentations. For instance, patients can be both impulsive (tremendous risk takers) and compulsive (methodical list makers). Some may be able to focus endlessly on the details of a video game but unable to sit through a 30-minute business meeting.

The *DSM* dutifully lists the individual symptoms that constitute the ADHD diagnosis, but the clinician's ability to appreciate the totality of the individual symptoms through recognizing typical life patterns is of equal importance.

ZEROING IN ON A POSSIBLE ADHD DIAGNOSIS

Once a diagnosis of ADHD is likely or probable, the clinician should consider the key elements of ADHD and determine whether the patient exhibits these tendencies to a significant level. Many people are occasionally impulsive, disorganized, distractible, or hyperactive; however, impulsivity, disorganization, distractibility, and hyperactivity strongly characterize and underline the life of the patient with ADHD, and this pattern of behavior causes the patient problems both at work and at home. Rating scales, discussed later in this chapter, can help clinicians evaluate the level of ADHD symptoms, but the initial diagnostic interview may provide important clues about the pervasiveness and intensiveness of such symptoms.

Evaluating the Level of Impulsivity

Impulsivity can be difficult to evaluate in the office, where individuals usually feel more constrained and may not exhibit their typical behavior, at least initially. However, self-controlled behavior lasts only so long, and some observations can be made about the patient during the diagnostic interview.

Impulsive patients may interrupt frequently or make it hard for the clinician to complete a thought. They may exhibit extreme impatience; if the clinician is delayed, the patient may alert the staff that he or she is indignant about having to wait. Ironically, at the next visit the same patient may be 30 minutes late and see no reason for anyone to express dismay. Other common impulsive acts are temper outbursts and blurting out unfiltered comments.

There are also less obvious elements of impulsivity. Kim, a 16-year-old high school sophomore, was brought to the emergency room with self-inflicted lacerations. She reported having a fight with her boyfriend that afternoon. Frustrated and feeling little consolation from her friends or family, Kim told the consulting psychiatrist that she used a razor to superficially cut her left forearm. "When I cut, I don't plan to. At the moment, it seems like a good idea."

Leslie, a thin, 56-year-old woman, presented for care because of conflict with her current husband. Quite bright, Leslie shielded her intelligence with a regressed, childlike demeanor. Ten minutes into the initial interview she disclosed that she frequently shoplifted, and her several arrests and subsequent punishments were the major source of tension between her and her bewildered husband. In language similar to Kim, Leslie reported that her behavior was triggered by a sense of anxiety and a need for excitement. The larceny was never performed with much planning. "I never know when the feeling will come over me, but I kind of like living on the edge. I never know when they will get me." For Leslie, getting caught was both ominous and exciting.

Confronted with these stories, the evaluating physician suspected that Kim's cutting and Leslie's shoplifting could be the most visible hints of the ADHD iceberg. Kim was found to have had difficulties in school from day one. Her father was alcoholic and her brother was on probation for a drug trafficking charge. In contrast, Leslie had been a fine student. She had a bachelor's degree in language education but had never been able to sustain meaningful employment. In her thirties, she was hospitalized for cocaine abuse. Over the years, Leslie had multiple relationships yet few friends. Neither Kim nor Leslie had a relevant medical history, and neither had bipolar disorder or major depression.

During the diagnostic process, the doctor spoke with Kim's mother and Leslie's husband to obtain their perspectives. Rating scales designed to determine levels of anxiety, depression, and ADHD (discussed later in this chapter) were administered. Educational videos about ADHD were shown to both women and both identified with the video's descriptions of other patients with ADHD.

In the end, the cutting and shoplifting *did* represent impulsive symptoms of ADHD combined type in both women. Future chapters will discuss treatment responses, but it is interesting to note that once given treatment for ADHD, these women with the same diagnosis had very different responses. For Kim, medications diminished her sense of angst and urgency, and she rarely cut again. Leslie also noted initial improvement and years into treatment continued to feel that medications improved her mood. However, despite treatment, her shoplifting and consequent arrests continued.

Evaluating the Level of Disorganization

How inattentive does an individual need to be to meet the criteria for an ADHD diagnosis? Among the cardinal conditions of inattention is disorganization, which in the context of ADHD can cause considerable problems. The clinician must identify lifelong patterns rather than occasional lapses.

Consider Alex, a talented lacrosse player at a local university. Three years into college, Alex had changed his major four times. He had few credits and little direction.

Alex presented to his doctor in a severe crisis. In the previous year, he had been placed on academic probation. Among other lapses, he had handed in an important paper 2 weeks late because he misplaced the syllabus that provided the paper's due date. Instead of checking with the professor or a classmate, he gambled and guessed the wrong date. Alex was warned that his poor grades jeopardized his lacrosse scholarship; in order to continue at the college, he needed to perform better. Despite these warnings, 2 weeks later Alex misplaced another assignment and forgot to start a third. This time Alex's professors were unmoved, and the dean judged that Alex's behavior was volitional. Upon permanent dismissal, Alex was told that he was "not ready" to navigate the complicated maze of academic life. Panicked, Alex sought psychiatric help.

Alex's doctor listened to the story and began developing a differential diagnosis. Alex appeared to be legitimately upset. He knew that forfeiting the scholarship made the prospect of completing his education unlikely. When asked why he was seeking help at such a late date, Alex conceded that he was advised to see a professional several times but never got around to it. "My parents never wanted me to take medications for anything. They thought I would test positive and be kicked off the team."

Alex had struggled throughout high school but got by due to his great athletic prowess and one semester of summer school. He was adopted and was never given background on his biological parents. He had never abused street drugs but had become more reliant on chewing tobacco. "I feel more focused and more into the game when I dip."

Rating scales were given to Alex and both he and his mother endorsed many of the items on the Conners Scale. His mother, energized that there might be a name and a remedy for Alex, collected his old report cards and delivered them to the psychiatrist. His third-, fifth-, and sixth-grade teachers had complained about Alex's disorganization. When asked about these issues, Alex's father quipped, "He reminds me of Pigpen from the Charlie Brown cartoon, but Pigpen's room is probably cleaner." ADHD combined type was diagnosed.

Evaluating the Level of Distractibility

Distractibility, the inability to shift attention efficiently from one topic to another, can be detected during a diagnostic workup. Distractible individuals report that they frequently start one project and move to another before the first one is done. They are often intensely frustrated by this trait. Ian is a case in point.

After their child, Paul, was diagnosed with ADHD, Ian's wife Thao pleaded with him to get evaluated. For several years he balked at the idea, as he was uncomfortable with becoming a patient and submitting to regular appointments, co-pays, and answering to anyone other than himself. One day he changed his mind and he and Thao presented to their son's doctor.

Ian: I think it's time you examined me.

Doctor: Why now? I've known you for 5 years. We've talked about your son twenty times.

Ian: I know, but last month I took Paul's medication and I could not believe how much better I was. That week I promised my wife that I would organize the garage—something I have been promising her forever. On Saturday, I did not have his medication. I did start working in the garage, but within a few minutes I was at the store doing something totally unrelated. Then I got my car washed, a haircut, and went to the driving range.

Thao: I got so mad at him that on Sunday he took Paul's medication again.

Doctor: The entire dose?

Ian: Yes, and I spent the next 8 hours in the garage.

Thao: I was so happy until I looked at what he had gotten done. Nothing! He spent the whole day organizing two drawers. He didn't touch anything else.

The diagnostic workup confirmed the presence of ADHD. Ian's case is instructive on many levels. Most importantly, his history demonstrates distractibility. Second, although they should not, patients who suspect that they have ADHD often experiment with other people's medication, but because dosages are variable from person to person, this is not an effective way to make the diagnosis. In Ian's case, the dose was adjusted so that he wasn't too distracted or overly focused.

Evaluating the Level of Hyperactivity

In some patients, their motor and cognitive hyperactivity is blatantly obvious, as with the person who sits down and then springs up and paces about the room and who may speak in very rapid sentences with confusing transitions from one subject to the next. If the person should sit down again, he or she often is still in motion, drumming the hands on the arm of the chair, making circles with the ankle and generally having the appearance of a person who cannot simply sit still.

Conversely, some individuals with ADHD can sustain their attention for long periods of time if they are interested in a specific topic. This can deflect the diagnostician from considering ADHD.

Dominic, a ninth grader, was referred for testing by his school counselor. During the evaluation the psychologist learned that school had been disastrous for Dom. Throughout grade school, Dom had been promoted from grade to grade despite minimal effort. His current social studies teacher reported that he required a great deal of individual attention. In English class, Dom displayed flashes of true creativity but more often appeared lost in thought. Dom was generally upbeat, but his guidance counselor knew that most of his peers found him odd and detached.

An attentional disorder was never considered because Dom could sit and work on his computer for hours with total absorption. He was a master video gamer and had developed and executed intricate gaming strategies that few adults in his life could fathom. In the past 3 years, Dom had compiled and catalogued a library of downloaded music that had few rivals.

When Dom was in fourth grade, a clinician wondered if he had Asperger's syndrome, a mild form of autism, and for 6 months Dom attended a social skills group. Since that time, however, Dom had had no testing or treatment.

At the start of their meeting, Dom's parents relayed that they did not believe Dom had "that ADD thing." Determined to stay neutral until all parts of the evaluation were completed, the doctor ordered a full battery of testing. Dom's full IQ was scored superior at 118. No learning disability was detected. A Millon Personality Profile did not reveal any significant personality problems and contrary to the doctor's expectation, Dom was quite poised when answering direct questions. ADHD rating scales were completed by Dom, his mother, and the counselor. Each rater returned the scales with elevated distractibility scores.

Dom's doctor concluded that Dom had ADHD predominately inattentive type. His ability to concentrate intensely on topics that particularly interested him at the expense of subjects he considered more mundane was explained to be "hyperfocus," a phenomenon seen with many ADHD individuals. Dom's ultimate success depended on balancing his time and interests between all disciplines. After the methodical evaluation and because the physician carefully listened to the family's concerns, Dom and his family accepted the diagnosis and enthusiastically chose to pursue treatment.

Forgetfulness: Is It ADHD or Dementia?

Forgetfulness is a common ADHD presentation, and adults with inattentive ADHD sometimes question if they have Alzheimer's disease. It is important to distinguish normal aging from dementia and from the forgetfulness associated with ADHD.

Most aging patients experience forgetfulness. Word-finding difficulties are common, and the demands of aging, like physical decline and worrying and caring for an aging spouse, can tax the cognitive strengths of even the most resilient. Yet these patients retain their sense of humor and can articulate their concerns. They do not lose psychological insight into their condition.

A healthy person may lose track of time and occasionally be late, but people with dementia come to forget that the device strapped on their wrist is a watch. Moderately demented patients are typically unaware of their increasing deficits. In contrast, patients with ADHD are painfully aware of their failings. They certainly know what a watch is but may forget to look at their wrist to note the time. In addition, the forgetful person with ADHD may misplace common household items many times a week.

The Comprehensive Evaluation

The diagnostic approach to ADHD depends on the venue. In single-clinician settings, obtaining the history of personal and family symptoms, identifying impairments, and using rating scales can be done during the initial visit. In clinics specializing in ADHD and related disorders, other rating scales are routinely given. These are best done by a psychometrician, who can administer the tests in a quiet place and pace the process so as not to overwhelm the patient. However, many ADHD scales are self-administered.

In this setting, it is best to use multiple ADHD rating scales to ensure internal consistency. It is also important to assess for common psychiatric comorbidities such as mood and anxiety disorders and substance abuse. Most ADHD rating scales assess the hyperactive and impulsive symptoms separately from the inattentive symptoms. Inattentive symptoms may not be appreciated until adolescence.

USING ADHD SCALES AND RATING SYSTEMS
TO AID IN DIAGNOSIS

ADHD rating scales (Table 1.2) are extremely useful in the diagnostic process and should be routinely employed as part of an initial ADHD assessment. Rating scales offer a rapid, inexpensive method to quantitatively and qualitatively assess ADHD symptoms. Some of the scales are clinician-administered; others are designed for patient self-assessment.

Rating scales have added value when they are also completed by the patient's spouse, parent, or coworker. These tests are easy to administer and can be completed quickly. Of course, clinicians should not rely solely upon rating scales, but rather use them alongside a comprehensive clinical interview.

The most common rating systems used for adults are: the Conners' Adult ADHD Rating Scales (CAARS; a similar scale is available for patients younger than 18), the Brown Attention Deficit Disorder Rating Scale for Adults, the Brown ADD Scale, the Wender Utah Rating Scale (WURS), the Adult ADHD Self-Report Scale (ASRS) Symptom Checklist, and the Adult Self-Report Scale V1.1 Screener.

Conners' Adult ADHD Rating Scales

The Conners' Adult ADHD Rating Scales (CAARS) were developed by C. Keith Conners, Drew Erhardt, and Elizabeth Sparrow, and they are offered by Multi-Health Systems, Inc., in North Tonawanda, New York.

There are actually several Conners' scales, including one form that is administered by the clinician. Another scale is a self-rating completed by the patient, and another is completed by someone who knows the patient, such as a parent or spouse. The self-report and the observer versions of the scale are offered in screening, short, or long versions.

TABLE 1.2
COMMON ADHD RATING SCALES

Name of Scale	For Adolescents	For Adults	Self-rater	Clinician-administered	Other raters (Teachers, parents, spouses, etc.)
Adult Self-Report Scale-V.1.1 (ASRS-V.1.1) Screener		√	√		
Adult ADHD Self-Report Scale (ASRS) Symptom Checklist			√	√ (Clinician scores and interprets scores)	
Brown ADD Scale		√	√		
Brown Attention-Deficit Disorder (ADD) Rating Scale for Adults		√		√	
Brown Attention-Deficit Disorder Scales for Adolescents	√		√	√	
Conners' Adult ADHD Rating Scales (CAARS)	√	√	√	√	√
Conners-Wells Adolescent Self Report Scale	√		√		
Copeland Symptom Checklist for Adult ADHD		√	√		√
Current Symptoms Scale		√	√		√
Vanderbilt ADHD Diagnostic Teacher Rating Scale	√		√		√
Wender Utah Rating Scale	√ (To determine ADHD retrospectively in childhood)		√		

The CAARS rating scale that is completed by the clinician provides a framework from which information can be derived. For example, the first question is "What is going on in your life that leads you to believe you have attention-deficit/hyperactivity disorder or ADHD?" The scale asks questions about the patient's childhood history, temperament, academic achievement as a child and adult, interpersonal relationships, and past and current psychiatric problems.

The Conners' scale is most popularly used in clinical evaluation of ADHD children. They are used in some adult ADHD clinical trials but have not yet become the standard.

Brown Attention-Deficit Disorder (ADD) Rating Scale for Adults

The Brown Attention-Deficit Disorder (ADD) Rating Scale for Adults, developed by Thomas Brown and available through The Psychological Corporation in San Antonio, Texas, is another very useful assessment tool. This scale, which is administered by the physician, elicits responses about the patients' symptoms at work and school, as well as the patient's psychiatric and health history and the history of close relatives. It was created prior to the publication of the *DSM-IV* and emphasizes cognitive symptoms related to adults, such as the ability to maintain attention, cope with frustration, and draw upon memory.

Another scale, the Brown ADD Scale (also developed by Dr. Brown and available through The Psychological Corporation) may be given to patients to respond on their own. Many patients like the interactivity of answering questions on a form that they can then give to the physician. This form has 40 items such as "starts tasks (e.g., paperwork, chores) but doesn't complete them." Patients rank each item from 0 to 3, with 0 meaning "never," 1 meaning "once a week or less," 2 meaning "once a week or less," and 3 meaning "almost daily."

Wender Utah Rating Scale

Developed by psychiatrists Paul Wender and Fred W. Reimherr, the Wender Utah Rating Scale (WURS) is a retrospective tool to help the physician determine whether ADHD symptoms were present when the adult was a child. This is a self-rating scale with responses that range from 0 (not at all) to 4 (very much). There are 61 items such as "When you were a child, you were active, restless, always on the go, and sloppy, disorganized." The scale also has individuals evaluate themselves on childhood problems such as headaches, stomachaches, and school problems such as "slow in learning to read" and "bad handwriting." This scale has been validated as useful and reliable in research studies. It can be viewed online at www.add-pediatrics.com/add/wender.html.

The Adult ADHD Self-Report Scale-V1.1 (ASRS-V1.1) Screener and the Adult ADHD Self-Report Scale (ASRS) Symptom Checklist

The short self-rating form known as the Adult ADHD Self-Report Scale-V1.1 (ASRS-V1.1) Screener was created by the Workgroup on Adult ADHD, including Dr. Len Adler at New York University Medical School and Drs. Ronald Kessler and Thomas Spencer at Harvard Medical School. (See Appendix B.) With this scale, patients self-assess on items for inattention and hyperactivity/impulsivity and they evaluate themselves on a scale of 0 (never), 1 (rarely), 2 (sometimes), 3 (often), and 4 (very often). The scale has been validated as reliable in patients who were screened positive as having ADHD and who were subsequently diagnosed in a clinical setting.

Adler, Kessler, and Spencer wrote the ASRS-V1.1 Screener in language and context relevant to adults. "How often do you have trouble wrapping up the full details of a project, once the challenging parts have been done?" They eliminated "double barrel" questions so that each inquiry specifically addresses a particular symptom. "How often do you have problems remembering appointments or obligations?" is another question in this scale. (See Appendix B to view this instrument.) In addition, the Adult Self-Report Scale (ASRS) Symptom Checklist is a lengthier two-part self-rating instrument, also developed by Drs. Adler, Kessler, and Spencer. The patient fills out both Part A and Part B and gives the scale to the clinician for further evaluation. (See the Adult Self-Report Scale (ASRS) Symptom Checklist as well as the scoring key in Appendix C.)

Other ADHD Scales

There are a variety of other scales that are sometimes helpful in the diagnosis of adult ADHD. The Copeland Symptom Checklist for Adult ADHD helps to assess symptoms as well as the impact of these symptoms on the patient. The Current Symptoms Scale asks patients to self-assess their behavior for the past 6 months. This scale includes two versions, one for the patient and another for an "informant" (a friend, spouse, or parent), to enable the physician to corroborate the patient's self-evaluation.

There are also some ADHD rating scales specifically designed to be used with adolescents, including the Brown Attention-Deficit Disorder Scales for Adolescents, the Conners-Wells Adolescent Self-Report Scale, and the Vanderbilt ADHD Diagnostic Teaching Rating Scale.

Other rating scales are available online. The subscriber-only website myADHD.com offers symptom checklists for adults and other rating forms, such as a Child and Adolescent Developmental History form. Web MD has helpful scales as well.

Depression Scales

The Zung Depression Scale is a self-administered assessment of mood. The Zung consists of 20 questions and it can be expeditiously scored. The patient is asked about appetite changes, feelings of self-worth, and suicidal thoughts—issues that are often overlooked in an interview. The Hamilton Depression Scale (HDS) is more commonly used in research settings. Unlike the Zung Scale, the HDS is designed to be clinician-administered and tends to be time-consuming. Convenience may be the most important feature when selecting which outpatient screening test to use.

Anxiety Scales

Anxiety disorders coexist with ADHD 25–50% of the time and should be identified early in the diagnostic process. Anxiety disorders can be screened using the MINI Patient Health Survey. The MINI is an abbreviated self-administered test that can be completed in less than 5 minutes. Patients are asked about symptoms of common anxiety conditions including panic disorder and social anxiety disorder. The same questionnaire assesses alcohol dependency and depression. For each disorder the MINI starts with a screening question. If the patient answers "no" to the questions, that particular diagnosis can be ruled out and the patient can proceed to questions for the next disorder (Sheehan et al., 1997).

EDUCATIONAL VIDEOS

Good clinical interviewing, the use of rating scales, and an ability to detect atypical ADHD presentations all contribute to accurate diagnosis. That said, the better informed a patient is, the easier it is for the clinician to obtain a full history. Several educational videos describe ADHD and feature personal accounts of adolescents and adults who have struggled with the condition (Young, 2005).

A valid diagnosis is essential in order to help the patient, and this chapter has covered the key elements of diagnosing ADHD, including considering the *DSM* criteria for ADHD, determining why the patient is in the office and actively listening to and observing the patient, asking targeted questions, taking a medical and psychosocial history, ordering laboratory tests to screen for potential mimicking disorders (such as thyroid disease), and using rating scales for ADHD, depression and anxiety.

Chapter 2

Coping With Comorbidities in Diagnosis and Treatment

PATIENTS WHO HAVE RESPONDED only minimally to therapeutic treatments for depression, anxiety, and many other disorders often have untreated ADHD. Conversely, patients with ADHD may not respond sufficiently to ADHD medications alone if they have a comorbid disorder. Often ADHD is the primary problem in comorbid conditions, but a careful identification of all major contributors to the patient's difficulties is needed for the best patient outcome. When ADHD appears to be at the core of the patient's problems, it usually needs to be treated first, followed by treatment for other comorbidities. This chapter discusses the prevalence of common comorbid conditions, methods of diagnosis, and techniques to sequence the course of treatment interventions.

Diagnosing ADHD and its comorbidities is comparable to manipulating a child's plastic toy: Inside a large egg is a smaller one, inside that egg is one even smaller. Until the therapist finally reaches the core—the smallest "egg" around which all the larger ones rest—the diagnostic and therapeutic job is not complete.

Preexisting ADHD predisposes adults to other conditions like anxiety, depression, and even personality disorders. Mental health clinicians should assess each symptom carefully, but in complicated comorbid cases, many professionals minimize the presence of ADHD. Using an "ADHD first" model, the clinician will discover that the true driver of psychiatric pathology may be different from what is usually considered.

Quite simply, the majority of patients with ADHD have cooccurring psychiatric conditions. In adolescents and adults, the development of an episode of anxiety or depression is among the most common reasons that ADHD is ultimately revealed. Usually the depression or anxiety is discovered and treated first, and only after further probing is the presence of ADHD revealed as well. In such cases, ADHD is not treated first, but at least it is eventually treated.

Assessing ADHD comorbidities requires an appreciation of common signs and symptoms and an understanding of the relative frequency of the likely suspects. For the clinician, this takes diagnostic skill, careful analytical thinking, and sometimes trial and error. Clinicians should sequence their treatment interventions based on when the comorbid symptoms present, how frequent these symptoms are, and how significantly they impair the patient's functioning.

Many patients with ADHD are comorbid for the following diagnoses: major depression, one or more anxiety disorders, bipolar disorder, antisocial personality disorder, oppositional defiant disorder (ODD), conduct disorder, and substance use disorders (covered in Chapter 8). In addition, some patients with ADHD also suffer from a chronic pain condition, such as fibromyalgia, chronic fatigue syndrome, or migraine headaches (covered in Chapter 11). Furthermore, some ADHD patients have comorbid eating disorders, such as bulimia nervosa or binge eating disorder. Patients with untreated ADHD may also have significantly greater difficulty with obesity and achieving weight loss than individuals without ADHD. Other ADHD patients struggle with learning disabilities.

Clinicians need to actively identify and address comorbidities early in the diagnostic process; untreated, these comorbidities will complicate and compromise outcome. In doing so, clinicians must appreciate the chronological progression of ADHD. Symptoms are typically first evident in latency-aged children, sometimes earlier. The core symptoms of distractibility and inattention compromise the developing child's ability to process information and accurately interpret the environment. During these crucial developmental years, children with undiagnosed ADHD often perform beneath expected levels both academically and interpersonally. It follows that anxiety (in the form of hypervigilance and ruminative thoughts) and depression (characterized by frustration and hopelessness) can result from childhood ADHD. The sum total of these multiple issues can negatively affect the patient throughout life if not diagnosed and treated.

Unfortunately, few psychiatric conditions have a proof-positive blood test and no patient comes equipped with an owner's manual. Symptoms overlap and diagnostic boundaries quickly blur. Although insurance companies demand that diagnosticians reduce symptom complexes into set categories, these distinctions are in fact manmade and quite arbitrary, even if they are helpful as guidelines. They are unhelpful when they are slavishly followed.

PREVALENCE OF COMORBIDITIES WITH ADHD

According to research on the comorbidity of ADHD and other psychiatric diagnoses, the lifetime prevalence of a variety of comorbidities among adults who have ADHD is significantly higher than among control individuals without ADHD (Biederman, 2004). For example, in Biederman's study of adult women with ADHD, the lifetime prevalence for multiple anxiety disorders (2 or more) was 52%. The prevalence was roughly 15% in women without ADHD. Similarly, 46% of men with ADHD had an anxiety disorder—36% more than nonafflicted controls. Table 2.1 details the most common lifetime comorbid conditions for adults with ADHD.

GETTING THE DIAGNOSIS RIGHT

Seeing a psychiatrist can be an ignominious experience for many patients. Waits are long, fees are high, and patients have to endure the bias against

TABLE 2.1
Common Lifetime Comorbid Conditions for Adults with ADHD

	Females With ADHD	Females Without ADHD	Males With ADHD	Males Without ADHD
Multiple anxiety disorders	52%	15%	46%	10%
Major depression	36%	6%	27%	4%
Antisocial personality disorder	7%	2%	17%	4%
Oppositional defiant disorder	27%	2%	32%	3%
Bipolar disorder	10%	3%	14%	4%
Drug dependence	19%	4%	28%	8%
Alcohol Dependence	19%	6%	34%	22%
Enuresis (bedwetting)	29%	3%	28%	14%

Adapted from Biederman, Joseph, M.D., "Impact of Comorbidity in Adults with Attention Deficit/Hyperactivity Disorder," *Journal of Clinical Psychiatry 65*, supplement 3 (2004): 5.

going to a "shrink." The clinician should appreciate the obstacles that patients face and recognize that their very presence in the waiting room already involves a high level of discomfort. "Distressed" patients can have any number of psychiatric symptoms: ADHD, psychosis, depression, anxiety, inattention, fatigue, substance abuse, behavioral disorders, dementia, or most likely, a combination of the above. Clinics specializing in one particular condition should not limit their purview to the favored diagnosis. The objective clinician should be open to *all* diagnostic options in the distressed patient.

Medical students are universally taught that "all that wheezes is not asthma." Psychiatry should extend this wisdom to include "all that is sad is not depression" and "all that is a mood swing is not bipolar disorder." Accurate diagnosis is paramount. In many offices, patients with ADHD may resemble typical patients with clinical depression; they may appear hopeless and despondent, but this distress, in fact, may be dejection that is associated with carrying the burden of ADHD for so many years.

IDENTIFYING COMORBIDITIES CAN BE CHALLENGING

Consider Bonnie, an agitated young patient who constantly blurted out comments and writhed about in her chair during her evaluation. She was easily irritated and appeared moody. At an ADHD clinic, Bonnie might have been viewed as hyperactive; a center specializing in mood disorders might have seen her as demonstrating manic behavior consistent with bipolar disorder. The truth may be that Bonnie had *both* ADHD and a mood disorder. If so, treatment for the ADHD alone would provide some level of mood elevation, but Bonnie would be unlikely to obtain maximum benefit unless the mood symptoms were specifically addressed.

ADHD With and Without Comorbidities

Psychiatry cannot readily be reduced to simple charts; however, Table 2.2 may help illustrate some key points about ADHD with or without comorbidities. In this chart, it is assumed that the patient does meet the criteria for ADHD.

KEY QUESTIONS CLINICIANS SHOULD ASK THEMSELVES IN DIAGNOSIS

Clinicians need to ask themselves the following questions to help with teasing out comorbidities that are present with the patient's primary problem:

- When did the key symptoms present and how frequent are they?
- Do these symptoms impede functioning?
- When there are multiple symptoms, which symptoms bother the patient most?
- Could these symptoms fit the criteria for two or more diagnoses?
- How was the patient treated for these symptoms in the past?

When did symptoms present and how frequent are they? It is important to consider *when* comorbid symptoms were initially apparent and whether they were and still are intermittent or chronic problems. For example,

TABLE 2.2
Considering ADHD and Comorbid Conditions

ADHD Alone	*ADHD With a Comorbid Condition*
Patient is occasionally moody or sad.	Patient has a frequent or constant pattern of depressed mood or depressed mood alternating with excessively elevated mood. Consider depression or bipolar disorder.
Patient is distressed about constantly losing items.	Patient is panicked over lost items and repeatedly remonstrates self as being stupid or useless. Consider anxiety disorder or depression.
Patient is reluctant or refuses to try new therapies or medications and argues with the therapist that they won't work.	Patient may be overcautious. If an adolescent, patient may have oppositional defiant disorder *or* may be resistant to authority, as many adolescents are.
Patient cannot pay attention in school or at business meetings.	Patient has particular trouble with math or reading skills in addition to inattention. Consider a learning disorder.
Patient regularly uses caffeine or nicotine.	Patient actively seeks out illicit substances to the extent that the use interferes with daily functioning. Consider a substance use disorder.

patients with ADHD alone have inattentive or hyperactivity symptoms that are traceable to their youth, but they have not demonstrated noteworthy depressive symptoms. In contrast, patients who suffer from ADHD and comorbid depression typically have ADHD symptoms that are longstanding and depressive symptoms that wax and wane for many years.

In most comorbid cases, ADHD symptoms become more apparent and prominent during periods of depression. Thus, preexisting ADHD is more likely to be to be overlooked if depressive episodes are infrequent. When a depression is unrelenting, the consideration of ADHD is usually only entertained after the patient has been through many different and usually unsuccessful antidepressant treatment regimens. Accordingly, clinicians should consider ADHD immediately for all patients who complain of depression, as ADHD is so commonly a concurrent issue.

Do these symptoms impede functioning? In order to sequence treatment, it is essential for the clinician to determine if the symptoms affect the patient's functioning at work as well as school and/or home. Patients with ADHD are impeded in all settings of their daily lives. If the symptoms *are* seriously impeding the patient's functioning, the clinician's next step is to determine their level of severity—in other words, to what extent the symptoms have an impact on the patient's ability to succeed in these areas.

For example, if the patient is typically hopeless, distractible, forgetful, *and* cannot perform her job, she may have a mood disorder and possibly ADHD as well. The clinician then must determine which problem to address first. Often antidepressant medications will improve the patient's mood and cognitive symptoms. If the distractibility and amotivation persists, the ADHD symptoms can be treated with gusto.

When there are multiple symptoms, which symptoms bother the patient most? Sometimes cognitive symptoms severely impede the patient, and if so, these are the treatment priority. For example, if a college student presents for treatment because she is disconsolate about her academic woes and exhibits some dysthymia, but her examination uncovers normal intelligence and a history of inattentiveness and impaired concentration, early treatment with ADHD medications may be preferable to treatment for depression.

In another situation, if a patient who clearly has symptoms of ADHD expresses extreme despair or suicidality, the depression needs to be addressed first, followed by ADHD treatment.

Could these symptoms fit the criteria for two or more diagnoses? Sometimes patients are hyperactive, restless, and agitated and the mental health professional needs to consider ADHD as well as an anxiety disorder, bipolar disorder, or other possible diagnoses. This can be a tricky process, because it is often difficult to distinguish core ADHD symptoms from the secondary issues that frequently result from a lifetime of inattention, distractibility, impulsivity, and hyperactivity. The key is to determine the most likely prevailing and distressing problem and treat it first.

How was the patient treated in the past? The patient's past treatment, rather than an abstract treatment algorithm, should drive the order of intervention. Many patients have already had trials of antidepressants. If the antidepressant did not remedy the patient's inattention and distractibility, there is no need for another expert to repeat the earlier failed experience, especially when ADHD is the primary diagnosis. Proceeding directly with a stimulant or atomoxetine is worthwhile, such as when the patient has the capability to do better work in school and pass classes, and the depression may abate. An antidepressant may be added to treat depressive symptoms if ADHD treatment alone is insufficient.

ADHD AND DEPRESSION

Frequently patients have both a depressive disorder and ADHD. Often, the clinician diagnoses and treats one of the conditions while the comorbidity goes unrecognized—sometimes for a very long time (Levin & Evans, 2001). This was the case with Nancy.

Nancy

Nancy, age 44, had been struggling for years. She frequently felt rejected, and her tears flowed at the slightest provocation. Nancy had been married for seventeen years, but she had now little libido and avoided intimate contact with her husband, Michael. Despite consuming large amounts of coffee and cola, she was always tired. In the past few years, Nancy had gained weight and returned to regular nicotine use. She smoked surreptitiously because her family objected to this habit, and she had tried and failed to quit smoking many times. The couple presented for treatment because of marital tension; Michael had distanced himself and felt alienated. He had engaged in two affairs in the past 3 years and freely reported that his wife's self-defeating behaviors repulsed him.

Nancy recounted that she was tempestuous in grade school and rebellious as a teenager. In her first year of college, Nancy's parents announced their divorce, and she aborted an unwanted pregnancy from a brief relationship. The next year she became romantically involved with a woman.

During this time, provoked by periods of extreme worry and depression, Nancy began superficially cutting herself on her arms and inner thigh.

When her counselor discovered the cutting behavior, Nancy was psychiatrically hospitalized. Afterwards, she became involved with a group therapy for survivors of childhood sexual abuse. Prior to the group experience, Nancy had no memories of any mistreatment during her childhood. Although Nancy had never previously spoken about any mistreatment in the past, within 2 months of starting the group she dramatically accused her father of sexual abuse and blamed her mother for failing to protect her. This "revelation" alienated her from her parents, but the camaraderie of the group fortified her.

During her late twenties, Nancy left her girlfriend, after which she met and then married Michael. She reestablished a relationship with her parents after conceding that the memories of childhood abuse were implanted during her earlier individual and group therapy. Nancy's life settled down in the first years of the marriage until the birth of her second child, when Nancy again became depressed. At her obstetrician's urging, Nancy sought therapy and was diagnosed with postpartum depression. Three weeks after starting sertraline (Zoloft), she noted that her crying bouts were fewer and her suicidal thoughts had abated, but she remained fatigued and unmotivated. She did little outside her home and performed the bare minimum for her young children. Her doctor increased the antidepressant dose, but Nancy noticed little added benefit. Over the next few months, other antidepressants gave similar underwhelming results.

Because of her apparent treatment-resistant depression, Nancy was referred to a depression research center for enrollment in an antidepressant clinical trial. There the psychiatrist confirmed that while Nancy's tearfulness had diminished, her energy was still low and her long-standing complaints about impaired memory, focus, and concentration remained. With Nancy's permission, the psychiatrist confirmed his findings with her family. The doctor diagnosed ADHD combined type and comorbid depression. Adderall XR was added to her current antidepressant, duloxetine (Cymbalta).

This medication combination proved to be effective. Nancy noted improved mood and increased energy. She cared for her children with greater ease. She no longer took daytime naps, and she began volunteering at her church. The Adderall decreased her appetite, and she also was motivated to exercise. As she lost weight, Nancy noticed a burgeoning sex drive, and her ability to initiate intimacy with Michael improved their overall relationship. Two years later, on the same medication regimen, Nancy's improvements were sustained.

Is ADHD a Factor in Treatment-Resistant Depression?

Nancy's case clearly illustrates that in depressed patients who are comorbid for ADHD, treating only the depression is inadequate. Standard treatment protocols exist to help clinicians negotiate this clinical conundrum. Interestingly, stimulants are recommended (late in the treatment process) as a way to potentiate the antidepressants, not as a treatment for comorbid ADHD.

Various studies show the cooccurrence of ADHD and depression to be 20–40% (Alpert, Maddocks, Nierenberg, O'Sullivan, Pava, Worthington, et al., 1996). My colleagues and I tried to answer the next logical question: What is the rate of ADHD in patients who failed a previous trial of antidepressants? This question essentially asks whether ADHD plays a role in treatment-resistant depression (TRD).

We recruited 40 patients who had at least one failed trial of antidepressant medications. The patients agreed to taper off their current treatment and take fluoxetine (Prozac) up to 40 mg/day. If their depressive symptoms responded in 6 weeks, they left the trial. The majority of patients did not improve and proceeded into the active phase of the trial. Here, half the patients received fluoxetine and Concerta and the other half received fluoxetine and placebo (Young, Amann, & Lenhardt, 2006).

After 8 weeks, both groups improved and no statistical difference between the two groups was found using the Hamilton Depression Scale. On a scale measuring quality of life however, the group treated with Concerta and fluoxetine reported greater satisfaction compared to the group treated with fluoxetine alone. The authors of the study said they suspected that a larger study may reveal an additive antidepressant effect (Young, Amann, & Lenhardt, 2006).

Perhaps the most important finding of the study was that 55% of the treatment resistant group met criteria for ADHD. In the control group, individuals without a known history of previous depression, only 12% had ADHD. Treatment-resistant depression is an area of intense interest and the central contribution that ADHD plays will certainly become recognized.

ADHD AND ANXIETY DISORDERS

Anxiety disorders are often linked to ADHD, based on research studies and the observations of many clinicians. In a study of 134 Canadian school-aged children, 11.2% of those with ADHD had obsessive-compulsive behaviors (a less impairing variation of obsessive-compulsive disorder) compared to less than 5% of the general population (Arnold, Ickowitz, Chen, & Schachar, 2005). Although this study was limited to children, it is also relevant to adolescents and adults with ADHD, as childhood anxiety conditions often extend into adolescence and adulthood. In one report, 20% of generalized anxiety disorder patients had ADHD (Fones, Pollack, Susswein, & Otto, 2000). Panic disorder has also been linked to adult ADHD.

Many of the same arguments about the central role that ADHD plays in depressive conditions apply to anxiety as well. Unlike depression, however, anxiety may paradoxically benefit the ADHD patient. Perfectionism is culturally valued in the United States, and constantly losing one's possessions or being unable to be punctual or stay on task is often considered unacceptable. To combat their inherent distractibility, the young person with ADHD can develop a heightened self-awareness (generalized anxiety) that can transform into personality rigidity or obsessive-compulsive behavior. As a result, the development of anxiety may be adaptive. Caring deeply enough about one's own deficiencies to alter behavior may be preferable to not having awareness of one's deficiencies and not caring at all.

Dana

Dana, a 33-year-old woman, presented in panic, overwhelmed with the criticisms from her new boss. She had symptoms of intense worry and feelings of doom. Her last three jobs had ended unhappily, and Dana dreaded the possibility of being fired again.

Dana's previous clinician had diagnosed and treated her for anxiety and had prescribed benzodiazepines (Valium-like agents) to quickly help Dana through a period of intense anxiety.

However, several key factors that were integral to Dana's diagnosis and treatment had been ignored in the past until she sought an evaluation from a new clinician; for example, the fact that Dana was always tardy, that she struggled mightily to master new tasks, and that her work performance was so deficient that she had been terminated from her last three jobs had never been considered as relevant factors. As a result, her prior diagnosis of anxiety disorder was not wrong, but it was insufficient.

A new comprehensive psychiatric history and the use of screening tests revealed that Dana was comorbid for *both* ADHD and generalized anxiety disorder. Like many with ADHD, Dana demonstrated stress intolerance in response to her long-standing problems with learning new routines, staying on task, and managing her time.

Focalin XR, an extended-release form of methylphenidate, was added to Dana's antianxiety medication and this combination allowed her to transition successfully into the new job. Her anxiety persisted however, and she became tolerant to the benzodiazepine dose. Her doctor introduced Celexa, a selective serotonin reuptake inhibitor (SSRI), but the sexual side effects of the drug quickly became intolerable. Atomoxetine (Strattera) was substituted for both agents and Dana sustained her improvement.

ADHD AND BIPOLAR DISORDER

Bipolar disorder consists of periodic mood swings. An estimated 1–2% of the adult population suffers from bipolar disorder, and of this population, 5–15% have rapid cycling of their moods. Bipolar disorder and ADHD share common features, and sometimes the diagnoses are confused. It is also possible for the patient to have *both* ADHD and bipolar disorder.

These common features of both ADHD and bipolar disorder are:

- Mood lability
- Bursts of energy
- Restlessness

- Talkativeness
- Racing thoughts
- Impatience
- Impulsivity
- Impaired judgment
- Irritability

Forms of Bipolar Disorder

Bipolar disorder has two variations, Type I and Type II. Type I is more severe; patients have alternating periods of normal mood (euthymia), depression, and mania. Manic episodes can be quite dramatic, and they are the distinguishing feature of bipolar disorder Type I. Manic episodes last from days to weeks and are characterized by severe racing thoughts, sleep disturbances, and impaired social judgment. In the most extreme circumstances of Type I mania, patients can be floridly psychotic. Depressive episodes inevitably follow, and they are clinically similar to unipolar depression.

Bipolar disorder Type II also includes mood episodes, but each phase is less severe than in Type I. Type II patients may become sad, but not hopeless; depressed, but not suicidal. Hypomanic patients have an inflated sense of self-importance, but not the outrageous grandiosity or psychosis seen with mania.

Differences Between ADHD and Bipolar Disorder

There are important differences between bipolar disorder and ADHD (Table 2.3). In general, ADHD has an earlier age of onset (childhood) compared to bipolar disorder (adolescence or adulthood). ADHD symptoms remain constant, rather than occurring episodically, as with bipolar disorder. ADHD is a problem of cognitive functioning; it is associated with learning disabilities and problems with processing new information and storing short-term memory. Cognitive difficulties are not linked to bipolar disorder. By estimates, ADHD is two to four times more common than bipolar disorder (Scheffer & Niskala Apps, 2005).

TABLE 2.3
Differences in Signs and Symptoms of ADHD and Bipolar Disorder

	ADHD Alone	*Bipolar Disorder Alone*
Hyperactivity	If present, a constant problem	Appear hyperactive only during mania
Mood swings	Rapid and brief but not severe	Mood swings last days to weeks
Difficulty with concentration	Constant problem	Intermittent problem
Euphoric moods	Not present	Present with mania
Delusions	Not present	May present with mania
Chronic irritability	Usually not present	Present
Frequently losing items	Common	Not common
Hallucinations	Not present	May occur with mania
Sleep disturbances	Chronic periods of insomnia and/or hypersomnia	Insomnia common in manic periods, rarely insomnia
Disorganization	A key and persistent feature	Not common unless patient is manic
Distractibility	A key and persistent feature	Not common unless patient is manic
Grandiosity	Not present	Common, especially during manic episodes
Self-esteem	Usually poor	Inappropriately high during manic periods
Racing thoughts	Often chronically present	Present, especially during manic episode
Impulsivity	Common feature	Present only during manic episodes
High-risk behaviors	May occur, but reason generally prevails	Present during mania, when risks may be extreme and life-threatening

During the manic phase, bipolar patients can suddenly develop a markedly decreased need for sleep. In contrast, adolescents and adults with ADHD may have trouble falling asleep, but once they overcome their initial insomnia, they generally sleep normally for 6 to 8 hours. Actively manic patients have irregular and very short sleep durations, sometimes not more than an hour or two at a time.

One of the characteristics of hyperactivity is excessive talking. However, manic patients can display pressured and rapid-fire speech, sometimes so rapid that others cannot follow them. With mania, periods of excessive talking occur intermittently, but the hyperactive ADHD patient is chronically verbose.

Many patients with ADHD have lifelong struggles that often result in low self-esteem; they tend to underestimate their own abilities and potential. In contrast, grandiosity is synonymous with the manic phase of bipolar disorder.

Distinguishing bipolar disorder from ADHD is one of the most important determinations in the diagnostic workup. Whereas clinicians may overemphasize ADHD in children (to the exclusion of bipolarity), with adults, many psychiatrists are more comfortable with the bipolar diagnosis. Even clinicians without diagnostic bias may find it hard to tell them apart. Nevertheless, because of the broad area of overlap, both ADHD and bipolar disorder should both be considered either alone or comorbidly in this patient population.

Medication for ADHD With Bipolar Disorder

Unless there is an active substance use disorder, patients who are comorbid for both ADHD and bipolar disorder, especially those with recent or current manic symptoms, should receive medications that stabilize mood. Divalproex sodium (Depakote) is frequently used. Lithium carbonate, carbamazepine (Equatrol), oxcarbazapine (Trileptal), and lamotrigine (Lamictal) are alternative choices, but none has been comprehensively researched for ADHD/bipolar comorbidity.

In my experience, ADHD/bipolar patients with stabilized mania can safely be given stimulant medications. Treating ADHD symptoms increases compliance for bipolar medications and gives the patient greater insight into nascent mania. Some clinicians believe that atomoxetine (Strattera) can destabilize manic patients in a manner not seen with stimulants (Patel & Sallee, 2005). However, this conclusion is based on a small sample and should not be overinterpreted.

Robert

Robert, age 47, presented with a primary complaint of depression. A military veteran, Robert had been diagnosed with bipolar Type II in the Veterans Administration (VA) system 9 years ago, but he did not receive a service-connected disability. Since his military discharge, he had been unable to hold a job. When he worked, he was often late or called in sick. When he did show up, his work quality was inconsistent—sometimes excellent and sometimes poor. Eventually he was either fired from a job or quit because he was bored.

Robert's personal relationships were also troubled. He had been divorced twice and had experienced a series of tumultuous relationships. His parents and sisters were angry at him because he had been arrested for hitting his wife while abusing alcohol.

Robert seemed sincere in his desire to secure help. Past physicians who had diagnosed him with bipolar disorder had treated him with the mood stabilizing agents lithium and divalproex sodium (Depakote). He noted no benefits with lithium, and the Depakote made his hair fall out. He had tried a course of antipsychotic medication but gained considerable weight and felt no better. Most recently, he had been taking lamotrigine (Lamictal), which calmed him and stabilized his mood swings but did not improve his lackluster motivation or his ability to start and finish projects.

While in the psychiatrist's office, Robert mentioned that his 11-year-old son had recently been diagnosed with ADHD and was having a favorable response to Metadate CD. Aware that ADHD often runs in families, the doctor suggested reevaluating Robert, this time giving him specific ADHD screening forms. The doctor found that Robert met the criteria for ADHD (hyperactive-impulsive subtype). He added atomoxetine (Strattera), a nonstimulant medication specifically approved for the treatment of ADHD, to Robert's lamotrigine.

Within weeks, Robert noticed a significant improvement. He was less easily provoked to anger and his impulsivity decreased. He was able to concentrate better, even on mundane tasks he would have never been able to continue in the recent past. He obtained a job and his employer was satisfied with his work. His relationship with his children improved considerably. Robert continued to improve for the next several months and even his skeptical family conceded that, after 6 months of treatment, he was performing better than in a long time. Robert's comorbidity of bipolar disorder and ADHD had troubled him for years, but at last he had gained the proper treatment.

ADHD AND MOOD LABILITY, INTERMITTENT EXPLOSIVE DISORDER, AND BORDERLINE PERSONALITY DISORDER

Some patients with ADHD overreact to social rejection or to even minor criticisms from others. In response to a rebuke, some respond with rage. Later, after the mood storm has passed, these patients may be genuinely perplexed about why others are resentful, angry, and wary of them, as they feel the problem is completely over. Therapists can help these patients recognize the effects of their rage on others, but often this insight is short-lived. Without frequent redirection, impulsive patients will fail to see the extent of the problem (or even minimize it), let alone endeavor to solve it.

Frequently, presentations of this type of mood instability may persuade the therapist that the patient has borderline personality disorder or intermittent explosive disorder. Treatment for intermittent explosive disorder usually demands a full neurological evaluation, including imaging the brain to rule out a temporal lobe brain tumor or lesion. Even if the neurological workup is negative, the patient is often placed on antiseizure medications.

These patients should be evaluated for ADHD hyperactive-impulsive type superimposed on a comorbid mood disorder, and treatment should include stimulants or atomoxetine. Antidepressants can modulate the patient's mood lability. Psychotherapy with a therapist knowledgeable about ADHD can allow patients to develop insights that are more valid.

ADHD AND ANTISOCIAL PERSONALITY DISORDERS, CONDUCT DISORDER, AND OPPOSITIONAL DEFIANT DISORDER

Stealing, vandalizing, and assaulting others are elements of ODD, conduct disorder, and antisocial personality disorder. These diagnoses are defined by the actions of individuals rather than by their symptoms or signs. Many individuals committing these acts come to the attention of law enforcement authorities and incarceration is not uncommon. The conditions are very often comorbid with ADHD.

In children and adolescents with these comorbidities, researchers have found that methylphenidate improves the oppositional and aggressive behavior as well as the ADHD symptoms. The addition of clonidine may be effective in decreasing aggressive tendencies. Therapy may also be helpful (Connor, Barkley, & Davis, 2000).

ADHD AND EATING DISORDERS

Some evidence indicates that patients with ADHD may also be more prone to eating disorders, such as binge eating disorder and bulimia nervosa. The National Institute of Mental Health reports that up to 5% of all adults in the United States have binge eating disorder. According to the National Institute of Mental Health, binge eating disorder is characterized by three or more of the following behaviors:

- Eating much faster than usual
- Eating that continues after the person is full
- Eating when the person is not hungry
- Eating that occurs when the person is alone, due to embarrassment over the large quantity of food consumed
- Feelings of self-disgust, depression, or guilt after overeating

In one published study, researchers treated six ADHD/bulimic patients with dextroamphetamine. Dramatically, the bingeing and purging behavior stopped (Dukarm, 2005). In five of the six cases, the patients had not previously been diagnosed with ADHD.

A study of 215 obese patients, Altfas (2002) described the universal difficulty many of the patients had losing weight. Notably, 27.4% of the patients studied had ADHD. Nearly half of the *severely* obese patients (42.6%) had ADHD.

Compared to their non-ADHD peers, obese patients with ADHD symptoms had significantly greater difficulty succeeding in a weight-loss clinic. Non-ADHD patients with the most severe form of obesity lost twice as much weight as the patients with ADHD symptoms. The failure at weight loss was not due to a lack of trying to lose weight: The patients with ADHD symptoms had gone to the weight-loss clinic more frequently and for longer periods than their peers. According to Altfas (2002, p. 7), the high prevalence of ADHD in obese and especially extremely obese individuals argues "that comorbid ADHD increases the health risks of obesity, and that extreme obesity, itself a stressful condition, adds burden to the profound impairments common in ADHD."

Binge eaters have some features in common with those with ADHD. Both groups perceive their world to be highly stressful. When asked about their behavior, many patients report that the bingeing is impulsive and sometimes spontaneously occurs in response to an upsetting event. Binge eaters are often highly distracted by food, and for some, the sight of a chocolate cake or another favorite food leads to the urgent desire to feed. The exact relationship between binge eating and ADHD is not established, but patients with ADHD are known to be at risk for overeating and obesity. In the extreme, patients may develop purging and advance to bulimia nervosa.

The role of stimulants for obesity treatment is checkered. In the past, the appetite-suppressing effects of stimulants were exploited, but their safety was questioned as individuals developed abuse and tolerance.

The true utility of stimulants in obese ADHD patients may be that they decrease impulsive overeating, motivate patients to exercise more regularly, and help them stick to a rational diet. Although stimulants do carry a minimal risk, especially among those with hypertension, cardiac disease, and type 2 diabetes, the ominous complications of obesity carry a larger risk. Stimulants are also less invasive than gastric bypass surgery, itself a nonreversible and risky procedure.

Some studies have shown efficacy with methylphenidate in treating bulimia nervosa and binge eating disorder. Other studies have shown the antidepressants citalopram (Celexa) and bupropion (Wellbutrin), as well as the novel antiepileptic topiramate (Topamax), to be effective in treating binge eating disorder (McElroy, 2003).

ADHD AND LEARNING DISABILITIES

Learning disabilities are deficits in acquiring reading, writing, mathematical, and listening skills. Learning disabilities are brain-based difficulties, usually genetic and most likely resulting from errors in the brain's hardwiring. The field of learning disabilities is a burgeoning one, and most research currently centers on school-age children. Few studies have followed the natural progression of learning disorders through the life cycle, and most psychiatrists treating adults do not assess for the condition at all. Adolescents with learning disabilities are much more likely to have school and interpersonal problems than others; they constitute nearly 40% of all high school dropouts (Kaplan & Sadock, 2003). As with ADHD, learning disabilities do not disappear simply because a person becomes an adolescent or adult. They still impair and impede individuals, especially at work, unless they receive useful assistance from others.

Reading disorders, sometimes referred to as dyslexia, may explain a patient's academic delays. Individuals with these types of verbal learning disorders are at greater risk for depression, anxiety, and ADHD. As many as 25% of children with reading disorders have ADHD. Students with mathematics disorders may have problems solving the most basic calculations.

The *DSM-IV* does not formally categorize nonverbal learning disorders (NVLDs), yet these problems are present in 5–10% of children with learning disabilities. NVLDs include such diverse deficits as impaired social skills, below-normal mathematical ability, and problems with organization. Many of these individuals have average to excellent verbal skills but have poor hand-eye coordination. Patients with NVLDs often misread social cues and may appear awkward with peers, a problem particularly evident in adolescence. This group is at increased risk of developing anxiety and depression (Reiff, 2005).

Patients identified with learning disabilities may benefit from occupational therapy, social skills groups, and alterations to the school curriculum. Inattention is common in most learning disabilities, but the patient may not have other ADHD symptoms. Individuals with learning disabilities are commonly misdiagnosed as having ADHD; this is one of the most common reasons for ADHD medication failure.

Although learning disabilities and ADHD are distinct clinical entities, they often coexist. When ADHD is comorbid, conventional treatment improves both symptom complexes.

Andrew

Andrew, a quiet and tentative 25-year-old, presented at the insistence of his parents. For the past 2 years, Andrew had worked a solitary job, picking up clinical samples from dental offices. His parents were concerned that Andrew was stagnating.

Andrew's psychologist elicited an extensive history. In elementary school, Andrew was fearful and preferred to stay home rather than play with friends. Throughout school, he struggled academically and was socially ostracized. He was perpetually unkempt, his hair was a bit greasy, and he seemed to react slowly in conversation. These traits made him an easy target for bullies.

Testing revealed Andrew's full-scale IQ to be average at 101, but subtests showed that his verbal IQ (a measure of language ability) was considerably higher than his performance IQ (a measure of the ability to use one's knowledge). He was diagnosed with a nonverbal learning disability and ADHD predominately inattentive type.

For several months, Andrew attended a social skills group for young adults. This experience provided a sense of camaraderie. The group leader modeled appropriate interpersonal behavior and Andrew benefited. Several months later a doctor introduced modafinil (Provigil) to Andrew's treatment. "My eyes opened up," Andrew reflected. "For the first time I could concentrate on what people said to me. I didn't have to pause as long when I heard something for the first time."

Both Andrew's group leader and his mother also noticed improvement. "Andrew seems to care more. I don't think he is as oblivious to what is going on around him. He remembers to wash his face before he leaves the house." His therapist offered that on medications, Andrew remembered fellow group member's names and was able to initiate conversations.

ADHD Medications May Help With Learning Disabilities

ADHD medications play a role in traditional learning disabilities as well. A child struggling with dyslexia will surely benefit if he can patiently sit and try to decipher the sentence structure. Students with both math learning disabilities and ADHD will still transpose numbers and be stumped about the order of mathematical functions, but they will find more success if their mind is not wandering during class. With treatment, they are less likely to rush through and arrive at the wrong answer. ADHD medications will not always be helpful for learning disabilities or learning disabilities comorbid with ADHD, but the potential benefits of these medications far exceed any risk.

Although adolescent and adult patients may be initially euphoric to discover that undiagnosed ADHD or learning disabilities largely contributed to their school problems in the past, their reaction is often bittersweet. They are gratified to learn they are not "stupid," but they are often angry that their teachers or other professionals did not explore the possibility of ADHD or learning disabilities in the face of their school failure. These feelings are valid to work through with the assistance of a psychologist.

WHEN THREE OR MORE COMORBIDITIES ARE PRESENT WITH ADHD

Some patients with ADHD have multiple comorbidities. It is not uncommon to find an adult patient with all of the following diagnoses: ADHD, bipolar disorder, generalized anxiety disorder, chronic fatigue syndrome, and a histrionic personality disorder. When sequencing treatment, be sure to identify the conditions that are most long-standing and most severe, and then make a clinical judgment about which diagnosis to address first.

Often one medication can suffice for two different diagnoses. For example, in the extreme case of the patient with ADHD, bipolar disorder, generalized anxiety disorder, chronic fatigue syndrome, and a histrionic personality disorder, a clinician could prescribe a long-acting stimulant. Lamictal could stabilize the patient's mood as well as treat the problem with fatigue. The mood stabilizer could be followed by an antidepressant. Modafinil (Provigil) might address low energy. Psychotherapy with a trained clinician might diminish the patient's theatrical behavior.

Potential side effects must be considered when sorting out the best medications for comorbid disorders. Clinicians need to be cautious about propelling mania with antidepressants in bipolar patients. Many women and most patients with binge eating disorders will resist medications that may cause weight gain. Conversely, adolescent boys wanting to fill out their frame may object to the anorectic effects of stimulants. Few patients want antidepressants to decrease their libido, but some will enjoy their enhanced staying powers.

Compliance is paramount, as is explaining to patients that the effects may take some time; the most accurate diagnosis is meaningless if the patient does not comply with treatment. Clearly, the clinician must weigh multiple factors when making treatment choices for comorbid patients.

Chapter 3

Patients Most Likely to Be Diagnosed: Those With ADHD Hyperactive-Impulsive Type

IN SOME CASES, THE DIAGNOSIS OF ADHD is arrived at with great difficulty and after a long and arduous process. The symptoms of patients in these cases are not obvious and do not "jump out" at the clinician as obvious ADHD symptoms, and thus the clinician may believe that the primary problem is depression, an anxiety disorder or another psychiatric diagnosis, and treat the patient accordingly. Yet the patient still struggles. Only after a painstaking review of past symptoms and treatments does it become apparent that ADHD might be the underlying problem.

Other cases are much more clear-cut, such as the troubled and troublesome adolescent, the adult bewildered by problems at work and home, and those who self-refer after researching the condition or having children diagnosed with ADHD. This chapter discusses these commonly seen patients.

The classic hyperactive and impulsive symptoms of ADHD are much "noisier" and dramatically affect patients and those around them. The consistent inability to sit still, omnipresent irritability, and general air of being overwhelmed by life are all problematic features that cause these patients to stand out in sharp relief to parents, teachers, legal authorities, and clinicians.

It is now clear that hyperactive and impulsive symptoms persist *beyond* childhood and the behaviors associated with this type of ADHD have public health implications. These patients overtly express their symptoms with clear behavioral patterns, among them substance use, driving problems, work and school failure, and run-ins with legal authorities. Many of them are adolescents, although some are young adults.

Identifying these patients is essential, as there is evidence that intervening early can forestall bad outcomes. The diagnosis and treatment of adolescents and adults with ADHD can save not only their lives, but also the lives of others, as successful treatment for ADHD usually decreases risky behavior such as drunk driving and unprotected sex. This chapter characterizes how these patients are viewed by their teachers and parents and how to alert primary-care doctors, mental health professionals, court officials, and employee-assistance professionals to suspect ADHD or some other treatable condition.

Increasingly, people who have endured troubled lives independently seek out an ADHD evaluation. Patients who pursue their own diagnosis have special characteristics. Many who question if they have ADHD do, in fact, have it. Others have ulterior motivations or rationales for obtaining the diagnosis. They may have used a family member's medication, responded well to it, and thus concluded that they have the condition. They may want the diagnosis as a means to excuse their current life predicament. A minority of self-referred patients want access to medication that might offer them an altered state or a decreased appetite. The clinician should be aware of these situations and remain vigilant in making the diagnosis and prescribing medications.

There are some behavioral indicators to watch out for among those who are likely to have ADHD. For example, teenagers or adults who have received more than two traffic tickets for speeding over the course of a 6- to 9-month period should be evaluated for ADHD regardless of whether they have other obvious symptoms. This dictum, if adopted by the nation's traffic courts, would do much to mitigate this major social concern. Similarly, adults who continue to use marijuana may have underlying ADHD. Alan was a case in point.

Alan came in for a psychiatric evaluation at the advice of his internist. By all accounts, Alan's life was going well. At 46, he was the head of his family's booming business and was a high-profile philanthropist. He was in good health and was supported by a thriving family. But for the past 2 years, Alan had struggled with insomnia. His doctor had tried to help Alan with various sleep medications, but nothing seemed to work. Alan reported, "I don't know what's wrong. I can't slow it down at night. I just can't fall asleep."

As he grew more comfortable in therapy, Alan shared with his doctor that for years he was addicted to marijuana. "I had been using nearly every night since college but when my oldest started high school 2 years ago, my wife absolutely insisted I stop because I could no longer hide it from him. Our house is large, but not big enough to keep up the deception. Now my wife thinks I have stopped, so I have had to distance myself from her. I smoke less but when I resist the temptation, I know I will be miserable in the evening and not sleep at night."

Alan's history was consistent with someone with ADHD. He was never an effective student. He was smart, but most of his teachers felt that he was aloof and spoiled. At a young age, Alan became obsessed with action. An expert skier, he hit the slopes whenever he could. As a teenager, he hang-glided and climbed mountains, and as an adult he pursued as much high adventure as he could afford. He socialized most evenings and rarely missed a chance to exercise. Marathons and iron-man competitions became his passion. Alan was not depressed and did not have a history of mania. This history, combined with the fact that Alan's son had ADHD, prompted the psychiatrist to consider the possibility that Alan had ADHD too. After an extensive workup, Alan was diagnosed with ADHD hyperactive type. Strattera was prescribed.

Alan reported remarkable results: "After I took the medication for about 10 days my brain rested and my sleep got much better. I was able to settle. Now I'm able to sit through a movie. I can be active during the day but I can have leisure time with my family. I can sleep on a predictable schedule and, most importantly, I finally stopped craving pot. I can't tell you what a relief this is. I risked so much, buying and smoking the stuff. I knew it was bad for my lungs yet I couldn't stop until I got my ADHD treated."

EARLY PRESENTATION: CHILDREN WITH HYPERACTIVE
AND IMPULSIVE SYMPTOMS

Patients who are chronically fidgety, nervous, and fast-talking and exhibit other classic behaviors such as a propensity to procrastinate or lose things may seem to cry out "ADHD." Patients with this overt form of ADHD are more likely to be referred at a younger age than patients who primarily present with a lack of focus and inattentiveness but few behavioral problems. Fortunately, both groups respond to treatment.

In childhood, hyperactive and impulsive symptoms are likely to be noticed by parents. As these kids age, the troublesome symptoms extend into school or the workplace. Hyperactive children and adolescents are notoriously reactive and may have little tolerance for peers. Fighting and pushing the limits of the school rules can be their part of their daily routine, and early on in their school careers these kids become "known."

Educational or guidance counselors have the option of viewing these students as "bad kids" in need of discipline or as troubled kids in need of assistance, counseling, and perhaps medication. Being referred by the schools is the most common path to diagnosis. In general, boys are more likely than girls to demonstrate hyperactivity and consequently boys are more likely to be diagnosed with ADHD. It is unclear what causes this difference in the presentation of hyperactivity between males and females. (See Chapter 7 for a more detailed discussion on gender issues.)

ADOLESCENTS WITH BEHAVIORAL ISSUES

Hyperactive and impulsive children with ADHD morph into adolescents with the same or more dramatic problems. If they have not been previously diagnosed with ADHD, their behavior may lead to a diagnosis in this life stage. These kids are adventurous and have little anxiety about the consequences of their behaviors. They may be quick to experiment with illegal substances, accumulate traffic tickets, and disown any stake in their own school success. Their behaviors always draw the attention of their elders. The diagnosis of these kids is very important because medication and therapy can significantly turn around their lives and help to prevent the serious consequences suffered by those who continue undiagnosed.

Brett: Hyperactive From the Start

Following his conviction for a second breaking-and-entering charge, 22-year-old Brett was diagnosed with ADHD. His mother, a high-school teacher, reflected on her son's youth: "I think he was different from his first breath. When I was pregnant with him, he kicked me nonstop. He never slowed down. He was colicky as a baby and nothing we did—change his formula, give him stomach medicines—ever helped. In first grade, Brett bit his teacher badly and was always getting hurt or hurting someone else on the playground. He darted into the streets, and I can't count the number of near misses when he learned to ride his bike. I just couldn't keep up with him."

"Brett was always on the move. I could never let him near a pool—he had no fear that it could be dangerous. We were so scared that we paid more than $10,000 to pave over the swimming pool in the house we bought. I think he was smoking cigarettes at 12 and then I lost him. He was a great skateboarder and hung out with older kids who introduced him to marijuana and who knows what else. I think once he hit 14, he completely stopped listening to us. This week he was convicted of a burglary. Who knows what will happen next."

One problem with treating Brett was his resistance to taking medication; his mother was ambivalent about it as well. An unfortunate byproduct of the antidrug movement has been the failure to discriminate between doctor-prescribed medication and drugs of abuse. As a result, ADHD medications have become demonized. "I did not feel comfortable giving him a pill after he accused me of drugging him," said Brett's mother. "I felt I was giving him the wrong message. We spent so much time warning him about pot that we never were enthusiastic about giving him Ritalin. I knew that he was much calmer and got into less trouble when he took his Ritalin, but I never demanded that he take it."

Oppositional Behavior

Oppositional behavior is characteristic of many youth with hyperactivity and impulsivity. As many as 40% of children and adolescents with ADHD (the majority of them males) meet the formal diagnostic criteria of ODD or conduct disorder (CD). Adolescents with ODD have long-standing behaviors of temper tantrums, arguing, disrespecting or defying adults, and being angry, spiteful, and profane. Conduct disorder is a more severe condition that is characterized by actions such as stealing, fighting, lying, running away, truancy, fire-setting, and cruel coercion of others.

Adolescents in school detention, the juvenile court system, and other institutional settings have high rates of ADHD. Unfortunately, it may be only when the teenager is facing school expulsion or pending court action that professional evaluation is sought and the diagnosis of ADHD is considered. Approximately a quarter of these adolescents become adults with antisocial personality disorder. Researchers often separate ODD and CD from ADHD, but most clinicians are hard-pressed to find an ODD patient who does not have ADHD. Fortunately the converse is not true: Most patients with ADHD do not have ODD or CD.

Driving Infractions

Adolescents with untreated ADHD hyperactive type seek the thrill of speed and lack the fear of legal consequences. The accumulation of points and citations commonly begins with receipt of their driver's license and the police and court system take notice soon thereafter. In a study of 25 young adults ages 17–30 years old with ADHD and 23 controls of the same age without ADHD, those with ADHD had received significantly more speeding tickets (an average of 5 tickets) than the non-ADHD group (1 ticket). Two individuals in the ADHD group had their driver's licenses suspended, compared to one person in the non-ADHD control group (Barkley, Murphy, & Kwasnik, 1996).

Russell Barkley has extensively researched the driving impairments of teens and adults with ADHD. One study compared 105 teenagers and young adults with ADHD to 64 subjects without ADHD. Patients with ADHD had more than twice the risk for receiving traffic citations than the control group, especially for speeding. Of even greater concern, the ADHD group was significantly more likely to have severe accidents and be at fault (Barkley, 2004).

As with other ADHD behaviors, medications have been shown to be helpful. Using driving simulators, Cox, Merkel, Kovatchev, and Seward

(2000) showed that stimulant medications improved the decisions of young adults with ADHD. In a small study of 13 subjects (7 with ADHD and 6 without) whose average age was 22 years, the ADHD subjects on placebo drove significantly worse than the subjects who took Ritalin. Although larger studies are needed, it seems likely that the benefit of treatment with stimulants would accrue to other drivers as well.

Teenagers commonly drive in vehicles with other teenagers, whether they have ADHD or not. If alcohol or drugs are introduced, the risk of accidents, serious injury, and loss of life escalates exponentially. Given the public health concern about the safety of adolescent driving (let alone adolescents with ADHD), the Cox study offers important findings. Indirectly the study underlines the need to treat this population with medications in the evening, on weekends, and during the summer, times when adolescents are most likely to be behind the wheel.

Substance Use Disorder and Suicidality

The diagnosis of ADHD can explain an adolescent's self-defeating behaviors. Untreated adolescents with ADHD are at high risk for alcohol or drug abuse. According to Wilens (2004c), substance misuse starts earlier in adolescents with ADHD (on average at 19 years) than among their peers (on average 22 years).

An elegant study at the Massachusetts General Hospital found that stimulant treatment was protective against the later development of substance abuse (Faraone & Wilens, 2003, p. 13). The researchers concluded: "Although stimulant treatment for ADHD cannot prevent the subsequent development of substance use disorders, its protective effect is clear."

In 2003, Dr. Joseph Biederman, a prominent Harvard researcher, wrote in a *Journal of Clinical Psychiatry* article that "It is clear that ADHD itself, even without psychiatric comorbidities, is a risk factor for substance use disorder, and . . . that people with unmedicated ADHD are at 3 to 4 times the risk for developing substance use disorder as are those who are medicated" (Biederman, 2003a, p. 7).

Early treatment reduces the child's impulsivity and fearlessness — two features consistently seen in substance abusers. Substance abuse experts agree that intervention prior to the onset of substance abuse is beneficial. Of course, substance abuse can also be treated *after* it occurs, but prevention is the primary public health goal.

Adolescents with both ADHD and substance use disorders have a particularly lethal combination of problems. In a study of 314 male and 188 female adolescents with ADHD and substance use disorders, 55% of the males had attempted suicide. The numbers were lower in female youth (18%), but both groups far surpassed the risk in the general adolescent population (Kelly, Cornelius, & Clark, 2004).

DIFFICULTIES AND INSIGHTS ABOUT DELAYED DIAGNOSIS

Teachers of young children are usually sensitive to ADHD symptoms and are trained to encourage assessment by the school psychologist or other professional. Consequently, most students with ADHD hyperactive-impulsive subtype are identified by the time they are 7 or 8 years old, if not before then. However, sometimes the diagnosis is not as timely. There are a number of causes for delay in diagnosis.

A large percentage of children with ADHD do not have presenting symptoms until they are in junior high school or even high school. In these cases, ADHD symptoms that may have simmered undetected through elementary school ignite during the hormonal explosion that occurs at puberty. During these years teenagers often feel that they can do no wrong and that no one knows more than they do. ADHD teens thus lose some of the self-consciousness that previously dampened their impulsivity. When this sense of omniscience strikes, the adolescent can become behaviorally disinhibited and problematic behavior can emerge for the first time. Showing off to peers and displays of arrogance, disobedience, and self-absorption become evident. Unlike grade school teachers, instructors in junior high and high schools are less primed to look for ADHD, and they may not consider these behaviors to be signs of ADHD. Thus, they are less likely to recommend a full evaluation.

Intelligent students with ADHD are also vulnerable to delayed diagnosis. Adolescents with good memory, an intrinsic ability to problem-solve, and an awareness of their shortcomings may be better able to compensate for their concentration difficulties or impulsive thoughts. In general, individuals with high full-scale IQs are more likely to be diagnosed at an older age than their less talented cohorts.

Another impediment to early diagnosis is the adolescent's overall attitude about being diagnosed. Therapists are challenged daily by negative or cynical adolescents who sometimes bring to the session an attitude of "Treat me. . . . I dare you." They seem hostile and unworkable and may abruptly walk away from treatment. Clinicians can be caught in the middle between parents who implore that something be done and contrary adolescents who want anything that counters what the doctor or parents want. The doctor should be an advocate for treatment, but there is no magic bullet for these patients. That said, maintaining an open-door, accepting stance toward patients may yield dividends years later when patients return for treatment as adults. Delayed treatment is much better than no treatment at all, as the case of Jack illustrates.

Jack, a 23-year-old manager of a pizza franchise, reflected on his visit to our office when he was 16. "I was a son of a bitch, I was rude, but you guys were okay. For a few months I took the medication and I knew things went better. I just didn't want to admit it, so I stopped. You disagreed with me and told me, but nobody gave me a hard sell or preached that if I didn't take medication for my ADHD, my life would be over. I remember you giving me a brochure showing all the trouble that untreated kids with ADHD go through. After I got through high school I joined the Army and for 18 months I was stationed in Kuwait as a security guard. I was so bored and restless. I knew that I was not learning any skill. I was always late and got into trouble for not following orders. I thought about that brochure a lot. I came back to you because I knew you wouldn't say, 'I told you so.'"

INITIATING TREATMENT

Patients with undiagnosed ADHD often appear in the therapy office for the first time during a crisis or after a major life change. In easier times they may have managed their ADHD symptoms adequately without treatment, but some life circumstance, such as the development of a medical illness, a job change, or a relationship breakdown compels them to seek help. They may not suspect that ADHD is the significant contributing problem—rather, they are simply aware that something is wrong. In some cases these patients are referred by an employer, teacher, or family member or friend. Other times they initiate treatment solely on their own.

Outside Referrals

Some patients come to the therapist's office as a result of outside referrals, such as when an employer recommends or requires treatment or when another physician, such as a primary care physician, recommends that the patient see the therapist. The patient may have been told little other than that he or she *should* see a therapist, without the potential benefits of therapy having been explained. As a result, when a patient is seen for the first time as the result of an outside referral, it should be ascertained through talking with the patient if he or she feels there may be some benefit to therapy or that instead he or she is being coerced or misunderstood. If the patient feels forced into therapy, this issue should be discussed, which may enable the therapist to work to uncover what may underlie work problems and to create a mutual plan toward which both the patient and therapist can work toward.

There are many different reasons for an outside referral, and the patient's perceptions about these reasons are important. In the case of Mark, who worked at a parcel delivery service, he had difficulty with his work requirements and had asked the Employee Assistance office for help. This office had steered Mark to therapy.

For 10 years, Mark, 35, sorted packages at a large parcel-delivery service. He was able to perform the necessary repetitive tasks while still spending much of his time feeling very anxious and tense. He learned that the workday moved more quickly if he listened to music on his headphones, and although this was officially against regulation, Mark's supervisor never questioned his routine. Mark had a good work record and a remote affability. After the retirement of two managers he was promoted and given a substantial raise.

In his new job Mark was required to supervise others and interact frequently with his new boss. His shortcomings quickly became apparent. He was impatient when he had to listen to the concerns of his small team. He had a difficult time learning the software required to do shift scheduling, and when the phones rang constantly Mark was uncharacteristically irritable with his customers. He found sitting behind a desk for 8 hours intolerable.

Mark's boss became annoyed when her calls were not returned promptly or at all, and Mark was defensive when she made suggestions. Within months, Mark's irascibility placed him in real danger of being fired. He was given the option of returning to sorting mail, but he liked the higher pay and schedule flexibility that came with the supervisory position.

In frustration, Mark went to his Employee Assistance Plan. The counselor had recently attended a seminar about ADHD in the workplace and quickly raised the possibility that Mark had hyperactive and impulsive symptoms. He suggested that Mark pursue an evaluation. A specialist confirmed the diagnosis and treatment was initiated within a week of the EAP appointment.

Treatment significantly improved Mark's functioning. In retrospect, it was clear that Mark had had ADHD all along, but in his original job he had been able to camouflage his symptoms. It wasn't until his promotion had required him to use different skill sets that his deficits became apparent.

Self-Referrals

Many adults who are ultimately diagnosed with ADHD learned about the condition not from their doctor but via other avenues. Most then try to find a doctor who can address their ADHD needs. In a 2004 review of the medical records kept by 100 psychiatrists and primary-care doctors, 95% of the primary-care practitioners' patients with ADHD and 91% of the psychiatrists' patients were self-referrals (Faraone, Spencer, Montano, & Biederman, 2004). Thus, in many cases, the patients suspected that ADHD was a problem before their previous doctors did. Further, many of these ADHD patients had complained of their symptoms for years before their official diagnosis. Fifty-six percent of the patients who were not diagnosed with ADHD prior to their self-referral had complained of symptoms that were virtually identical to the symptoms that the new doctors listed as reasons for suspecting ADHD, such as poor concentration, general disorganization, the tendency to leave projects unfinished, problems with time management, impulsive behavior, and so forth. The researchers also reported that self-referred patients had sound reasons for seeking an ADHD evaluation, including their symptoms and signs as well as poor school or work performance.

Faraone and colleagues' (2004) review also indicated that primary-care practitioners were the least likely to diagnose ADHD in adult patients, compared to other physicians. This study validates previously discussed findings that doctors are often behind the curve in responding to their patient's ADHD needs. This compares unfavorably to illnesses like diabetes, hypertension, and obesity, where doctors are often passionate about their patients' need for treatment.

Patients who suspect that they have ADHD self-refer for several key reasons. Sometimes one of their children or another relative has been diagnosed with ADHD, and the patient identifies the same symptoms in him- or herself. Other times patients see a television advertisement for an ADHD medication that treats symptoms they recognize in themselves. In other cases, patients are serendipitously educated by a television program or a magazine or Internet article they happen to stumble across.

ADHD DIAGNOSES IN FAMILY MEMBERS

Many studies support the powerful genetic transmission of ADHD; if a child has ADHD, the parents are also likely candidates. When parents are told that their children have ADHD, many gradually recognize their own previously undiagnosed ADHD symptoms. For Eva, a young mother in her early thirties, this realization was an epiphany. She recounted a visit with her daughter's pediatrician Dr. Hassett:

"Dr. Hassett was talking about Amber's having trouble sitting still and he commented that she was constantly in motion. Together we read her teacher's report that complained that Amber wasn't listening to instructions and not staying up with the class. Then the doctor told me Amber probably had ADD and this would explain why it was so hard for her to pay attention in school. It could explain why she was getting such bad grades."

"Then he started telling me about choosing a medication, but I actually heard only maybe half of what he said because I was thinking about the angry exchange I'd had with the doctor's receptionist earlier. Then I was distracted by the scenic mountain pattern on the wallpaper in his office—it made me think about the vacation we took last summer to the mountains, which made me think about where we should go *this* summer."

"After a couple of minutes Dr. Hassett stopped and said, very quietly, 'Eva, are you *hearing* what I'm saying to you? You're as distracted as your daughter.'"

"I was jolted—he was right. I noticed then that I was swinging my right leg rather wildly, and I willed myself to stop it as he continued to talk, but a minute later I was tapping my toes again. I became obsessed with the idea that maybe we both had it. I went to ADHD websites. My husband was reluctant to put Amber on the medications but he respected Dr. Hassett's opinion, so we did start the medications and counseling for Amber. She behaved much better and her teachers were relieved."

Once the crisis with Eva's daughter was averted, the burden of day-to-day life returned. Although Eva's husband tolerated his daughter's taking medications, he strongly disapproved of Eva's pursuing treatment. Eva remained convinced that the fidgetiness and distractibility Dr. Hassett had observed was emblematic of her long-standing ADHD, but she chose to avoid a family confrontation. Months passed without much happening.

However, Eva's good friend Julie refused to let the subject dissolve. Sensing Eva's drift, she gave her friend a new article about ADHD as well as a copy of *Driven to Distraction* for her birthday. She emailed Eva a link to the attention deficit disorder website, and she insisted that they attend a local support group for adult ADHD. Refusing to allow Eva to dismiss the possibility that she had a medically treatable condition, Julie worked with Eva to develop strategies to disarm her husband's obstructionism.

Ten months later Julie's efforts paid off, and Eva located an adult ADHD specialist. After a full evaluation the clinician confirmed ADHD hyperactive/impulsive type. Fortunately, her husband's bluster proved short-lived, and Eva's successful treatment improved her ability to listen, focus, and parent Amber.

Sometimes people self-refer because they have read about ADHD in a magazine or on the Internet. Other times they have seen a program about ADHD on television or noticed an advertisement from a pharmaceutical company. These chance encounters prompt a critical "aha!" moment, when patients wonder to themselves: "Wait a minute—this is me! I have those symptoms, too! I forget things more than other people. I lose items more than others seem to and I blurt out embarrassing remarks without thinking. Could I possibly have ADHD?"

Because of their distractibility or out of fear of mental health professionals, these individuals may ruminate for weeks or months before making a move to see a mental health professional. They may also doubt that improvement is even *possible*, as so many adults with ADHD have been told their entire lives that their symptoms were their own fault. Self-blame keeps many patients from seeking an evaluation and it is also one of the issues that must be addressed during treatment. ADHD therapists must be unambivalent about asserting that the patient is not to be faulted for having ADHD yet simultaneously emphasize that it is the patient's responsibility to learn about the condition and obtain the best treatment.

STAYING DISCIPLINED WITH THE DIAGNOSIS

Self-referred patients may have other psychiatric disorders in addition to ADHD, or they may have *no* discernible disorders. A thorough screening is always in order, and it must not only take into account the patient's concern that ADHD may be present, but also consider the full spectrum of possibilities—including the absence of any psychiatric problems.

Other times self-referred patients have disorders other than ADHD, and in some cases they still insist on being prescribed ADHD medications. One such patient was Laurie, whose clear agenda differed from that of her doctor.

> **Doctor:** Laurie, you've come to see me to find out if you have ADHD. We've discussed your symptoms and I have reviewed your psychiatric history. You responded to many of our questionnaires, in-

cluding those that specifically assess ADHD. We've also run some medical laboratory tests, all of which came out normal. Based on all of the information I gathered, I think the major problem you have is with your temper and mood swings. I think you have bipolar disorder. I do not think you have ADHD. You did well in school, and you function well most of the time. You do have periods when you get very depressed and you have had two episodes when you might have been manic. I think you have a recurrence of your depression and I can't rule out the possibility that you have bipolar disorder. The best treatments for depression are antidepressants. That's where I think we should begin.

Laurie: I think you're wrong. My friend has ADHD and I know this is my problem. I know Adderall will help me—I've taken hers and it's helped.

Doctor: Laurie, I understand your concern. However, I am convinced that treating you for ADHD would not only be inappropriate but could also be harmful. A stimulant could make you more likely to have another manic episode. I don't want that to happen, and I don't think you do, either. You need to be treated for the problem that you do have. Depression and bipolar disorder are very treatable.

Laurie: I'm not going to get fat! On Adderall I had no appetite. The medications you talk about cause weight gain. No way!

Laurie left the office angry and cursing that her effort had been a waste of time. She did not return phone calls. However, 3 weeks later her husband called to offer an update and ask for advice. Laurie had been hospitalized following a suicide attempt. In the hospital, she again was diagnosed with a mood disorder and again was resisting treatment. She maintained that she would not take any medication that had potential for weight gain. The doctor advised the husband that Laurie urgently needed treatment, and he should try to convince Laurie to work with the hospital staff and then return to treatment as an outpatient after her discharge from the hospital. He also told the husband that it would be best if he conveyed to Laurie that, although some medications do cause weight gain, others result in little or no increase in weight. But more important than weight gain or loss was the goal of feeling well enough that she would not wish to try suicide again.

With the support and encouragement of her husband, Laurie agreed to comply with taking her medication.

Shortly after she was discharged from the hospital, Laurie returned to her psychiatrist's care. The antidepressants had improved her mood and this time she was contrite.

Laurie: I might owe you an apology.
Doctor: How's that?
Laurie: I thought I would be able to convince you that I needed ADHD medications. I know that they would have helped me curb my appetite. I answered the ADD questionnaires according to what I thought would give me an ADD diagnosis. I guess I didn't convince you.

Laurie did end up doing well on antidepressants and over the years her medication was adjusted to minimize weight gain. She never tried to obtain inappropriate medications again.

As noted earlier, patients exhibiting hyperactivity, distractibility, and behavior that antagonizes other members of society are likely to be noticed and often are referred for a mental health evaluation—if not in childhood, then often in adolescence. Many adults with problematic behaviors may be referred as well, such as by their EAP programs at work.

Yet many professionals are deeply ambivalent about providing help. Psychiatrist and educator Birgit Amann (2005) summed it up: "When I speak to pediatricians and family doctors who treat so many of these kids, half of them believe that kids will outgrow their ADHD. We would never tell a diabetic not to take her insulin. We need to approach this disorder the same way." Regardless of whether these patients appear in our offices due to court mandates, referral from educators, or simply on their own, we as mental health professionals must not squander our opportunity to help these at-risk individuals.

Chapter 4

Patients Least Likely to Be Diagnosed: Those With ADHD Inattentive Type and ADHD Combined Type

LAUREN'S FRIENDS AND FAMILY described her as "bubbly" and "vivacious." A 46-year-old dental assistant, she was warm, generous, and rarely critical of others. Her sincerity and concern for the well-being of others was never questioned. But her friends and family had complaints, too: Lauren was frequently late to appointments. She often forgot having met people previously. Her tendency to lose important items like her cell phone and car keys not only exasperated her but also affected her family, friends, and the people with whom she worked.

In exasperation over her inability to get to work on time, Lauren's boss denied her a raise, but because of her loyalty and diligence, he did not fire her. Lauren's husband, Carl, an accountant who valued order and punctuality, was frequently frustrated by Lauren's missteps. For example, she once had left Carl stranded at a car dealership 40 miles from their home, causing him to miss an important business meeting. Lauren explained that she had not forgotten about the ride home and agreed that Carl *had* reminded her earlier in the morning about picking him up, but she had become distracted at their child's school and lost all track of time.

To Carl's further dismay, Lauren could not be reached because she had left her cell phone at home. This episode was emblematic of their relationship. The marriage survived because of Lauren's good humor and Carl's passive amicability, but these recurrent situations took a toll.

Lauren also faced a perpetual battle paying off her credit card debts. She rarely kept track of her impulsive purchases, and when asked about them, she couldn't recall nor justify why she had bought these items or even where most of them were in her home.

Despite her problems with impulsiveness, forgetfulness, procrastination, and inattentiveness to others, Lauren appeared to lead a relatively stable life. She was married, had two children, and had worked at the dental office for almost 10 years. This, along with Lauren's cheery outlook, belied her inner struggle. She knew that she often disappointed others, and her friends, family, and coworkers had little faith in her reliability. All had tired of her excuses and reassurances that things would be better "the next time."

Lauren did not have dementia or a personality disorder. She had no history of grandiosity, racing thoughts, or psychosis, and the absence of mania made it unlikely that she had bipolar disorder or any other significant psychiatric diagnoses. But Lauren's symptoms continued to impinge on her work and family life, distressing both her and the people around her.

This chapter describes patients like Lauren, who suffer from ADHD inattentive or combined type. These two categories represent the majority of adults with ADHD. These patients are unfocused and distractible. Individuals with ADHD combined type may have residual hyperactivity, but, as the cases in this chapter illustrate, inattention and distractibility can be the most debilitating symptoms. Often viewed by others as simply silly or lazy, many of these patients go undiagnosed.

Whereas the majority of patients with ADHD hyperactive-impulsive type are boys and men, ADHD inattentive type and ADHD combined type appear more commonly in females. Instead of being hyperactive and restless, these patients are plagued with lethargy, fatigue, and extreme distractibility. In a study of 454 boys and 417 girls with ADHD, the girls were 2.2 times more likely than the boys to be diagnosed as predominantly inattentive (Biederman & Faraone, 2004).

Because inattentiveness wreaks less overt havoc than impulsivity or hyperactivity, parents and teachers are less likely to take notice of it. These patients quietly underperform, and although their symptoms are sometimes problematic to those around them, they usually have fewer (or no) antisocial tendencies than their noisier hyperactive-impulsive type counterparts.

Because inattentive children and adolescents with ADHD often go undiagnosed, they grow up feeling that these symptoms are a natural part of them. Children with inattentive ADHD progress through adolescence and adulthood with many of the same problems as those without ADHD, but they appear to be at a greater risk for developing a poor self-concept and concurrent anxiety and depression.

Among patients with core complaints of inattention, distractibility, or fatigue, there are several key groups that clinicians should carefully monitor. These include daydreamers, underperformers in school (without behavioral problems), and those with refractory depression and anxiety.

Impulsivity, inattentiveness, and distractibility are essential features of the ADHD diagnosis. To the public, hyperactivity is synonymous with ADHD—it is after all, the "H" in "ADHD"—and many inattentive patients with ADHD summarily reject the diagnosis because they do not identify with this particular symptom. Clinicians must emphasize that hyperactivity is not the definitive feature of ADHD. As the cases in this chapter demonstrate, inattentive ADHD can be extremely disabling. As the criteria for ADHD are reconstituted over the next few years for the DSM-V, this "deceptive labeling" will need to be clarified.

Patty was diagnosed with ADHD inattentive type after years of struggling. Her diagnosis was predicated on her doctor's observations of her extreme distractibility, inability to quickly pick up instructions, long-standing learning problems, and the formal diagnostic process outlined in Chapter 1.

"I was always called an airhead," Patty recalled, "so I collected blonde jokes and told them to others to deflect criticism. On some level it was self-deprecating fun, but on another level, the need to disarm people all the time was draining." She continued: "I always knew I was smart, but no one ever took me seriously because I was so inattentive that I missed half of what was being said." Her distractibility and poor eye contact made others feel she was disinterested and aloof when, in fact, she was neither.

GETTING BY WITH ADHD

Most people are linear thinkers, navigating their thoughts from point A to point B and so on. In contrast, people with ADHD may start at point A and then think about another subject altogether, later rebounding to point D of the first topic. Some individuals have referred to this thought pattern as a "bouncing brain." It is not mania and it is not aberrant behavior, but rather a way of thinking that characterizes most people with ADHD, particularly those with ADHD inattentive or combined type.

Such thought patterns can work well in multitasking and highly creative individuals who have others to plan and carry out the mundane details of their lives, such as paying bills or keeping appointments. Most people with ADHD, however, do not have the luxury of hiring an executive staff and need to learn how to manage their own lives.

As a result, individuals with ADHD usually have to work harder to adapt to their non-ADHD physical and psychological environment. They often instinctively begin doing this from an early age.

TYPES OF PEOPLE WHO MAY MISS BEING DIAGNOSED

Inattentive or combined ADHD patients are not belligerent or aggressive, which may be the major reason they have eluded detection for ADHD. The hallmark of ADHD inattentive type is daydreaming. Individuals may have a lackadaisical and drifty persona and usually struggle quietly. Patients with the combined type may struggle somewhat less quietly, especially when their hyperactivity is roughly equivalent to their inattentiveness. Typically, both groups try hard to comply with the rules of society and their workplace, but somehow they do not fit in.

Undiagnosed inattentive and combined type ADHD patients are common in clinical practice. Clinicians are advised to take special note of the underperforming student or overwhelmed worker, individuals with mild comorbidities such as anxiety and depression, sufferers of chronic pain conditions that are nonresponsive to medical treatment, and adults who have no children and thus lack an "early detection system" that might alert them to the presence of genetically transmitted ADHD.

Underperforming Students, Overwhelmed Workers

ADHD is a brain-based condition unrelated to intelligence. Gifted people can have the condition, as can those less well-wired. ADHD does not discriminate by IQ. Therapists, however, should be keen to gifted or highly talented individuals who are nowhere close to living up to their potential — the math prodigy who is clerking at a convenience store, for example, or the D student who receives high aptitude testing scores. Other times people with undiagnosed inattentive ADHD have plodded along on the slow track while often others around them have covered for them. For example, colleagues may make allowances for forgetting and losing items when they personally like the individual.

After years of conditioning, inattentive ADHD patients can default to an immersed belief of low self-expectation. Appropriate diagnosis and treatment can challenge that belief. Consider Colleen, whose family friend, a psychologist, identified Colleen's brilliance but surmised that inattention interfered with her achievement. When, after many months of gentle encouragement, Colleen finally acceded to seek help, the diagnosis of ADHD inattentive type was confirmed.

"When I was given Concerta, the fog lifted," Colleen said. "I could slow down and focus. I did not interrupt others and I could follow a conversation. I no longer had to have friends cover for me. People took me seriously for the first time. More importantly, I started taking myself seriously." In the following years, Colleen went back to school and completed her master's degree in education. She is now an elementary school principal and is in the running to become a superintendent. What Colleen had that most others do not was an advocate — someone who recognized her aptitude and underperformance and encouraged her not to accept the status quo. For Colleen, the detection and treatment of her ADHD was transforming, much like new glasses are for a myopic person who has squinted her entire life.

Patients With Mild Comorbidities Such as Anxiety and Depression

The greatest risk factor for the development of one psychiatric condition is having another psychiatric condition. All forms of ADHD run with many other psychiatric disorders, and as patients grow older, their clinical presentations become more complicated. Comorbidity is the rule, not the exception, with ADHD.

The clinician should consider inattentive ADHD in situations where conventional treatment for depression or anxiety does not yield good results. Oftentimes inattentive ADHD is overlooked or unappreciated because the patient's overwhelming complaint is depression, and it becomes the sole focus of treatment. The clinician prescribes various antidepressants to little avail, and the patient remains depressed. When patients are comorbid for *both* ADHD and depression, adding a stimulant or atomoxetine (Strattera) can address the underlying inattentive symptoms, allowing the antidepressant to act more effectively on the mood symptoms. This combination can offer the patient remarkable relief.

Eating-disordered patients and patients who self-mutilate (cutters), also often have profiles of inattention and impulsivity and may meet criteria for ADHD. Clinicians will often miss the underlying ADHD if they do not appreciate the symptoms of distractibility and inattention that run with the self-defeating and impulsive behavior.

Patients With Chronic Pain Conditions

Somatic complaints like fibromyalgia, irritable bowel syndrome, and chronic fatigue syndrome are associated with ADHD inattentive type. This association is relatively uncharted territory but represents a large number of patients. My experience has shown that if the ADHD is pharmacologically addressed, typically with mixed amphetamine salts, the patient's physical complaints will often remit. (This association is further elaborated in Chapter 11.)

People Who Don't Have Children with ADHD (Or Don't Have Children)

Many adults and some adolescents are diagnosed with ADHD because a child in the family is first diagnosed with the disorder. When a clinician explains to the family that symptoms such as impulsivity, distractibility, and disorganization are supportive of an ADHD diagnosis, most parents want to learn more about the condition. They research the condition by scouring books, websites, educational videos, and other resources, and not uncommonly they come to the revelation that they too have had the problems for years. However, sometimes adults with ADHD have children who do not have ADHD—or who have not been diagnosed with ADHD. In addition, some childless individuals have ADHD.

Today, conversations about adult ADHD are generally patient-initiated, rather than therapist-initiated. This will change as more clinicians become aware of the condition or treatment experience. The goal for ADHD educators is to encourage doctors to make a habit of inquiring about concentration, patience, and distractibility, just as they ask about vaccination, weight management, and hypertension.

ADULT CASES: COMPENSATING FOR ADHD

Adults with ADHD inattentive or combined type have, of course, had the condition for many years, and most have developed methods to cope with their symptoms. For example, Lauren, the patient discussed at the beginning of this chapter, compensated for her frequent tardiness by working late and working hard. She learned to counteract the exasperation of others by adopting an appealing demeanor that made it difficult for others to remain angry with her. Other people develop rigid rules and self-discipline as a way of regulating their distractibility. Delores, a 42-year-old postal worker, had a strict rule that she would not buy a new purse unless it had a zippered inside pocket. Her therapist initially perceived this as compulsive behavior, but through discussion, he discovered that Delores had to overcompensate for her deficits. "I learned, not soon enough," she said, "that if I didn't put my keys in the special designated spot every night, they would be hopelessly lost every morning."

The following case studies illustrate other such coping strategies among adults with ADHD inattentive and combined types.

Tom: Obsessive-Compulsive Traits

Tom was a 55-year-old accounting clerk in the local community hospital. For 22 years, his job provided him with a good salary and excellent benefits, and for most of this time Tom had performed his job adequately. Routine and persistence, virtues emphasized from his early days in Catholic school, served him well. His compulsive strategies of checking and rechecking his work mitigated his frequent clerical mistakes. Overall Tom liked work, finding the camaraderie and banter comfortable, and his boss appreciated his loyalty.

Over time, however, Tom's work environment changed. His boss retired and was replaced by a young female MBA. With new management came new operating procedures. Tom's rigid behaviors, which had served him well earlier in his career, now proved counterproductive. He had trouble learning new accounting software — he had done things "his way" for so long that he could not tolerate the change. His supervisor also repeatedly warned Tom about his sexually suggestive humor; what was acceptable in the workplace had changed over the years, and so must his language.

Ultimately, Tom could not adapt to the new workplace expectations, and soon he was dismissed. Devastated by the firing, Tom worked minimally for several years. He found several part-time positions (clerking at a hardware store, delivering for a pharmacy), but none proved to be a good fit. Tom's wife became impatient and he became increasingly depressed. Their family doctor prescribed antidepressants. As little improvement was realized over the months of treatment, Tom was referred for a psychiatric evaluation.

Based on his school history (report cards detailed his distractibility and stubbornness as far back as second grade), his family history, and his responses to the Adult ADHD Self-Report Scale Cases (ASRS) Scale–v.1.1 Symptom Checklist, Tom was diagnosed with ADHD combined type. The psychiatrist also noted that Tom's medical workup was negative and antidepressant medications were unhelpful. He was prescribed modafinil (Provigil) and was also referred to a psychotherapist.

In psychotherapy, Tom garnered support and encouragement. He and his therapist decided that he should exploit his virtues (tenacity and a fondness for routine) rather than focus on his deficits (rigidity and resistance to change). The options for retraining middle-aged men were not many, but after much deliberation, Tom began a rigorous 12-month vocational course to become a hair stylist.

The perseverance and preoccupation with exactness that distinguished Tom early in his accounting career helped him get through the surprisingly intense demands of barber school. With great effort, he learned to cut and color, and to his great relief, he passed the state certification exam on the first try. Soon he found work in a busy shop not far from his old hospital job, and his precise haircuts soon won him a dedicated following.

Jeannie: Beauty as Adaptation

Jeannie, 29, had been treated since high school with various therapies and medications for chronic depression. Strikingly attractive, Jeannie always gravitated towards jobs in cosmetic retail. One opportunity followed another, yet one disappointment led to another. Keeping herself impeccable was instinctive; keeping a spreadsheet updated was impossible. Jeannie became irritable when multiple tasks were asked of her. Over the years her many jobs created a clear pattern. She would interview well and was frequently recruited to perform a job that pushed the limits of her experience. Each job would start well but sour within a year or so. More than once, Jeannie left a job with bitterness directed at her employer.

Jeannie's beauty was a fundamental part of her persona, synonymous with how others described her. Yet in her many years of therapy, her physical presentation and the role it played in her life were never really discussed. When the new therapist raised the issue, Jeannie initially signaled an unwillingness to explore the topic. With gentle encouragement, however, she became intrigued and soon wanted to talk about it extensively.

Jeannie had learned early on that her beauty translated into a type of power. Throughout school, girlfriends competed for her friendship. Male teachers and supervisors would relax rules for her. In the business world, coworkers would ingratiate themselves. She learned quickly that personal meetings were more successful than telephone contacts. She had destructive affairs with two male managers. On some level, Jeannie was aware of her magnetism, but somehow she was ashamed of it as well. It seemed unearned to her.

In therapy Jeannie spoke of her overweight but talented sister, who was overlooked frequently by supervisors. Her twin brother, from whom she had grown apart, was unemployed, unambitious, and cocaine-addicted. Neither of her siblings viewed the world as particularly warm or welcoming. Jeannie had had more opportunities than either her brother or sister, but like both of them, she had little to show for it.

Jeannie was screened for ADHD and a comprehensive evaluation of her school history and screening tests supported the diagnosis. With the addition of an ADHD medication and continued treatment of her depressed mood, Jeannie improved. She became more punctual. She became more effective in updating her database and in managing multiple tasks.

As had been Jeannie's pattern in the past, another desirable position opened up for her. Three years subsequent to psychotherapy, and with continued treatment with Adderall XR, Jeanie sustained a job as regional manager for a national cosmetic retail firm. She credited the stimulant for much of her functional improvement, but maintained that insights she reached about the role her beauty played in her adaptation added great understanding to her daily life.

ADOLESCENTS: THE IMPORTANCE OF EARLY AND ACCURATE DIAGNOSIS

Often, patients ultimately diagnosed with ADHD inattentive type present for evaluation because of other issues, and they receive their ADHD diagnosis by happenstance. Jake, age 16, was a brilliant student about to enter the eleventh grade. In general, school had been easy for him. He had always tested well and barely had to work to obtain his grades. He enjoyed many friendships and participated in several school clubs.

Amidst many stresses, Jake's performance began to change in his junior year. His parents finalized their divorce, his grandfather passed away, and a school friend died in an auto accident. Jake's homework assignments went uncompleted and the most important project of the school year, a formal research paper, was barely begun. Jake had difficulty getting out of bed and dropped his participation in school clubs.

Alarmed, Jake's parents pressured him to seek help. One therapist, aware of his recent losses, raised the possibility of depression, but Jake did not bite. He denied feeling sad. The death of his classmate upset him, but Jake insisted that he was more concerned about the effect on his friends than on himself. His grandfather had suffered from Alzheimer's disease, and Jake said he felt that this death was merciful, not tragic. Finally, he told the therapist that he had anticipated his parent's divorce for years and was relieved that it had finally happened.

When Jake's mother informed the therapist that she had found a trail of gay Internet sites on his computer, Jake was embarrassed but forthright. He readily identified that he was gay but firmly denied that he was psychologically struggling with it. "I've known for years," he said comfortably, "and I think my parents have known as well, but they were kind of afraid to ask." Despite Jake's assertions that he was not depressed, Jake's doctor concluded that all these major life incidents must in some way be contributing to Jake's poor scholastic performance. An antidepressant was prescribed and Jake took the medication willingly.

After two full rounds of antidepressant medications and several months of psychotherapy, Jake showed no noticeable improvement. Psychological testing was performed and revealed elevated rates of inattention and anxiety but little evidence of hyperactivity or depression. The testing also noted that Jake was constantly fatigued, and no medical problem or sleep disturbance could explain this troubling symptom. A preliminary diagnosis of ADHD inattentive type was made and Dexedrine was prescribed three times daily. Jake had an immediate positive response.

Jake's ADHD was not evident earlier in his school life because he used his innate intelligence to compensate for his inattention and distractibility. Through much of school he did well by default. Complicated concepts came naturally to him. Geometry just sank in. He had a photographic memory and unlike his fellow college-bound peers, he never really had to study. The particular demands of his junior-year research paper, however, forced Jake and those around him to critically assess his inability to focus and concentrate. This writing project required a different skill set than a chemistry or math class. Planning, making deadlines, and researching the project to the specifications of his teacher proved too boring. His "depression" was really demoralization caused by his poor performance in the important class. This realization demotivated and overwhelmed him.

In contrast to Jake, many adolescents with inattentive ADHD perform poorly throughout school. Students with average aptitudes cannot easily compensate for their symptoms. At some point, however, almost all inattentive students "hit the wall" and are no longer able to do their work according to the prevailing standard. Students may reach their limit in grade school, high school, or even later in their education.

In Jake's case, major depression and an adjustment disorder related to his parents' divorce or the deaths of his friend and grandfather were judged inaccurately to be causative of his decline. Other therapists might have insisted that Jake's nascent homosexuality was driving his behavioral change. Jake's symptoms could also have been explained as adolescent forgetfulness or anger. Although they generally do not like it, most adults will accept a certain level of unreliability and turbulence among adolescents, and allowances are made for this behavior.

Jake's case is instructive for a number of reasons. First, students with good grades *can* have ADHD. Second, a sudden downturn in grades does *not* always mean that the patient has clinical depression. Third, not all teens feel depressed when or if their alternative sexual orientation is revealed. Finally, ADHD may be a factor even when it does not seem a likely diagnosis at first blush.

Looking back on his troubled high school year, Jake, now a successful graduate student, is gratified that the ADHD diagnosis was made in high school. He reflected that the timely intervention provided him dramatic help. His functioning in school and other domains of his life was forever improved.

Whether he was treated or not, Jake's raw intelligence ensured some level of academic success. Usually individuals with undiagnosed inattentive or combined ADHD do not pursue their education. They may have received poor grades or they may have convinced themselves that they are not cut out to succeed. Some attend college, only to drop out in the first or second semester. But for many ADHD students, college may actually be easier than their earlier education.

Melissa, an excellent athlete with severe combined ADHD, recounted how high school was more challenging than college. "In high school I had so much pressure on me to do well so I could compete for a Big Ten scholarship. It always felt like make or break. I will never forget how horrible it was to start studying for final exams in May and have to review material from late August when school started. I could not remember anything, I had lost most of my notes through plain disorganization, and I was panicked that I would end up academically ineligible for a scholarship."

College semesters move much more quickly. Unlike high school, college courses tend not to emphasize tasks that require memory and organization. Thus, the risk of disorganization and "memory failure" is less. For these reasons, it is important for clinicians to emphasize to high school students that college is not necessarily off limits. Higher education is, of course, not easy, and the loose structure of campus life presents different challenges to ADHD students. But many ADHD students can perform well in college despite these challenges. The clinician should advise ADHD students to prepare by visiting the college and learning about the social and academic life of the campus. It also should be noted that patients taking medication should not consume alcohol or use other drugs, and they must be warned against doing so.

CONSIDERING FUNCTIONALITY: ARE PATIENTS DOING AS WELL AS THEY COULD BE?

Sometimes patients report that they feel better after beginning treatment, and yet they do not appear to be functioning much better. Hailey, age 29, was a case in point. Hailey struggled in high school and never became connected to her therapist. She spent most of her early twenties traveling the country in search of happiness. She could not find contentment in college and no job held her interest for long. At age 24, pregnant and broke, Hailey returned to her parent's home with the precondition that she get treatment. With nowhere to turn, she agreed to the demand.

On Hailey's initial visit, her psychiatrist inquired about her motivation and attention. "I can't get excited about anything. I start a project and I lose interest as soon as I get frustrated. When I drive, I never remember to get off at the right exit." When asked about her activity, she reported "feeling so restless that I can't ever sit still." Her parents agreed that the symptoms had been present since grade school. ADHD combined type was diagnosed and stimulant medications were started after her son was born.

Within weeks, Hailey saw improvement. "I can now get out of bed. I'm not so grumpy. Mostly I notice that I'm not so damn depressed." Yet 3 years into treatment, Hailey had made little progress in building her life. She still could not sustain close friendships, her relationship with her mother remained tumultuous, and she made little effort to get trained or educated. Hailey reluctantly agreed that her progress was minimal: "I guess I expected more of myself. I do feel so much better. I can't imagine my life as it was before I got treated, but I am disappointed with myself."

Her father lamented, "I think Hailey's treatment has been successful, in that she does not feel as desperate, and I'm so glad for that, but I can't see her building an independent life for herself and her child."

Hailey's outcome is instructive. The most accurate assessment of a patient's outcome considers both how the patient is feeling and how the patient is functioning. Treatment that improves feeling also usually improves functioning. In Hailey's case this was not so. With some patients, such as Hailey, the clinician must concede that the patient's functioning is unlikely to improve further. Her cognitive deficits may benefit through psychotherapy and coaching, rather than through psychiatric intervention.

WHY PATIENTS WITH INATTENTIVE AND COMBINED ADHD NEED TREATMENT

Patients with inattentive and combined ADHD usually function adequately in society, without exhibiting substance abuse, law enforcement problems, or serious behavioral issues. It is reasonable to question if they should receive treatment at all. But the answer is yes, treatment really does matter.

Like individuals with other mental health problems, patients with ADHD may figure out ways of limiting the impact of their symptoms on others. Yet the failure to perceive these symptoms does not mean that they do not exist and are not harmful to the individual. As clinicians, we wouldn't decide to leave a teenage patient's depression untreated simply because it had escaped the notice of the patient's parents and teachers. Similarly, we cannot ignore ADHD patients who appear to function adequately in their daily lives. Their symptoms, however well-masked, will still take their toll.

ADHD, like hypertension or diabetes, can be viewed on a severity continuum; some patients are severely affected by their symptoms, others less so. Often ADHD inattentive type is thought to be less impairing than the hyperactive variant, but this is misleading. Like many of the patients introduced in this chapter, inattentive ADHD patients may appear at first glance not to be impaired, but a closer evaluation usually reveals that even mild ADHD symptoms are introducing chaos and despair into their lives.

The effects of untreated ADHD extend beyond the individual to spouses, families, coworkers, and others. When an individual with ADHD is diagnosed and treated, the layers of symptoms that prevented full functioning can be peeled away. This relieves the individual and others from the frustration and harm caused by the spillover effects of ADHD. Symptoms may continue on a residual basis, but with medication and either coaching or therapy, they can be much improved.

Diagnosis Can Be Liberating

Many people with ADHD struggle valiantly to manage their daily lives and have worked out a few effective ways to cope with their symptoms. These compensations can take the form of relentless double-checking or recruiting other individuals to assist them in managing their lives. It has been my experience, however, that without medication treatment, these patients continue to underperform relative to their potential. Therapy in the form of coaching—a form of very individualized therapy that is tailored to the person's specific needs (see Chapter 10)—also provides considerable benefits.

Many people with ADHD report that, once they have been diagnosed and treated, they feel like worlds of opportunities have opened up to them.

They are able to use the full range of their intelligence and talents instead of wasting time backtracking to find lost objects or to resolve problems created by their impulsive acts. Instead, they can become productive and sharpen their focus on what happens at work and at home.

An End to Self-Blame

Most people with ADHD self-blame for their symptoms. Even when they think that the behavior is normal for themselves, they know that others disapprove of their forgetfulness, inattentiveness, and impulsivity. The burden of guilt and self-blame that is carried by many adolescents and adults with undiagnosed ADHD can be very difficult to bear, as they assume that the reasons for their lateness, procrastination, and impulsivity are character defects that could only be remedied by trying much harder. Many individuals with undiagnosed ADHD report having been chided repeatedly about their shortcomings. Since childhood, they have heard that if they try harder everything would come out right. If you hear something long enough, you start to believe it.

Unfortunately, "trying harder" is usually insufficient by itself to overcome the symptoms of ADHD. What is needed instead is treatment in the form of medication and therapy. Many patients benefit greatly from coaching. Other therapies and strategies, such as cognitive-behavioral therapy (CBT) and exercise, also can enable success. These therapies and an array of other strategies are discussed later in this book.

It is also important for doctors and other mental health professionals to avoid letting patients adopt a victim mentality and ascribe all their problems in life solely to their ADHD. Patients need to be told that ADHD is an explanation for behavior, not an excuse, and that treatment and the development of adaptive coping mechanisms are both essential.

Chapter 5

Reasons for Misdiagnosis

DESPITE ITS HIGH PREVALENCE, ADHD continues to be underdiagnosed. The question lingers: Why? This chapter speculates about why ADHD is so often overlooked and what can be done to change the therapeutic landscape. It is possible that ADHD is still considered a "fluffy" or fake diagnosis by many clinicians, just as many people, including physicians, once thought that depressed people were "faking it" or trying to get attention. Many physicians also continue to cling to the idea that ADHD is limited to children and is somehow magically resolved with the onset of puberty. These are just some of the reasons why ADHD is often not diagnosed.

ADULT ADHD IS WHERE DEPRESSION WAS THIRTY YEARS AGO

The general perception held about ADHD today is very similar to the common attitudes toward clinical depression a generation ago. In the 1970s and 1980s, much of the general public believed that the severely depressed should just try to "get it together." Most clinicians practicing at the time did not understand the sheer impossibility of "looking on the bright side" for a person suffering from clinical depression. Few physicians prescribed antidepressants, although the various classes of antidepressants have been available for many years.

Fast forward to 2006. Today, many people have a general understanding that depression is more than a passing mood. They now accept that it is a serious problem that requires treatment. They realize that depression transcends the sadness of a transient mood. It is a generally accepted dictum that depression is real and treatable — and that it *should* be treated. Acceptance of ADHD, however, lies in stark contrast to that of depression.

There are also many misperceptions about ADHD. Many physicians and much of the general public explain away ADHD symptoms by asserting that nearly everyone is forgetful, impulsive, or inattentive at times. What they do not understand is that for the person who has ADHD, these symptoms are pronounced, form a clear pattern, and cause impairment of daily functioning. Just as feeling sad once in a while is not the same as a clinical depression, losing one's car keys once a year is not the same as losing them almost every day, making the person late for work. In addition, just as people with depression need treatment, so do people with ADHD.

Like other medical conditions, ADHD is best viewed on a continuum of severity. Some people have severe hypertension and some have mild hypertension. Some diabetics require high doses of insulin; others can get by merely with changes in their diet, oral medication, and exercise patterns. Depression is similar in its variability: Some people are mildly depressed whereas others are suicidal or even psychotic. Many gains have been made in educating professionals and the public about depression. There is every reason to believe that similar strides will be made with ADHD.

The following list details some of the key reasons for misdiagnosis and missed diagnosis of ADHD.

- There is a general belief that children with ADHD will outgrow the illness. Thus, ADHD is considered a pediatric problem. Yet more than half of children with ADHD continue to suffer from symptoms into adolescence and adulthood. In addition, many adults with ADHD were never diagnosed as children, despite their symptoms. In this situation, relying on a past diagnosis to initiate or perpetuate treatment is circular logic.

- Many clinicians do not acknowledge ADHD as a valid diagnosis in anyone of any age. Some skeptics see it as a scheme created by pharmaceutical companies to sell medications. Others have more benign views, but many believe ADHD is not a valid condition.
- Many clinicians persist in assuming that ADHD is a problem limited to males. As a result, many girls and women with ADHD remain undetected. According to the Centers for Disease Control and Prevention, boys are twice as likely to be diagnosed as girls, although this ratio has fallen in recent years (Visser and Lesesne, 2005).
- Primary-care physicians and some psychiatrists are reluctant to treat adolescent and adult ADHD compared to other disorders such as depression or generalized anxiety disorder because they feel inadequate to the task or undertrained.
- Key medications for treating ADHD are Schedule II drugs, and doctors may suspect that patients who self-refer seek stimulants for illicit purposes. Doctors may feel their medical license will be jeopardized if they become involved with these patients.
- Some doctors are concerned about creating an addictive problem in patients by prescribing scheduled psychostimulants. This is rarely a valid fear unless patients have a prior substance abuse problem. In fact, the opposite may be true: Some studies indicate that treatment for ADHD in children and adolescents may be protective against future substance abuse (Faraone & Wilens, 2003).
- Sensationalistic media reports about medications used to treat ADHD frighten and confuse people, including some physicians. The general lack of publicly circulated information about adult ADHD—with the exception of periodic dramatic media reports—means most laypeople are unaware of the disorder. As a result, people with undiagnosed ADHD often blame themselves for their symptoms. Yet without treatment, they cannot improve.
- Some feel that medicating ADHD symptoms is tantamount to suppressing an individual's uniqueness, much as some used to believe that depression or bipolar disorder should not be treated lest it somehow hamstring innate creativity.

These issues are addressed in greater depth in the following sections.

BELIEF THAT PATIENTS WITH ADHD WILL "OUTGROW" IT

Many physicians, as well as much of the general lay public, scoff at the notion that adults could suffer from ADHD. The pervasive belief is that ADHD is a childhood problem and is outgrown at some point between puberty and adulthood. In the 1970s Dr. Paul Wender at the University of Utah began describing ADHD among adult populations, but the myth that ADHD is a pediatric problem persists.

Taking Wender's lead, researchers such as Weiss and Trokenberg Hechtman (1993) followed up on subjects who were diagnosed with ADHD as children. Interviews with these ADHD subjects were conducted when they were adolescents (mean age 13.4 years) and again when they were young adults (mean age 25.1 years). The study indicated that many young adults who had ADHD as adolescents still had a significantly higher rate of continued symptoms. For example, 66% of the adults had at least one symptom that continued to be troublesome (poor concentration, impulsivity, explosiveness, or restlessness).

Weiss and Trokenberg Hechtman (1993) reviewed other studies in addition to their own, and concluded that in about half the cases of children diagnosed with ADHD, these individuals had mild residual symptoms as adults. Half of them felt that they could self-manage their symptoms. The other half reported more severely disabling symptoms with which they continued to struggle. This seminal research clarified that, for many people with childhood ADHD, the mere passage of time does not neutralize the impairing nature of the symptoms.

SKEPTICISM ABOUT THE VALIDITY OF ADHD

Some physicians, psychologists, and educated laypeople continue to believe that ADHD is not a "real" diagnosis or is overdiagnosed in patients who are either malingering or have other psychiatric problems such as major depressive disorder, bipolar disorder, or generalized anxiety disorder. Often the doubters are well-meaning clinicians influenced by ideas from the mainstream media touting the latest "train wreck" headline about overdiagnosis and overmedication for ADHD, or editorials that challenge whether ADHD is a valid diagnosis at all.

A growing body of work supports the claim that ADHD is a unique medical condition and is not a variant of depression or anxiety. Two methods that prove that a psychiatric condition is valid are genetic studies and brain imaging. ADHD has proven to be valid on both these levels. Dr. Stephen Faraone (2002) and his colleagues have extensively researched the genetics of the condition and have shown that ADHD begets more ADHD. Adult relatives of children with ADHD have elevated rates of ADHD as do child relatives of adults with ADHD. Seven genes that code for the mechanism of dopamine transmission have been identified.

Some studies have revealed differences between ADHD brains and non-ADHD brains (Bush, 2002). By combining advanced brain imaging techniques such as single photon emission computed tomography (SPECT) or positronic emission tomography (PET) with neuropsychological measures, the current data suggest that the areas of abnormality in the ADHD brain lie within the prefrontal cortex and the caudate. While these techniques are not well enough developed at this point to make the diagnosis of an individual with ADHD, they might become sophisticated enough to assist clinicians with diagnosis in the near-future. But it is clear that, even in these early days of imaging and genetic research, the overwhelming evidence supports the validity of ADHD as a distinct clinical diagnosis.

THE GENDER BIAS

Female adolescents and adults are frequently not diagnosed with ADHD, unless they self-refer, because for many years ADHD was perceived as a disorder limited to males. Many clinicians continue to cling to this belief. That girls and women could also suffer from impulsivity, distractibility, and inattentiveness and meet ADHD criteria is still in some circles a novel idea.

Authors such as Solden (1995) and Quinn and Nadeau (2002) have championed the idea that ADHD is a disorder that crosses sexes. This has led a number of writers and researchers to look at this particular phenomenon (Young, 2002).

Girls and women have often been underdiagnosed with ADHD because they are less likely to exhibit hyperactivity than males. Inattentive females, although they may seem drifty and dreamy, do not usually demonstrate "acting out" behaviors that are noticed by others. Rather, they quietly underperform, slipping through the cracks and avoiding the radar of mental health or law enforcement professionals. Because they do not disturb or distress others, these females often receive little attention, although they are among the groups that most dramatically benefit from treatment. (For a more detailed discussion of gender bias in ADHD diagnosis, see Chapters 4 and 7.)

LACK OF CONFIDENCE IN DIAGNOSING AND TREATING ADULT ADHD

There is a significant shortage of psychiatrists in North America and abroad. As a result, much of the burden of mental health care falls to pediatricians, family doctors, and internists. Yet most primary-care training residencies do not devote adequate time to psychiatric issues, and very few teach the concept of ADHD as a lifelong disorder. Although many nonpsychiatrists are comfortable diagnosing and treating psychiatric illnesses like major depression or anxiety disorders, this comfort does not extend to ADHD management, and ADHD patients consistently complain that they have difficulty accessing clinicians comfortable with treatment issues. This is unfortunate, as primary-care doctors are often in an ideal position to intervene.

Primary-Care Doctors: A Survey of Their Feelings About Adult ADHD

A 2003 survey of 400 physicians conducted by Harris Interactive for New York University School of Medicine revealed that part of primary physicians' reticence to approach ADHD stems from a dearth of information (New York University School of Medicine, 2003). The respondents were doctors who treated at least 30 patients a week with any combination of ADHD, bipolar disorder, depression, generalized anxiety disorder, and obsessive-compulsive disorder. These family-practice, general-practice, and internal-medicine physicians could be presumed to have a greater interest in and knowledge about psychiatric illness than the average primary-care doctor who concentrates on treating patients with common illnesses such as hypertension or diabetes.

The survey showed that, despite their exposure to ADHD, almost half the doctors (48%) said they did *not* feel confident in treating adult ADHD. In addition, 65% of the doctors said they would defer to a specialist in treating adult ADHD, but only 2% said they would defer to a specialist if they believed that the patient had depression and 3% said they would send a patient to a specialist for generalized anxiety. The survey did not ask if these physicians knew of an ADHD specialist to whom they could refer, although it has been my observation that many do not.

Most of the surveyed doctors reported that they did not feel sufficiently knowledgeable about adult ADHD, and only 34% said they were "very knowledgeable" or "extremely knowledgeable." In contrast, 92% of the doctors believed that they were very knowledgeable or extremely knowledgeable about depression, as were 83% of the doctors about generalized anxiety. Clearly, more education about ADHD is needed among primary-care physicians to shore up their knowledge base and their confidence levels.

Primary-care physicians are often at the forefront of opportunities to flag possible ADHD in patients, in part because everyone, child through adult, needs to see a physician at some point. Often the time allotted to each patient is brief; however, if primary-care physicians appreciated the impact of the condition, they could efficiently initiate treatment or make a referral to a psychiatrist or other mental health professional who could provide needed diagnostic precision and treatment.

It is essential that the clinicians to whom the primary-care physician is referring—whether they are psychiatrists, psychologists, social workers, or therapists—be aware of the differential diagnosis of these patients.

Potential Impact of Primary-Care Doctors' Refusing to Treat Adult ADHD

Of course, there is nothing wrong with referring a patient to a specialist when a doctor feels uncomfortable with the diagnosis or treatment of a medical problem. However, there are several problems with this from the patient's perspective. Some patients' health insurance makes it very difficult for them to see a specialist, and co-payments for mental health visits may be higher than seeing the primary-care doctor.

Some patients will refuse to see a psychiatrist because of their own negative stereotypical views of psychiatry and their assumption that a person must be "crazy" to need to see a psychiatrist. These biases die hard and are perpetuated in the media and sometimes among nonpsychiatric physicians as well.

CONCERN THAT SELF-REFERRED PATIENTS MAY BE DRUG-SEEKERS

Clinicians' concerns that self-referred patients may be seeking to obtain scheduled, potentially abusable drugs like amphetamines is another obstacle to care. This fear should not be summarily dismissed; however, neither should it be assumed that most adolescents and adults who think they have ADHD are devious drug-seekers. Nevertheless, the fear of being manipulated by a street-savvy drug abuser allows an ambivalent clinician to avoid the clinical challenge of ADHD altogether.

Certain safeguards can be implemented to avoid being placed in a compromising position. Nonstimulant drugs are now available; atomoxetine (Strattera) has virtually no abuse potential and may be used first-line in all patients, particularly those with a history of past or current substance abuse. More nonstimulant mediations are under development and their arrival will negate this clinical dilemma. If the patient is actively disappointed or argumentative and tries to convince the doctor to prescribe a scheduled drug with no valid reason (e.g., a relative with ADHD had very good results with a scheduled drug), the drug-seeking suspicion may be reasonable.

CONCERNS ABOUT MISUSE OF MEDICATIONS

Physicians' fears about drug-seeking and diversion have some validity. In three separate studies, 16–34% of students with ADHD had been approached to sell, give away, or trade their stimulant medication (Molina & Pelham, 2003; Musser, Ahmann, Theye, Mundt, Broste, & Mheller-Rizner, 1998; Poulin, 2001). Teenagers and young adults taking prescribed stimulants may be goaded by their peers, who are curious about what the drug "feels" like. Their friends may plead with them that a few diverted capsules are inconsequential and harmless. Insecure adolescents with ADHD, wanting to be accepted and excessively eager to please their friends, may reluctantly comply with these demands and allow their few friends access. Physicians should anticipate this predicament and prepare teenagers to deflect such an advance by advising them that they should not advertise their ADHD diagnosis or treatment to peers and others.

More jaded adolescents may be willing to exchange their stimulant medications for cash in a very calculated manner. Physicians who suspect that adolescents are either giving away or selling their medications may be able to enlist the help of the teenager's parents by putting the parents in charge of dispensing all medications. Doctors may request that parents keep track of the number of pills in the bottle and physically dispense the drug to observe compliance.

As with all prescribed medications, physicians need to ensure that patients and their parents fully understand the implications of taking a controlled substance. The family needs to be informed that the stimulants are federally regulated and the physician's office cannot tolerate malfeasance.

That said, most teenagers do not succumb to this temptation, and if they do, it often is not done recurrently. Again, the potential for misuse should not be a reason to deny or avoid treatment. No aspect of practicing medicine is free from risk.

When the Potential Drug-Seeking Patient Is an Adult

Adult patients who abuse stimulants generally have a past history of substance abuse (Biederman, 1995). Physicians disagree on whether and when stimulants should be prescribed to patients with such a past history, but as a general rule it may be best to consider nonstimulants as the medication of first choice. Chapter 9 covers this subject in greater depth.

FEAR THAT PRESCRIBING STIMULANTS COULD CREATE
A SUBSTANCE ABUSE PROBLEM

Another reason some physicians avoid ADHD diagnosis and treatment is their concern that in prescribing stimulants, they may inadvertently create addictive behaviors in some patients. Understandably, clinicians do not want to cause harm to their patients or become involved in questionable clinical practices. However, available research tends to be reassuring. Substance abuse or dependency is usually only a potential problem in patients with a history of substance abuse.

More surprising is that several studies have clearly indicated that stimulants apparently act as a preventive mechanism against substance abuse in some patients with ADHD (Biederman, Wilens, Mick, Spencer, & Faraone, 1999; Faraone & Wilens, 2003). In a study that was jointly funded by the National Institute of Mental Health and the National Institute on Drug Abuse, researchers at Harvard Medical School, Massachusetts General Hospital, and the Harvard School of Public Health found that 25% of the ADHD adolescents who had been taking stimulants had substance abuse problems, compared to 75% of the nonmedicated boys with ADHD. Furthermore, the rate of substance abuse among the medicated boys with ADHD (25%) was close to the rate of substance abuse among non-ADHD boys (18%). The finding that stimulants served as a protective factor *against* substance abuse in these adolescent males needs to be appreciated by clinicians and parents.

SENSATIONAL MEDIA REPORTS FRIGHTEN
AND CONFUSE PEOPLE

Omnipresent and conflicting media reports often interfere with the free flow of information on ADHD diagnosis and treatment. Clinicians and the general public are frequently exposed to reports that breathlessly assert that too many American children are "on" Ritalin or similar medications. The tacit message is that the medical profession is unnecessarily drugging children and that such medications may cause current or long-term harm. The argument that many children are overdiagnosed with ADHD is a fallacy, as are the deductions that the treatments are dangerous, poorly arrived at, and invalid in adolescents and adults.

The Role of "Big Pharma"

In the last 10 years, as the prices of prescription medications have increased and the controversy about the prudence of importing drugs from other countries resonates on cable news and op-ed pages, editorialists frequently assail the pharmaceutical industry for allegedly inventing illness in order to create a market for their medications. Indeed, many people who take drugs like Viagra do so only to enhance their sexual performance and not because they have true medical conditions. But like many complicated issues, the truth is somewhere in the middle. Although the media has lambasted them for exaggerating the prevalence of ADHD, companies that produce ADHD medications have done a responsible job of educating physicians and the public.

Ideally, educating physicians is the job of the nation's medical schools, but when a condition like ADHD becomes fully appreciated after most doctors have completed their formal medical education, the responsibility of disseminating information falls increasingly to the private sector. Big pharmaceutical companies, now highly regulated by trade organizations and the government, have effectively drawn attention to these conditions by producing good medications, spurring research, and appealing to the public through advertisements. Although this system is imperfect, the more that is known about ADHD in adolescents and adults, the more patients can access care, and most importantly, the less people will suffer from untreated illness.

The Public's Lack of Accurate Information About Adult ADHD

In contrast to the proliferation of stories about childhood ADHD, for the most part, there is insufficient information available about adult ADHD. Many people have heard about childhood ADHD, especially if they are the parent of a child who has been diagnosed, but individuals without children often know little or nothing about the disorder. Consequently, childless adults with ADHD often go undetected.

Many undiagnosed adults with ADHD blame themselves for their symptoms. A lifetime of frustration inevitably erodes self-esteem. The title of one of the first books on adult ADHD, *You Mean I'm not Crazy, Stupid, or Lazy*, (Kelly & Ramundo, 1996) inevitably provokes a knowing response among ADHD sufferers because it so succinctly defines the inner thoughts of those afflicted. Only accurate diagnosis and treatment can offer them any hope of true liberation.

FEAR THAT MEDICATING PATIENTS WITH ADHD WILL IMPAIR THEIR UNIQUENESS

Some individuals express the fear that medications for ADHD will somehow "zombify" a person or take away his or her unique personality. They do not understand that personality is not changed by medication, psychotherapy, or coaching. Indeed, ADHD symptoms often mask individuals' true personality and impede them from achieving their goals. Adolescents and adults with ADHD who are diagnosed and treated ultimately can be liberated to optimize their true selves.

II

ADHD Patient Populations

Chapter 6

Adolescents and Young Adults

THE STRAINS AND OVERALL CONFUSION that the onset of puberty brings (generally between the ages of 11 and 14 years), as well as the general turmoil of adolescence itself, can make the ADHD diagnosis even more challenging, as clinicians must differentiate normal adolescent behavior from ADHD symptoms. In adolescence, the body and brain are altered by physical changes and hormonal surges, and ADHD symptoms become even more daunting and difficult to address. Furthermore, whereas adults with ADHD have had time to adapt to the symptoms of inattentiveness, disorganization, impulsivity, and hyperactivity, adolescent patients have far less sophisticated compensatory skills.

In addition, young adult males and females in their late teens and early twenties often struggle with conflicts at work, as well as with relationships and at home. When ADHD is present and untreated, the symptoms of disorganization and distractibility can lead to failure in college or at work and romantic relationships may be turbulent. This chapter offers examples of adolescent and young adults whose undiagnosed ADHD has presented

113

major obstacles to their success, but whose subsequent diagnosis and treatment provided them with much brighter futures.

Sometimes parents of teenagers suspect that their children have ADHD but they cannot find a clinician to concur. Parents with this belief may arm themselves with supporting claims from teachers, academic counselors, and sometimes even the adolescents themselves. Although it is important to fully evaluate these concerns, clinicians should not overlook the possibility that the teenager may be exhibiting typical adolescent behavior—possibly at the outer edges of the normal range, but normal nonetheless. Still, many parents report frustration that they are not truly "heard" by the clinician. It is one thing for clinicians to disagree with parents after hearing their concerns and altogether another thing to quickly dismiss these concerns, sometimes in an overtly patronizing manner, without really listening to the people expressing them.

In other cases, parents, teachers, and others attribute the adolescent's symptoms to other problems, such as depression. Indeed, the high prevalence of major depression in adolescents has been better publicized in recent years. Of course, it may be true that the adolescent is depressed, but in some cases, the primary problem is ADHD. It is a clinician's challenge to sort out these complicated conditions.

Clinical expertise is also needed to decipher the thorny issue of which adolescents receive the ADHD diagnosis. Cynics refer to ADHD as a disorder of the affluent, pursued by overeager parents interested in optimizing their child's school achievement. At the same time, other critics reduce ADHD as a diagnosis clinicians give to less privileged children to explain their behavior and a method to control their behavior with medications. The last part of this chapter considers the role race and class play in the likelihood of getting the ADHD diagnosis.

ADOLESCENT ADHD SYMPTOMS VARY

As with adults, adolescent ADHD is not a "one size fits all" presentation. Some adolescents may be successful in school but struggle with social relationships. Others may have friends—sometimes approved of by their parents, sometimes not—but perform below their potential in school.

Some may attract the attention of law enforcement and school authorities; others may quietly suffer unnoticed.

Clinicians should also be mindful that female adolescents with ADHD may present differently than their male cohorts. As discussed in Chapter 7, girls and women are more likely to exhibit internalizing symptoms, whereas boys and men are more likely to externalize. In addition, female adolescents are more likely to be comorbid for other psychiatric conditions, such as depression and anxiety, and to have greater problems with teacher relationships than teenage boys (Rucklidge & Tannock, 2001).

By the process of asking questions and carefully listening to what the teenager says (or leaves out), the therapist can begin to develop a strategy to overcome the normal treatment resistance exhibited by most adolescents. Discovering what is important to the adolescent, whether it is music, a girlfriend or boyfriend, or a simple goal such as being left alone by one's parents, can lead to aligning therapeutic goals with what the patients think they truly need. For example, if adolescents believe the main problem is that their parents are constantly annoying them, the therapist may agree that parents sometimes can be very intrusive, and that the therapist and the adolescent together can work together to find ways to convince the parents to do some backing off.

At the same time, the therapist should not allow adolescent patients to think that they have no problems and that the only real problems are in the minds of others. However, a tacit acceptance on the part of the adolescent that there *may* be some problems other than those specifically identified by others may follow with the therapist's seeking to understand and assist the adolescent with his or her own goals.

DISTRESSED ADOLESCENTS: IS BEHAVIOR NORMAL OR NOT?

Distressed is perhaps the best word to describe troubled adolescents before a thorough diagnostic evaluation occurs. *Distress* connotes angst and dissatisfaction but does not presuppose a diagnosis. Distressed adolescents may be ornery and easily angered; they may also display oppositional behavior.

Often, parents bring their distressed adolescent in for evaluation because of a singular crisis. This can involve academic or behavioral problems including school failure, sexual promiscuity, or substance abuse. Commonly the teenager has exhibited other negative behaviors, such as aggression, shoplifting, or extreme passivity. He or she may be in trouble with the law. Such behaviors may be indicative of ADHD. Adolescents with ADHD frequently behave impulsively, which may be a combination of a drive for novelty and disinhibition.

In his book *ADHD in Adolescents: Diagnosis and Treatment*, Arthur L. Robin (1998) described teenage impulsivity in this manner:

Behaviorally, *the impulsive teenager has to have things right now, and thus acts on a whim. He or she does whatever pops into mind, becoming a victim of the moment, blurting things out, opting for short-term pleasure despite long-term pain, and not considering the consequences of actions before taking them. It is difficult for them to regulate their behavior in accordance with external or internal standards or rules.* Cognitively, *the impulsive adolescent rushes through schoolwork, overlooking crucial details, making careless mistakes, and writing sloppily. He or she cannot slow down [the] cognitive tempo.* Emotionally, *impulsive teenagers become easily frustrated, agitated, moody, and/or emotionally overactive, losing their temper, and having angry and/or violent outbursts which may be accompanied by aggressive physical and verbal responses, directed either at others or at oneself (e.g., suicidal behaviors).* (p. 17)

Mental health professionals who diagnose and treat adolescents with ADHD must be able to distinguish normal adolescent behavior from ADHD. Table 6.1 offers some general guidance on this issue.

Diagnostically, the clinician must consider whether the distress is an expression of normal adolescence, an adjustment disorder to a life circumstance, depression or another mood disorder, oppositional defiant disorder, ADHD, or a combination of the above.

Many distressed adolescents present with a previous ADHD diagnosis, but the new clinician should not assume that the earlier diagnosis was accurate. For all new patients, complete diagnostic testing should be reviewed and accepted only if it is timely and was properly executed.

Clinicians should also note that even if the past ADHD diagnosis was accurate, the adolescent's new presentation may be different. Adolescence

TABLE 6.1
Normal Adolescent Behavior Versus ADHD Symptoms

Adolescent Without ADHD	*Adolescent With ADHD*
May forget to do homework once or twice a month	Frequently forgets to do homework, as often as several times a week (or daily)
Changes his mind (even several times) about wishing to go on a family outing	Changes his mind on many things, as often as daily
Delays taking out the garbage	Never or rarely takes out the garbage, despite many reminders
Has a stormy argument with a friend	Has frequent arguments with peers; may have few or even no friends
Gets a traffic ticket	Receives two or more traffic tickets, especially for speeding, over a 2- to 3-month period
May try drugs or alcohol	May abuse drugs or alcohol, especially if ADHD is undiagnosed or untreated
Loses her watch	Loses her watch as well as her comb, cell phone, purse, and other items all in the same week
May start smoking before age 15	At greater risk for smoking initiation before age 15

brings with it many comorbidities not present in childhood, such as depression, substance use, or anxiety. Prudence dictates keeping an open mind and an acknowledgement that the presentation is fluid and looks and acts differently throughout the patient's first 2 decades of life.

GATHERING COLLATERAL INFORMATION

For the adolescent's initial evaluation, parents should be asked to bring in a sampling of their teenager's report cards since grade school. Young adults may be able to obtain old report cards from their parents. These can assist clinicians in assessing for historical patterns and any recent trends. Much can be derived from teacher comments. A student's failure to follow directions may be a sign of inattention. Frequently blurting out answers and making inappropriate social comments are signs of impulsivity. Supporting clues about disorganization may yield from reports that homework often was (or still is) lost or not turned in.

When the child previously has been professionally evaluated, the clinician should ask the adolescent and parents to sign permission for the clinician to receive all prior reports. Including the teenager in this process builds trust and respect and ensures that the best available background information is used to develop the patient's full picture.

Collateral sources can also be very helpful in providing a clearer view of the adolescent, which is why it is important for the clinician to determine if there are other adults with whom the teenager frequently interacts, such as a coach or a music teacher. In these cases, it is an excellent idea to obtain the permission of the adolescent and parents to speak to these other adults about the teenager's behavior. Emphasize beforehand that these other adults will be consulted about both strengths and areas in need of improvement, and that discussions will not solely focus on negative features of the adolescent.

MAINTAINING A NEUTRAL OR POSITIVE DEMEANOR

The therapist's demeanor while asking these questions is very important. To avoid sounding accusatory or condemning, the questions should be asked in a neutral tone of voice, so that the adolescent does not feel like he or she is being grilled by a police officer. In addition, the questions should be interspersed with innocuous and non-threatening comments that can put the adolescent more at ease. Rather than asking the questions one after the other, the therapist can intercede comments about the weather, the lateness of the day or other comments that may help put the adolescent more at ease.

When possible, brief positive comments should be made. For example, with the question, "How many grades have you failed?" if the teenager responds with "none," the therapist can state that it can be hard for many people with ADHD to do well in school, and it is a good sign and to his or her credit that the teenager has been able to stay on track with his or her peers.

With the question, "How many times do your parents have to tell you to do something before you actually do it?", the therapist might note that teenagers (and many other people) cannot seem to hear it when they are told to do boring work, yet their hearing suddenly becomes excellent if someone whispers that a popular rock star is in town.

CONSIDERING OTHER MEDICAL PROBLEMS

When clinicians evaluate adolescents and young adults for ADHD, conditions that mimic ADHD symptoms should be considered. Thyroid disease, nutritional deficiencies, and anemia are not common among American adolescents but they do occur. Primary-care physicians can conduct simple laboratory tests to identify these medical problems. If impulsive temper outbursts are evident, an electroencephalogram (EEG) can assess whether a seizure disorder may be a factor in the adolescent's behavior. By ruling out these medical problems, the clinician can proceed to determine if ADHD or other psychiatric problems are present. Height, weight, and blood pressure should be charted, as many of the medications that may be prescribed can affect these parameters. (For more information on medications, see Chapter 9.)

RATING SCALES AND TESTING

Many ADHD rating scales, which assess *DSM-IV* symptoms, are self-administered, inexpensive, and can be completed within 5 or 10 minutes. Popular rating scales for adolescents include the Brown Attention Deficit Disorder Scales for Adolescents, the Conners-Wells Adolescent Self-Report Scale, and the Vanderbilt ADHD Diagnostic Teacher Rating Scale. Given the high rates of comorbid depression, mood assessment is also necessary. The Childhood Depression Inventory (CDI) should be given routinely to adolescents.

These rating scales should be given to all adolescents who present for mental health treatment, not just those who are suspected of having ADHD. This allows clinicians to discover hidden ADHD histories and, just as importantly, assures that the rating scales are not elevated in every adolescent seen.

It should also be noted that self-rating scales are only as valid as the effort of the person completing them. If the teenager is ambivalent about the entire process and completes the scales half-heartedly, they offer little value. In these cases, the clinician needs to rely on the patient's history, clinical examination, and input from collateral sources like teachers and parents. Rating scales for adults are discussed in Chapter 1.

Screening for learning disabilities is typically not done in initial evaluations, perhaps because there is little consensus as to how this should be undertaken. Learning disabilities are pinpoint cognitive deficits such as problems with calculations, sequencing, or reading (Feinstein, 1991). They can exist within the context of normal or above-average intelligence. Estimates are that 20% of adolescents with ADHD also have a learning disability (Shaywitz & Shaywitz, 1989). Learning disabilities can be very disruptive to students, so identifying them is essential to understanding an adolescent struggling with school problems. Coupled with the ADHD symptoms of inattention and distractibility, learning disabilities minimize a child's chance of school success.

The formal diagnosis of specific learning disabilities belongs in the hands of a neuropsychologist, but screening for learning disabilities during an ADHD evaluation helps the clinician make an effective referral. The Wide Range Aptitude Test (WRAT) is a 40- to 60-minute test that can be administered to adolescents older than 16. The WRAT assesses non-contextual reading, spelling, and mathematical aptitude. The overall score correlates rather well with IQ. A learning disability is suggested if a substantial discrepancy is seen between the subtests—for example, if the patient tests high on reading and spelling but extremely low on math. In this situation, further testing for learning disabilities is indicated, and a referral to an educational psychologist is essential. The use of the WRAT early in the diagnostic process is time- and cost-efficient. It is not definitive, but if the results are normal, the clinician knows there is no need to refer the adolescent for a full neuropsychological evaluation. (See Chapter 2 for more about learning disabilities.)

Adolescents and young adults with ADHD often know failure better than success. They may feel undirected and struggle with making good decisions about their future. The goal of counseling is to help guide them and deter them from repeating past mistakes. Tests designed to assess aptitudes and interests, such as the Campbell Interest and Skill Survey (CISS), can be very effective. The CISS is software-based and generates a report for the patient and clinician to use. In plain language, adolescents can see how their aptitudes match with their interests. This information can help guide school and job selection. This type of testing is often among the most appreciated parts of the evaluation by the adolescent.

INTERVIEWING STRATEGIES AND DEVELOPING RAPPORT

During the initial evaluation, it may be advisable to meet with the teenager alone first, and then meet with the parents in his or her presence. Meeting the parents before meeting the adolescent jeopardizes the therapeutic alliance, as some teenagers will be suspicious that their parents will use the time to complain about them, share stories of indiscretion, or otherwise "misrepresent" their concerns. Adolescents are often concrete rather than abstract thinkers, and assuring them of confidentiality is less meaningful than showing them by action. Taking tangible steps to demonstrate the importance of confidentiality strengthens the therapeutic alliance and increases the likelihood of long-term cooperation. That said, parents should have access to the therapist, and the ideal situation is to meet with the entire family if the adolescent feels comfortable with it.

During the initial interview, before ADHD has been ruled in or out, it is important to remember that negativity is developmentally normal for adolescents. When a toddler is asked if she wants something, she may respond with a resounding "no," even if she wants the item, simply because she has learned that saying "no" holds power over others. This type of behavior is also common in adolescence. For example, if the therapist asks the teenager what concerns him most, he may overtly deny any problems. Some teenagers plead complete ignorance as to why they are there. This response may dismay the parents, as they might have been discussing all the relevant issues on the ride to the doctor's office. The parent's exasperated response allows the teenager to point out, as if on cue, that Mom should be the identified patient, not him. Of course, there is sometimes truth here, but the clinician cannot get distracted.

A more productive question might be, "Why do you think your parents brought you here?" or "What do you think your parents (or teachers) think is your main problem?" This question leads adolescents to describing how they believe others perceive them. It can also disarm them into talking about what is *really* bothering them, which may be quite different from what bothers the parents. Although adolescents may deny that their parents' conceptualization of the problem is correct, this opening question allows reticent teenagers to start talking about the symptoms that truly do bother them, and this information is clearly useful in the diagnostic and treatment process.

In addition to establishing rapport, the clinician must use the interview to ask questions that will elicit critical information pertaining to the ADHD diagnosis. The following questions, based on the extensive data collected on this group, can be penetrating and may provide rapid information.

- *How many traffic tickets have you received in the past 3 or 4 months?* Do not ask *if* they have received any tickets, but rather assume that tickets have been received. If you are wrong and the answer is "zero," the teenager will tell you. Two or more traffic tickets in several months is generally beyond the norm for the non-ADHD teenager. Adolescents with ADHD are notorious for having driving problems. They are almost seven times as likely as their non-ADHD peers to be in two or more car accidents and they are about four times as likely to be at fault in the accident. In addition, they have a greater risk of suffering from severe injuries (60% of teens with ADHD versus 17% of teens without ADHD; Barkley, Guevremont, Anastopoulos, DuPaul, & Shelton, 1993). Treatment can often provide significant improvement in driving behavior.
- *How many grades have you failed?* Studies indicate that adolescents and young adults with ADHD have an increased risk of failing grades

(about 29% compared to 10% of controls). Research has also indicated that about 46% of adolescents with ADHD are suspended from school, versus about 15% of controls (Barkley, DuPaul, & McMurray, 1990; Fischer, Barkley, Edelbrock, & Smallish, 1990). Again, treatment can often turn around an unhappy situation.

- *How many times in the past week have you lost your house keys/cell phone/watch/purse/backpack?* Choose one. If the teenager has lost the item more than once in a week, this is a sign of disorganization.

- *At what age did you start smoking?* Adolescents with ADHD are significantly more likely to smoke than others. For example, in one study, 25% of adolescents with ADHD began smoking before age 15, compared to 9% of controls (Milberger, Biederman, Faraone, Chen, & Jones, 1997).

- *If you could receive $500 now or $1000 two weeks from now, which would you choose?* This question is not diagnostic, but it can separate those with impulsive tendencies from their more restrained peers. ADHD individuals are not known for their ability to delay gratification. Some teens, however, may see through this question and know that $1000 is the "right" answer.

- *On average, how many times do your parents tell you to take out the garbage or wash the dishes before you actually do it?* Most teenagers might need to be told once or twice, but ultimately they complete the task. Adolescents with ADHD may be told three or four times and still never get the task done. Unlike non-ADHD teens, who consciously postpone their actions, ADHD teens often legitimately forget that the request was made. Many parents of ADHD children fear that their child cannot hear and arrange for an evaluation. Inevitably the audiologist finds that the neurological ability to hear is fine. The problem is that the child is too distracted to listen.

- *How many times in your life have you broken a bone, including fingers and toes?* The average adolescent may have experienced one fracture whereas the teenager with ADHD may have had multiple orthopedic interventions. (Of course, not having had any broken bones does not rule out ADHD.) If the adolescent reports fractures, ask about the circumstances. Did it occur as a result of carelessness (slamming the door on oneself) or risk-taking behavior (fighting)? This information may help with diagnosis and add to a more dimensional understanding of the patient's life.

- **How many times have you been hospitalized for injuries?** Adolescents and young adults with ADHD are more likely than those without ADHD to have been hospitalized for injuries, and the reasons for any hospitalizations should be explored.

- **How many times have the police come to your home or called your parents because of something you were accused of doing?** If the teenager says none, this does not rule out ADHD. However, if law enforcement officials have contacted the parents even once, this may indicate that impulsive behavior has led to trouble for the adolescent.

- **About how many screaming arguments have you had with friends in the past few weeks? How many with your parents?** Adolescents without ADHD may argue with both friends and family, but frequent or daily arguments need to be explored as a possible indicator of ADHD, as failure to comply with reasonable requests is more frequent among adolescents with ADHD. Many adolescents with ADHD are argumentative, especially when they also have oppositional defiant disorder.

- **When you are given a school assignment, like a term paper, when do you start working on it?** The average adolescent may start a day before or a few days before the assignment is due. The average teenager with ADHD may start at midnight the night before — or never get around to writing it at all.

- **How many times in the past few months did you do your homework but not turn it in?** The average adolescent without ADHD may say once or twice, but the average teenager with ADHD will, if honest, report many more incidences. If the teen says none or once, refer to the information from the report cards. For example, the therapist might say, "When you were in sixth grade, your teacher said you almost never turned in your homework. Now that you are a year older, have things changed?"

- **If you wanted to plan a party or barbecue, how much time would you need to plan the event?** The average adolescent or young adult without ADHD might say a few days or a few weeks, whereas the average

teenager with ADHD would start planning as soon as the thought oc-curred, although the plan probably would never actually be carried out.
- *At what age did you start having sex?* Teens with ADHD are more likely to initiate sex before age 15 than their peers. They are also less likely to use contraceptives and more likely to contract sexually trans-mitted diseases.

Establishing and maintaining rapport, as well as careful interviewing, are critical parts of initiating successful therapy. But optimizing the chances of a positive outcome is also dependent on the adolescent's per-ceiving an advantage to treatment. Distressed parents may readily see the benefits of an improved ability on the part of their child to take out the trash when asked or to raise a grade point average, but if the adolescent's goals do not match treatment goals, progress will move slowly, if at all.

DEALING WITH RESISTANCE OR RELUCTANCE

Adults who present for ADHD evaluation are often willing and enthusi-astic. Not so for adolescents. Many resent being identified as different from their peers, and many also resist the idea of taking medication, even when their parents are fervently in favor of it (or especially when their parents are fervently in favor of it).

Common adolescent and young adult mindsets can also obstruct ther-apy. The "there is nothing wrong with me" attitude, familiar to all who have raised, taught, or treated adolescents, results from primitive psycho-logical defenses. These types of attitudes, typical of many adolescents but much more pronounced in those with ADHD, must be taken into account by mental health professionals. Appropriate therapeutic responses to the following schema are discussed in this section.

- I'm young and should enjoy myself now.
- Other people (like my parents) are mean to me.
- Everyone is making a big deal out of nothing (even when the problems are car accidents, substance abuse, school failure, and so forth).
- I need excitement and there's nothing wrong with that (despite near misses of severe injuries and sometimes harm to others).

I'm young and should enjoy myself now. Young people should enjoy themselves. However, patients who seem to believe that this prerogative equates to an exemption from completing any boring task are abdicating their basic personal responsibility. Although in and of itself this is not diagnostic of ADHD, the clinician should challenge comments that represent immaturity beyond that expected of the average teenager.

For example: "You say that cleaning your room and preparing a meal occasionally is too much to expect from a 16-year-old. Do you really feel this way?" Faced with this direct question, most adolescents will distance themselves from the statement, insisting that although they do not like having to perform these tasks, they understand their responsibility and realize they could perform the task. In contrast, adolescents without much insight may endorse the therapist's statement, perhaps revealing a rationalization of their long-standing ADHD-related problems with initiation and motivation.

Other people are mean to me. It is very common for adolescents to blame others for the consequences of their own behavior and to think in a magical way that if only their parents would give them more money/freedom/ a car, everything in their lives would be perfect. Externalization is not the sole domain of the young, and many adults also share this mindset— if they had a better job, nicer spouse, bigger house, and so forth, *then* their lives would be ideal. It is hard work for the therapist to encourage adolescents to think less about the looming world and instead focus on changing what they control, not what they don't. Adolescents with ADHD may also be more prone than others to have grandiose ideas of how wealth (or power or status) could make them idyllically happy.

When adolescents believe that the expectations of others are unreasonable, clinicians should explore specifically what they perceive these expectations to be and how and why they are unjust. Sometimes the act of verbalizing immature and unreasonable thoughts can jolt adolescents into realizing that it is their own beliefs about others that are unfair.

Everyone is making a big deal out of nothing. It is common for adolescents to assume that their parents, teachers, and others have exaggerated the significance of their behavior. "Yes, I stayed out all night and did get into an accident that totaled the car, but that happens to a lot of people."

Or, "Yes, I am getting bad grades now, but it is just a temporary situation and very soon, probably tomorrow, I am going to sit down and study until my eyes bleed."

Accepting that adolescents are prone to melodrama, the therapist should try to make the youngster recognize his or her cognitive distortion. The therapist may wish to obliquely reference another patient, describing the behaviors and life direction of the adolescent patient but changing them just enough that the patient does not immediately realize that the example mirrors his or her own situation. The therapist can then ask the patient, "Do you think that the person I just described is going to achieve his goals by continuing this behavior?" If the adolescent says no, the therapist can then point out why and how the patient's own behavior is preventing him or her from achieving the goals that are important, just as the behavior of the hypothetical teenager is preventing him from achieving goals.

I need excitement and there's nothing wrong with that. Teenagers and young adults with ADHD need more stimulation and novelty than other adolescents. When they report being easily bored, they are usually telling the truth. Untreated teens with ADHD are more likely than other adolescents to place themselves in vulnerable and sometimes dangerous circumstances. These adolescents drive fast, experiment readily, and are attracted to associating with "bad boys" (regardless of their gender).

Even when treatment is effective, the drive for novelty may not vanish altogether; however, hopefully more positive outlets, such as active physical sports or hobbies, will fulfill the need for excitement. Medication can also help patients overcome the need for constant and intense sensation-seeking without deducting from the pleasure that teens can take in life.

Tactics of Uncooperative Adolescents

Most clinicians are experienced in diagnosing and treating difficult or resistant patients, but adolescents may be particularly challenging, whether they have ADHD or not. This is especially true when they are convinced that there is nothing wrong with them and that the problem instead lies with their parents, teachers, or virtually everyone else but themselves. Yet it is crucial for the clinician to obtain the information needed to make a diagnosis as well as to create a treatment plan.

Teenage patients' negative attitude may manifest in the following behaviors:

- Refusing to speak to the therapist
- Using abusive, profane, or insulting language
- Arguing with the mental health professional
- Agreeing to everything the doctor requests (but complying with nothing)
- Insisting there is no problem and that it's really others who need therapy

REFUSING TO SPEAK TO THE THERAPIST

Disarming or positive comments to the adolescent or young adult may break the ice, but with the implacable, stubborn teenager, arms folded across his chest and jaw set, other tactics may be in order. Keep in mind that sometimes, no matter how effective a clinician is, the adolescent may believe that he or she will ultimately "win" by refusing to answer questions— even those with simple "yes" or "no" responses.

Talking about what the adolescent would rather be doing instead of getting a psychiatric diagnosis may help. For example, asking the adolescent if she would rather be talking with her friends on the phone or going to the movies can help to break the ice and also acknowledges the teenager's true feelings.

A tactic of reverse psychology may also be effective, such as telling the adolescent girl clad in all black that she appears to be a "girly girl." It is difficult for a teenager to remain silent when she believes she is perceived as the opposite of what she is striving for. Such a strategy can surely backfire, but in some cases it is a risk worth taking.

Another strategy is to remark, "You are certainly a person of few words—or rather, no words at all." If the adolescent wishes to be oppositional, it would be hard to *not* speak at this point.

Some therapists use other approaches to deactivate an adolescent's defenses; for example, they will tell a teenager that because the adolescent has never met the therapist before and does not know him, it is okay to refuse to talk about something or even to lie about it. The therapist then adds that if the teenager wishes to talk about what is *really* going on, he or she should just say so and that will be fine, too. The response to the therapist's offer can be productive. Many adolescents are so conditioned to adults' insisting that they provide immediate, factual responses that when they are told they may withhold information or even lie, they become intrigued. The unusual offer can actually have the clinician's desired effect; most teenagers, when comfortable, cannot *stop* talking about how they truly feel. The information that the adolescent provides is important, not only to make a diagnosis but also to build the tenuous alliance.

USING ABUSIVE, PROFANE, OR INSULTING LANGUAGE

In some cases, adolescents or young adults will resort to the use of demeaning or abusive language, including profanity. Every clinician has heard offensive language and many do not consider it troubling. Often it is not the words themselves that are most offensive but rather the tone of voice and the volume that are disturbing. No one, including therapists, enjoys being on the receiving end of a screaming tirade, although sometimes it represents something of a breakthrough.

Adolescents today are more likely to use excessive profanity than teenagers of even a decade ago. However, when it is clear that the language is purposely being used to upset or intimidate the therapist, one tactic is to simply ask the adolescent to speak more politely. If this fails, one countertactic is to use the same language on the adolescent, to excess, to point out how annoying and silly it is. For example, if the teenager insists, "I don't fucking want to be here," the therapist can respond with a comment such as, "You are fucking here to get some fucking help to overcome your fucking symptoms that you have fucking complained about to your parents." (The use of the profane adjective before the word *parents* is discretionary.)

If the teenager is not using profanity or shouting but is instead being snide, sarcastic, and insulting, there are a variety of tactics the therapist may employ. Witty therapists may gain the respect of the adolescent by making sarcastic remarks in response, although the remarks should be mild and not cutting. Other therapists may wish to observe that the patient seems very angry about something and wonder aloud what could be going on to engender such hostility. The therapist may consider asking the patient if it is something about him or herself that disturbs the teenager. It is unlikely that the therapist is the problem, but if he or she is, asking the question can obtain important information. Sometimes being silly can open doors, as when the therapist asks the adolescent if she loathes people who wear navy blue (or whatever color clothing the therapist is wearing) or striped ties. Most teens would be startled out of their practiced hostility by such a question and the discussion can be free-floating for a short period until the therapist guides the adolescent back to the reasons why he or she is in the office.

ARGUING WITH THE MENTAL HEALTH PROFESSIONAL

Many adolescents seem almost hard-wired to argue with just about everyone and about just about everything. If the arguments are extremely heated, particularly over minor issues, this may indicate ODD, which is often comorbid with ADHD. One possible disarming tactic is to say to the adolescent, "You really like to argue, don't you?" to which the negative response would be to deny that tendency and consequently to stop arguing. This tactic may effectively inhibit argumentative responses long enough to obtain some useful information that can help the therapist to diagnose the teenager.

AGREEING TO EVERYTHING THE DOCTOR REQUESTS
(BUT COMPLYING WITH NOTHING)

Some adolescents and young adults are very compliant while in the therapist's office, agreeing to everything that the mental health professional wishes, whether it is to take medication, go to psychotherapy, or perform certain tasks. Then they leave the office and do not comply with anything that they have just agreed to do. These passive-aggressive patients can be difficult to manage. Keep in mind that adolescents actively seek control, and if they can be persuaded that taking medication or performing other tasks will provide *them* with increased control, they may become intrigued enough to follow through with what the doctor has suggested.

One way for adolescents to exhibit their defiance is to refuse to take their medication or to pretend to take it. Initially parents should administer prescribed medication to their adolescent children, but if the adolescent is defiant, he or she may still find ways to avoid taking it. "Cheeking" the drug, like a chipmunk storing an acorn and then spitting it out later, is a favored approach to avoid taking medication.

Fortunately, one of the attributes of stimulant medications is the quick onset of action, and the patient need not make a lengthy investment of time before he or she sees benefits. If the patient will agree to take at least one or two pills, a difference is usually noted. Once adolescents see these gains accrue, they will usually become less oppositional and more independent.

INSISTING THERE IS NO PROBLEM

Most adolescents and some young adults spend a good deal of time lamenting their parents' intelligence and judgment. At best, parents are considered annoying and unreasonable. Thus, if the parent believes that the child may have ADHD and needs help, the adolescent may summarily reject the notion. Adolescents without ADHD may also heartily disagree with their parents, but the disputes are more heated and frequent when the adolescent has ADHD.

In such situations, the therapeutic intervention is to align with the parent and work with the adolescent's objections. An exchange with 15-year-old Len demonstrates this approach.

> **Doctor:** Your parents are concerned that you are not doing as well as you could. If we work together maybe there is something we can do to help you feel and function better.
> **Len:** If you think I have ADD, join the club. That problem is my Dad's, not mine.
> **Doctor:** Well, that might be the case. If he agrees, what if we evaluate your Dad at the same time as we look at you?
> **Len:** Hmm. . . .

Such an offer may be very encouraging to the patient. It allows him to save face and proceed with less resistance while delivering the added benefit of letting the doctor learn more about Len's family.

Patients Who Are Cooperative but Confused

Not all teenagers and young adults are resistant to treatment. Some adolescents, whether they have ADHD or not, may realize that they have a problem and sincerely cooperate with the mental health professional. However, like many adults, adolescents often experience fear, which they may or may not express. These concerns are important to identify and discuss in order to effectively treat the adolescent. Common fears include:

- Fear that their friends will discover they are being treated.
- Fear that medication will change them or cause loss of control.
- Fear that they are incapable of change and it is hopeless to try.
- Fear that their problem is their fault.

FEAR THAT THEIR FRIENDS WILL DISCOVER THEY ARE BEING TREATED

Many adolescents, especially in early adolescence (age 11–14), appear to be in a permanent state of embarrassment. Their parents embarrass them, their siblings embarrass them, and they worry a great deal about what others think about them. If adolescents have never seen a mental health professional before (or even if they have had prior treatment, especially as a child), they may fear that someone will see them in the psychiatrist's waiting room and that the whole school will "find out."

These fears can be assuaged in several ways. One way is for the therapist to state that some teenagers are a little worried about seeing a therapist because they think that others may tease them, although not everyone feels this way. The therapist can assure the adolescent that everything that is said in therapy is held in complete confidence "by law." If adolescents are worried that they may see one of their peers in the waiting room, the therapist can use the opportunity to full advantage.

Molly, 13, started her session with uncharacteristic silence.

Doctor: You seem so quiet. Are you okay?
Molly: Christy, a girl from my school, saw me come in here.
Doctor: Where did you see her?
Molly: In the waiting room.

Doctor: What was she doing there?

Molly: I guess waiting too. Her mom told the receptionist they were there to see Lisa [another therapist].

Doctor: Then she saw you, but you also saw her.

Molly: So what?

Doctor: Well, didn't you also wonder why *she* was here?

Molly: Oh!

Doctor: Molly, there is no shame in you being here, but if Christy tells other kids that she saw you here, they will ask her how she knows and what she was doing here herself. She will have to tell them.

Molly: Yeah, I get it now.

Doctor: It's in her interest to respect your privacy and in your best interest to always respect hers.

Molly: Yes, I guess so.

This is also a good time to explore with the young teenager apprehensions about "being labeled." Inquire about this specific concern. If the teenager says that only "crazy people" see therapists, the therapist should counter by explaining that people who go to therapy are willing to do something to help themselves feel better. Normalizing behavior, when appropriate, can be fundamentally therapeutic to all patients who have trepidation about the therapeutic process.

FEAR THAT MEDICATION WILL CHANGE THEM OR CAUSE LOSS OF CONTROL

Another common fear for many adolescents (and some young adults) is that ADHD medications will somehow change their basic personality. They fear losing their emotions, their spontaneity, and even their self-control. Before a diagnosis is made, it is unclear which, if any, medications are appropriate. However, it is still a good idea to address these common fears about all psychiatric medications.

In fact, a few patients, particularly those on methylphenidate, report feeling blunted or dulled. Usually this side effect is addressed by changing to another medication. Patients and their families need to be informed about potential side effects; it is unethical not to give a full picture. They also need to be instructed that most patients who succeed with medication are freed from their long-standing symptoms and obtain greater control and mastery over their lives. Believing that medications will be helpful requires a leap of faith that may be difficult for many people considering treatment, especially adolescents. The doctor can assure the adolescent patient that the lowest possible dose of medication is given to start, and that if there are any side effects, they should be reported.

Because of confidentiality concerns, therapists cannot directly introduce adolescent patients to others who have succeeded with treatment. However, the therapist can transmit true stories (while maintaining confidentiality) that may engage a particular teenager. Kids considering treatment appreciate hearing of, for example, student athletes who become more mentally "in the game" after beginning medication treatment. Even more powerfully, some ADHD coaches "out" themselves and share their personal treatment experiences, good and bad.

FEAR THAT THEY ARE INCAPABLE OF CHANGE AND IT IS HOPELESS TO TRY

This fatalistic concern may be the greatest obstacle to overcome in seeking to obtain information about an adolescent to determine the diagnosis. It is tied closely with the self-blaming covered in the next section. Even before the therapist is sure that ADHD is the teenager's problem, it is important to infuse hope into the process and to tell the adolescent that although things may look glum now, nearly everyone can feel better.

Sometimes adolescents will respond to nonidentifying anecdotes.

> **Doctor:** I know you feel really bad, but I wish you were a fly on the wall earlier today when I saw another patient. About 7 or 8 years ago, he was a teenager sitting in the same seat where you are right now, and he felt pretty crappy. Like you, he kept losing his papers and forgetting when major examinations were scheduled. He was really depressed and thought I was kind of a jerk.
> **Patient:** Yeah, I believe that.
> **Doctor:** He did get treated and now he is doing great. He's a student at Notre Dame. He has a girlfriend. They are just about to leave to spend their junior year abroad in Spain.

Patient: But he still has to see you.

Doctor: Yeah, but he does do better on medications, and I only see him twice a year for medication checks. He no longer needs to talk to a therapist.

The goal is not to con patients but rather to encourage them. Sometimes they don't listen, but sometimes, even years later, they tell you that they appreciated your encouragement. Every therapist who has followed patients with ADHD can reference a similarly inspiring story.

FEAR THAT THEIR PROBLEM IS THEIR FAULT

Like many adults with ADHD, adolescents may believe that it's their own fault that they procrastinate, lose items, act impulsively, and exhibit other behaviors common to the condition. Over the years, teachers and parents may have blamed them, and some adolescents subsequently have internalized this guilt. The teenage years are a time of great narcissism; adolescents feel that if they have a problem, they *should* be able to solve it. If they have experienced failed attempts to change, even teenagers who do not tend to self-blame may feel tried and convicted in the court of adolescent law.

As a result, it is important to explain to adolescents that ADHD is a medical condition that many people have. It is not a psychological weakness but rather a biological illness that can be addressed with medications and therapy. At the same time, it is also important to convey that although it is not their fault, ADHD is an *explanation* and not an excuse. Once they are diagnosed, it becomes their responsibility to control their symptoms. There are no free passes with having ADHD. They may be allowed some accommodations—for example, they may be given more time to complete exams—but homework must still be completed and household tasks must still be performed.

INVOLVING THE PARENTS IN DIAGNOSIS AND TREATMENT

It can be helpful to establish the underlying reasons why the parents have agreed that the child needs diagnosis and possibly treatment as well. Different parents will have different reasons for making the initial appointment, but some of the most common include:

- School problems (poor grades, failures, suspensions, and expulsions)
- Acting-out behaviors
- Awareness that the child is not "growing out of it"
- Substance abuse
- Problems with peers
- Driving problems (such as multiple speeding tickets or car accidents)
- Sexual promiscuity

School Problems

Although school difficulties, including poor grades, failures, suspension, and expulsion, do not inevitably mean the teenager has ADHD, these problems are extremely common among ADHD adolescents. Information on the circumstances of the school problems needs to be gathered to determine whether they are due to ADHD or another psychiatric disorder such as depression or an undiagnosed learning disability. This information can be elicited from both the parents and the teenager. Corroboration from the school may also be helpful.

Poor grades and even school failure are common among untreated adolescents with ADHD. The responsibilities that occur with junior high school and high school, such as constant changing of classes, are much greater and more confusing than is common in elementary school. More abstract thinking in school and on homework is expected subsequent to elementary school, which can be extremely difficult for the distractible and impulsive adolescent with ADHD. In addition, the social demands from peers can be overwhelming. Without treatment, it is difficult for the teenager with ADHD to cope with his or her school responsibilities.

Again, it is important to determine whether the school problems are due to ADHD or to some other problem, such as a learning disability. Students with ADHD tend to globally underperform relative to their intellectual capabilities; students with learning disabilities tend to have a particular weakness in the context of otherwise normal accomplishment.

Other times behavioral issues are the main problem, often leading to suspension or expulsion. In one case, Annette, age 13, was suspended a week into her first year of middle school. She said that a boy in school "got in her face" and she became angry. She kicked him in the groin, and when he was lying on the ground, she kicked him again. She claimed she did not understand what she had done wrong and reported that she was "only defending" herself. The exasperated principal told Annette's parents that she needed some "help." He did not know that Annette had been diagnosed with ADHD predominately hyperactive-impulsive type and that throughout grade school she was treated with medications.

Annette was also trying to adjust to her parents' finalized divorce. Her problems in school continued. She cheated on tests without remorse. She teased heavy students and berated less popular ones. She openly defied teachers and counselors. Physical fights, often vicious, were not uncommon.

Acting-Out Behaviors

Annette's fighting is rather typical of teenagers with ADHD who also have oppositional defiant disorder (ODD). Adolescents with ODD engage in constant arguments with their frustrated parents. In one study, 87 males aged 12–18 with both ADHD and ODD were compared to 32 controls. The researchers found a significantly greater level of anger and negative communication between the teenagers with ADHD and ODD and their parents (Edwards, Barkley, Laneri, Fletcher, & Melevia, 2001).

Adolescents with both ADHD and ODD may vandalize and steal property. Some have explosive tempers and lash out at their siblings and even their parents. It is important for therapists to understand the stress that this unpredictable threat brings to these families. Part of therapy involves helping families develop plans for the next time they feel threatened by their child. The family's response should be determined in advance and the adolescent should be forewarned that acting out will have negative consequences, including the involvement of the police, if necessary.

ODD carries a poorer prognosis than ADHD. Many adolescent ADHD boys receive both diagnoses, but once the ADHD is treated, the oppositional symptoms may improve. Therapists should resist giving an ODD diagnosis unless a convincing long-standing history of oppositional behavior is evident and concurrent ADHD is treated. Adolescents given an ODD diagnosis are often regarded differently and more negatively by teachers and others than those who are given an ADHD diagnosis. The patient given an ADHD diagnosis is often regarded with a much more hopeful outlook than the patient with ODD. However, sometimes an ODD diagnosis is needed because it is the most realistic and logical diagnosis, as with Rob.

Rob was 4 when he first was seen by his pediatrician and diagnosed with low intelligence. In grade school he was supremely anxious, and by the time he was in fifth grade, his mother was being called into school to reassure him while he was in class. At this time he clearly met the criteria for ADHD combined type. His social anxiety levels remained high throughout middle school, but at home Rob did not act out or cause disruption. His interests turned to computer games, and he could spend hours online lost in interactive fantasy games. Rob did poorly academically, and multiple trials of medications proved ineffective.

Desperate, his parents sought help from different professionals. Behavioral plans were developed, but they did not yield quick benefits. A system of rewards and punishments did not help either, nor did positive reinforcement of good behavior. Efforts to limit Rob's on-line gaming were met with fierce resistance; on one occasion Rob struck his father after he disconnected the TV cable connection. The police were summoned and Rob's parents were distraught as they watched him fight the officers. He was arrested and detained overnight. Frustrated with Rob's lack of progress, the therapist diagnosed oppositional defiant disorder.

Feeling hopeless, Rob's parents no longer had the energy to limit his computer privileges. He refused to engage in therapy, although he did remain on Strattera. Eventually the situation calmed. Weeks, and then months, passed without incident. Rob's school performance did not improve much, although the Strattera did ameliorate his anxiety and forgetfulness. Without the fear of losing his computer access, Rob did not feel or act threatened. No further discussion of ODD was made until a year later when Rob's parents tried to enroll him in a boarding school. While reviewing his records, the school discovered Rob's ODD diagnosis and rejected his application.

Fortunately, Rob continued to improve and the ODD diagnosis did not seem to interfere with other plans. However, his story is cautionary to clinicians: Make the diagnosis of ODD only if the patient's history supports it. Rob did not have ODD—his oppositional behavior appeared only when he perceived that his freedom was being curtailed. Clinicians must also note that if oppositional symptoms surface in the context of ADHD, the ADHD must be fully treated.

Awareness That the Child Is Not "Growing Out of It"

Regardless of whether or not the teenager was previously diagnosed with ADHD, the parents may have believed that the behavior was a "stage" that the adolescent was going through and that the behavior eventually would improve as the child gained more maturity. Some parents believe what many doctors used to believe (and in some cases, still believe): that ADHD is inevitably outgrown. Now it is known that in most cases, the symptoms of ADHD continue through adulthood. In fact, the behavior may worsen during adolescence, and the tension between the teenager and family may escalate as a result of behaviors such as stealing, lying, developing friendships with a "bad crowd," and so forth.

Substance Abuse

Untreated adolescents and young adults with ADHD are more likely to engage in drug and alcohol abuse than treated teenagers who have ADHD. If the crisis that led the parents to bring the child in for a diagnosis is a problem with drug or alcohol abuse, the possibility of ADHD should be considered. (See Chapter 8 for more about issues of substance abuse and ADHD.)

Problems with Peers

It can be hard for adolescents to be a good friend when they have ADHD. Peers may assume that the procrastination, constant forgetting, and other characteristic behaviors of ADHD are indicators that the individual does not really care about them. Teenagers with ADHD may also struggle with dating relationships. Sadly, many teenagers with ADHD have few or no friends.

Of course, other psychiatric problems may also impede peer relationships; thus, having problems with peers alone is insufficient to diagnose ADHD.

Driving Problems

Many studies have demonstrated that teenagers with ADHD have more car accidents than their non-ADHD peers and are more likely to obtain traffic tickets, especially for speeding (Barkley, Murphy, & Kwasnik, 1996).

Studies also indicate that these accidents are not due to a lack of knowledge: Tests of adolescents with and without ADHD indicate that both groups have about the same level of driving knowledge. However, the adolescents with ADHD fail to apply what they know, whether it is in a driving simulator test or on the actual road. (In these studies, the ADHD adolescents who were taking medication suspended the medication during the study so that the effect of untreated ADHD could be observed.) Fortunately, stimulants have been shown to improve concentration as well as decrease distractibility, two important factors in driving skills.

Sexual Promiscuity

Some studies show that many teenagers engage in sexual activities. However, adolescents with ADHD are more likely than their non-ADHD peers to seek sex with others. Of course, not all teenagers who are sexually active have ADHD, and there are many other psychiatric diagnoses that may be present or comorbid in the teenager.

Sex with three or more partners in a year is indicative of a problem that needs to be addressed immediately—both for the safety of the teenager as well as those with whom the teenager is in sexual contact. At the least, the parent should ensure that the adolescent is familiar with contraceptives and knows the risks of sexually transmitted diseases (for example, many adolescents mistakenly believe that they cannot contract STDs through oral sex). The subject of oral sex is not one most parents are comfortable with, but it is better to inform the teenager than have him or her contract herpes or another STD.

If the clinician suspects that this topic has not been discussed by the parents, at least a brief mention to the adolescent of STDs and how they are contracted is in order.

Common Parental Fears

When the parents are the ones who have initiated treatment of their adolescent, there is a good chance that one or both of them acknowledge the existence of a problem. However, this is not always true. For example, they may have brought the child in for evaluation because of pressure from the school, an ex-spouse, or the court system. Parents who have been pressured to seek treatment for their adolescent may also fear mental health professionals, especially if they have had no prior experience with them. Of course, this can also be true even with parents who seek treatment for their adolescent on their own.

Most parents who are unfamiliar with the goals of mental health professionals are wary or even frightened by their adolescent's need for therapy. Although the parent is not the patient, these basic parental concerns should be addressed early in therapy to assuage fear, ease tension, and prevent them from prematurely withdrawing their child from therapy.

In most cases, the parents can be assured that although the child needs some help, many other children who had the same problem have been treated and now lead normal and happy lives. Parents also may be surprised and relieved to discover that other parents were also fearful or reluctant about therapy for the same reasons they are.

Some of the common fears parents may have include:

- Fear that bad parenting caused the adolescent's problems.
- Fear that others will discover that the adolescent has problems.
- Fear that the adolescent's problem is much worse than they had thought.

FEAR THAT BAD PARENTING CAUSED THE ADOLESCENT'S PROBLEMS

Probably the most common parental fear is that the therapist will pinpoint something the parents did wrong and blame them for creating the problems from which their child is suffering. They are worried that the therapist will say, "It's all your fault. If he had different parents, he would be just fine."

It is true that sometimes parents *have* made serious mistakes with their children. But it is important for the therapist to tell parents that the focus of treatment is on the present rather than on probing the past for what they might have done more effectively when their child was younger. The goal is to identify what the current behavior is and what to do about it. It is not about blaming or meting out punishment to the guilty.

Because of common media depictions of mental health professionals as cruel or even sadistic, some parents may worry that the therapist will insult or ridicule them. In the first session, much of this fear can be dispelled by treating the parents with respect and making it clear that their parental authority will not be impugned except in the event that there is evidence of physical or sexual abuse.

Although it is not a good idea to assure parents that they will never be criticized, as current parental behavior may be impeding the outcome of therapy or the child's responsiveness to change, it is important to make simple declarative statements such as "good parents can have children with problems" and "your bringing your child into the office indicates you want to help your teenager."

Another common fear of parents is that the therapist will decide that the parents require therapy themselves in order to be effective parents. Although this may be true in some cases, it is a subject that should be broached with extreme care, lest the parents become offended and remove the adolescent from treatment altogether despite therapeutic improvements.

As mentioned in earlier chapters, parents who have a child diagnosed with ADHD often come to the conclusion that they too may have the disorder. However, the parent's possible ADHD should not distract the therapist from the actual patient, the child.

FEAR THAT OTHERS WILL DISCOVER THAT THE ADOLESCENT
HAS PROBLEMS

Just as teenagers who see a therapist often worry that others will find out that they are in therapy, some parents are also worried that others will discover that they have a child with a problem. What if they run into someone they know in the waiting room? And what if that person tells others that they saw the parent in the waiting room of Dr. X, a child psychiatrist? Just as they might reassure adolescents who worry about peers' seeing them in the waiting room, clinicians should tell parents that their information will be held in the strictest of confidence. In the unlikely event that they see someone they know in the waiting room, they need not say why they are there, nor should they question others about the reasons for their presence.

FEAR THAT THE ADOLESCENT'S PROBLEM IS MUCH WORSE THAN
THEY HAD THOUGHT

Once they are in the therapist's office, parents may start to panic, fearing that the child has a severe problem such as drug addiction, schizophrenia, a multiple personality disorder, or criminal tendencies — something they may have seen on a made-for-TV movie or soap opera. Before they came to the office, they knew the child had some problems, but now they are concerned that the therapist will tell them, "Thank goodness you came in now — it was nearly too late to save your child." These fears are common but they are rarely realized. Parents should be assured that if the therapist identifies a serious psychiatric problem, he or she will notify the parents, but that such cases are rare.

Parents' Views on Medication

Some parents anticipate that a daily pill will readily solve their distressed child's problems, and physicians may feel pressure to prescribe medications immediately. "I came here for medication; you want to have him tested and go to therapy?" are words that echo in the psychiatrist's office.

Other parents fear that medications will harm their child in some way, and they reject the entire concept or try to convince the doctor to forego prescribing. These parents are usually amenable to less invasive treatments like psychotherapy. If they concede that more needs to be done, they are likely to pursue alternative "natural" treatments like vitamins and food supplements. Given that all families will have some type of bias, the clinician should evaluate each adolescent and family carefully to match treatment recommendations with what the family will find acceptable. That said, the most important goal for the clinician is to be honest about recommendations rather than say what others want to hear.

Benefits and Pitfalls in Involving Parents

The obvious primary benefit to involving the parents during diagnosis and treatment is that they are likely to encourage the teenager to continue treatment and to follow the recommendations of the mental health professional. If the parents believe that the adolescent is improving or likely to improve, they are also more likely to continue either authorizing or making direct payment for the bills.

However, there are downsides to involving parents that the therapist must manage. First, adolescents often worry that the therapist will reveal information they have shared in private sessions, despite the assurances they receive from the therapist. Second, the parents may err on one of two extremes—either pressing to be overly involved with the child's therapy or distancing themselves from it and seeing the therapist as someone whose job is to "fix" the child, much as a mechanic fixes their automobile. These ideas should be countered with realistic ideas about therapy.

ADOLESCENT FEMALES

Compared to teenage girls without ADHD, adolescent females with ADHD are more likely to have traffic accidents. They also have a greater prevalence of substance abuse. In a study comparing more than 100 adolescent girls and boys with and without ADHD, the researchers concluded that "overall, the females with ADHD were significantly more impaired than the female controls on most measures of psychosocial functioning, including levels of self-reported depression, anxiety, locus of control, self-esteem, over-all symptom distress, and stress levels. They showed more maladaptive attributional styles for negative events, a style that indicates a high risk for future psychological problems" (Rucklidge & Tannock, 2001, p. 538).

In addition, the teenage girls with ADHD had significantly more dis-satisfaction with their relationships with teachers than the female controls, and both their parents and their teachers perceived them as more im-paired than the parents and teachers of the control group. Disturbingly, 50% of the females with ADHD said they had suicidal thoughts to some degree and 25% reported past episodes of self-harm.

These statistics suggest that clinicians should not consider teenage girls with ADHD at lower risk than teenage boys. In some ways, they may be in greater need of treatment.

ADOLESCENT MALES

Adolescent and young adult males with symptoms that typify ADHD are a difficult group to treat, yet treatment is essential in order to help them decrease the risk for making impulsive choices that can be ruinous.

Chris, age 20, typified the angry young man with ADHD. He had pre-viously been prescribed Concerta in high school, but he stopped taking his medication when he reached age 18. The last two years had been dis-astrous for Chris. Moody and unwilling to talk, he barely graduated from high school. His attempts at community college were tepid; most assign-ments were not completed. His father had arranged several jobs that Chris, unable to motivate himself, promptly lost. His driver's license was suspended because of many speeding tickets that he had received and discarded, unpaid.

Chris's problems intensified after his 19th birthday. Provoked by a childish disagreement, he slammed his older brother into a sharp fence, fracturing his wrist. Their father, frustrated and furious, called the police, who removed Chris and filed domestic assault charges. At arraignment, the judge forbade him any contact with his family. Chris stayed with friends, who quickly tired of his broken promises. He sat around all day watching television or playing video games and made little effort to contribute meaningfully to expenses.

Within a few months, Chris became homeless and began selling and experimenting with street drugs. His life revolved around the subculture of Ecstasy and methamphetamine. One summer night after a drug exchange, he was robbed and beaten. The next morning a maintenance worker found him emaciated and injured. Gingerly, the man woke him up and oriented him. Chris later revealed this terse conversation to be pivotal in his recovery.

Chris called his parents and begged them to allow him to return home. He promised he would reconstitute. With trepidation and bitter memories of broken promises, they allowed him to return if he agreed to treatment.

Chris resented all authority, and his parent's ultimatum did not inspire him. He came to therapy but did not talk. He had his antidepressant prescriptions filled but did not take them regularly.

Chris' father, a powerful man who owned several car dealerships, became enraged at his son's continued downward spiral. The father blasted the therapist: "I don't think any of you know what you are doing." The assault injured the earnest therapist, who shared the parent's frustration but also knew that in his current belligerent state, Chris was unworkable in therapy. However, lacking a good alternative, they pressed on.

In therapy, Chris and his doctor reviewed his past aptitude testing (which was superior) and the consistent comments that his teachers had made about him since grade school (he was underperforming). They contrasted his relative success in middle school with his failure in high school. They discussed childhood friends who had moved on with their lives and some, like Chris, who had not. Finally, he relented.

"I know I did better when I was on Concerta a few years ago," he said. "I just hate that I have to take it."

Reluctantly Chris agreed to add a stimulant to the antidepressant he was haphazardly taking. He became motivated and focused. His reflex to oppose all things related to authority softened. The turbulent relationship with his therapist mellowed. Chris returned to community college part-time and gained momentum with success. Several years later, his parents attended his graduation from the state university.

CONSIDERING THE CASE OF BRANDON

Sometimes adolescents are diagnosed with depression or anxiety when their prevailing underlying problem is ADHD, as with Brandon. If patients are not responsive to therapies for depression or anxiety, consider the possibility of ADHD. At the urging of his mother, Brandon presented for treatment late in his junior year of high school. His grades were too poor to gain acceptance into the university of his choice. He was upset that he would have to attend the local community college, which he described as a "loser school." Brandon's father was an Ivy League–educated attorney, and his sister was thriving at the state university. Brandon's friends planned to attend prestigious schools and he worried he would be left behind.

Brandon told the therapist that he was constantly worried and could not concentrate in classes. He was so preoccupied with doing well on examinations that he could not focus on his teacher's instructions. He also thwarted his own efforts; besides finding it difficult to study, he often did not complete homework. Since middle school, his grades had rarely been above a C.

Brandon reported that he felt sad all the time, but he still enjoyed skateboarding with his friends, playing soccer, and hanging out with his soccer teammates and his girlfriend. His physician diagnosed depression and prescribed fluoxetine (Prozac). A month later, Brandon's condition remained unchanged, and the fluoxetine dose was doubled. Within a week, Brandon complained of agitation and delayed ejaculation, so his physician switched him to mirtazapine (Remeron), another antidepressant. On this medication, Brandon gained 15 pounds, intensifying his despair. Subsequent antidepressants proved no more effective and Brandon and his parents lost faith in a medical approach. Off medications, Brandon lost the weight he had gained, but his problems persisted.

Three years later, Brandon, now age 20 and thoroughly demoralized, was watching television when he saw an advertisement for a new ADHD medication. Brandon identified closely with the ad's description, so he visited the product website. There he completed an ADHD self-test and endorsed many of the questions. He shared this finding with his mother, who agreed that Brandon had many ADHD characteristics. They contacted the Attention Deficit Disorder Association (ADDA) and were directed to an ADHD specialist.

Through careful history-taking, the new doctor learned that Brandon's problems had worsened after high school graduation. His girlfriend broke up with him, and his friends moved on. To Brandon's dismay, community college was as frustrating as high school had been. He lamented that prestige was reserved for his friends attending big-name schools. Tensions with his hard-driving father complicated matters; his father had long ago concluded that Brandon was lazy and self-defeating. They alternated between yelling at and ignoring each other.

After a complete evaluation, the doctor concurred that Brandon had ADHD combined type. Aware that antidepressants had not worked in the past, the psychiatrist recommended a trial of methylphenidate (Concerta). Brandon lived far from a qualified therapist, so the doctor introduced him to an ADHD coach, who conducted twice-weekly telephone sessions. (For more about coaching, see Chapter 10.)

Brandon noticed an improvement within the first few doses of the Concerta, and within several months, he was functioning dramatically better. His coach kept him motivated and structured. His grades rose significantly at the community college, and within two semesters, he transferred to a regional university. Two years later, Brandon graduated from college and entered a master's program. Not surprisingly, Brandon's relationship with his father improved.

Brandon was not comorbid for depression. His initial diagnosis had been wrong and the antidepressant treatment had done him more harm than good. His main problem was ADHD, and until it was treated, Brandon remained mired in failed behaviors.

ADHD has derailed the lives of many adolescent and young adult males like Chris and Brandon. Some have happy endings to their story; others, not buoyed by wealthy parents, end up in jail, attacked on the street, or even killed. Their lives often involve substance abuse, crime, and despair. With surging testosterone superimposed on hyperactive-impulsive ADHD, a delayed or prolonged adolescence, the adoption of a macho grandiosity ("no one can tell me what to do!"), or all of the above, these patients present great challenges for therapists, as well as great rewards when they achieve success as a result of treatment.

Simply telling an adolescent or young adult male with ADHD to *stop* performing negative actions (like drinking, failing to take medication, and so forth) usually does not work. Nor is it effective to direct the recalcitrant male to *start* performing positive acts, like showing up for work or school on time or thinking twice before blurting out comments that offend others. As with Chris, some patients must "hit bottom" before being startled into the realization that they must change.

Following are some key points to keep in mind when treating adolescent or young adult males with ADHD:

* Give the patient a reason to comply with your advice.
* Accept that rebellion and refusal to comply with recommendations is common.
* Explain to parents that the patient must experience the negative consequences of his actions.
* Remember that sometimes nothing works.

Give the Patient a Reason to Comply With Your Advice

More so than with other patients, clinicians must actively motivate male adolescents and young adults to follow their professional advice and take medication. Telling the patient that his parents want him to take the medication is a compelling reason for many young males *not to* take it. Pointing out that he may improve his grades if he takes his medication may also be ignored if he does not care about school or grades. Instead, therapists must look at the situation from the patient's perspective to find a good reason for him to follow professional advice.

For example, if discussion with the adolescent or young adult reveals that he is interested in video games, the therapist can explain that the improved concentration that medications for ADHD often provide will result in improving his game. Adolescents involved in sports may be interested in the experience of athletes treated for ADHD. Young men considering treatment often connect to stories about doing better in school or receiving promotions at work. Some are intrigued at the promise of improving their relationships.

For example, Brad was diagnosed with ADHD after several years of antidepressant treatment. At first he had trouble tolerating ADHD medications, but about a month into modafinil treatment, he renewed his relationship with Marla, his girlfriend of 4 years. She offered, "We're doing so much better. Brad pays attention to me; we can actually talk and have fun. Before, we would talk and I thought he heard what I said, but he obviously didn't. He'd ask me a minute later about something I had just told him. It is much more fulfilling now." Brad sat by listening, amused and contented by Marla's comments.

Accept That Rebellion and Refusal to Comply With Recommendations Are Common

All therapists are familiar with adolescent rebellion and the problem behaviors that young adult males may exhibit, especially when they have ADHD. However, knowing this and dealing with it are two different things. It is important to remember that even when therapists offer their best advice, couched in the most convincing language possible and using the patient's own frame of reference, patients may still ignore or argue with the therapist's recommendations.

Jeremy was 15 when his parents brought him in for a full evaluation. He was diagnosed with ADHD and a learning disability. Although Jeremy's family accepted the diagnoses, Jeremy did not. He left the appointment with hostility, accusing the doctor of not understanding him and misdiagnosing his condition.

Jeremy returned 6 years later. His mean-spirited parting words, delivered years earlier, were still remembered by his doctor, but apparently Jeremy held no hard feelings. He reported that he was ready for treatment. In the intervening years, he had seen his friends surpass him at school and work. He reported that now he was serious about ADHD treatment.

Jeremy started medications and thrived. Within months, he lamented that he had "wasted" the past 6 years.

His doctor finally asked him, "I'm glad you are better, but why did you come back to me for treatment? You were so bitter when you left."

"Then, I was mad at everyone," Jeremy said thoughtfully. "But you told me I could always come back if I ever wanted to." Impishly he added, "I didn't know where else I could go."

This case shows the importance of developing a philosophy of patience; words delivered today may pay dividends years later. Therapists reinforced solely by immediate therapeutic turnarounds will inevitably be disappointed.

Explain to Parents That the Patient Must Experience the Negative Consequences of His Actions

Parents of difficult young men with ADHD may feel the need to help their sons whether they are 16 or 26. Some parents go to extremes to keep their children out of trouble or even out of jail. These "helicopter parents" are vigilant and omnipresent; they swoop in to save their child. They have needed to help with homework (and probably completed many of the school projects themselves), run interference with grandparents during temper tantrums, and entertain their child's friends as a way to compensate for their child's poor social skills. As their child enters adolescence and young adulthood, helicopter parents may pay their child's traffic tickets, rent, and utility bills. They construe that good parenting means that they remain responsible for their son's protection, safety, and happiness.

The therapist must acknowledge that rescue is an inherent reflex that parents have for their children. Too often, therapists self-righteously blame parents for being overinvolved or "enabling" their children's behavior. This tone is unproductive, because good parents instinctively aid their children, whatever their age. Praising, rather than admonishing, long-standing parental commitment is a humane and therapeutic approach.

Still, counseling the ADHD family requires advising the family that their children sometimes may *need* to suffer the consequences of their turbulent behavior if they are to become motivated to change. Sometimes it is the therapist's unpleasant job to suggest to parents that their children, like Chris, may need to hit bottom before they can rise again.

Undoubtedly, however, this strategy can backfire, so it must be the family's decision to limit their intervention. Additionally, emphasizing that the decision is in the hands of the family helps protect the therapist from being in a compromised position if anything dire happens.

This task can be accomplished without violating the adolescent's confidentiality. For example, the therapist can opine to Tim, a 16-year-old with ADHD, and his parents that Tim's behavior probably will not change as long as he is guaranteed that his parents will rush in like the cavalry to save him every time he gets into trouble. The therapist must also be careful not to give a mixed message. "You tell me I have to change my behavior," Tim argues. "But you also say I have a medical disorder, ADHD, that makes me act impulsively. Which is it?"

Tim is right, of course. It is hard to find the area between compassion and responsibility. Temper outbursts and poor social judgment are part and parcel of ADHD and the adolescent should not be blamed for his condition. The answer to Tim's question is that once a treatment regimen is established, behavioral changes are easier to make. He is responsible for taking his medications and following the treatment plan.

The therapist should also help the patient reflect on the patterns of dependency that have developed over the years. The goals should be for the patient to acknowledge and honor his parents' historic efforts and to adopt behaviors that promote healthy separation and individuation.

Remember That Sometimes Nothing Works

Despite the efforts of experienced and nuanced therapists, sometimes nothing seems to influence patients. They stop their medication, resist advice, and eventually reject treatment altogether.

Ultimately, the patient—not his parents—determines success. Young patients accept their condition on a different schedule than their therapists or parents do. As in Jeremy's case, the realization may not occur instantly. Still, the therapist has the responsibility to tell the patient what he *needs* to hear, not what he wants to hear. Therapeutic relationships must be cultivated and sympathy must be generous, but in order to avoid failure, the therapist must convey to the adolescent and young adult patient the gravity of the condition and the lifelong responsibility that caring for ADHD demands from him.

RACE AND ADHD

Among the issues that are debated about ADHD is whether certain racial or ethnic groups are more likely to receive the diagnosis of ADHD than others. Some commentators assert that the diagnosis is more likely to be considered in poor or African American communities, where they believe that children are more likely to be labeled with ADHD or another diagnosis. This argument is generally advanced on the distorted premise that ADHD treatment is designed to control those whose behavior is perceived as different than the mainstream of society. Other critics contend that ADHD is overdiagnosed in affluent suburban circles. This group has easier access to health care, particularly mental health care. According to this line of thinking, suburban families are interested in enhancing their loved one's daily functioning. ADHD medications allow greater concentration, focus and other cognitive tasks that improve academic competitiveness.

Data can be found in child studies to support both arguments. One recent survey found 5.65% of black boys had "clinically significant" ADHD symptoms compared to 4.33% of white and 3.06% of Hispanic boys, but the National Health Interview Survey indicated that 7.5% of whites, 5.7% of blacks and 3.5% of Hispanic families had been told that their child had ADHD. Income rather than race seems to be a more important variable in understanding prevalence. ADHD rates were higher (6.52 percent) in families making less than $20,000 per year. Families with higher incomes had a rate of 3.85% (Cuffe, 2003).

Teachers given random profiles of ADHD students were most likely to suspect white males of having ADHD rather than black males. Families of black troubled adolescents were less likely than white families to be suspicious that ADHD may be an explanation for their child's difficulties. In one survey, white families were two times more likely to pursue an evaluation. African American families were more likely to cite negative expectations, cost and the stigma of mental illness as reasons to avoid assessment (Bussing, 1995; Kelly & Raymond, 1997).

This finding may explain why treatment patterns differ by race. A 1997 federal study of medical expenditure revealed that 4.4% of whites, but only 1.7% of blacks were treated for ADHD. In a study of Maryland Medicaid recipients, of individuals with similar insurance coverage and access to the system, whites were twice as likely to have been prescribed psychotropic medications (Dey & Bloom, 2005).

Regardless of race, ADHD impairs individuals from attaining their potential. They are more likely to do poorly on achievement tests, repeat grades, and drop out entirely. Clinicians involved in triaging and assessing these adolescents should be blind to color and immune to the pressures of destructive sociological polemics. Diagnosing and treating people with ADHD, whether the intervention is at age 6 or 36, offers a ticket to personal liberation.

Chapter 7

Gender Issues: Considering Girls and Women

UNTIL THE LATTER PART OF THE 20th century, ADHD was assumed to be the province of boys—a problem they would outgrow during or shortly after the onset of puberty. Essentially, the unspoken fantasy was: Young man, we give you your junior high school diploma, and you give us back your ADHD. No one specifically stated that girls and women never had these symptoms, but it was just not on the "radar screen" of most mental health professionals treating females. Consequently, girls were rarely diagnosed with ADHD. Now considered a pedestrian concept, the idea that ADHD was limited to so few individuals (preadolescent males who were hyperactive) was not intellectually challenged at that time.

This chapter is devoted to issues related to adolescent girls and women with ADHD, including perceptions toward females with ADHD, common symptom clusters and presentation, the impact of female hormones on the escalation of ADHD symptoms, diagnostic issues to consider in females, and questions that elicit information from patients and help with diagnosis.

In the past, some experts believed that the ratio of male to female children with ADHD was about 9 to 1; however, now many experts believe that the ratio is more likely to be 3 males to every 1 female (National Women's Health Resource Center, 2003). As the condition is not transmitted by the sex chromosomes, the ratio may in fact be even lower. Yet boys are still diagnosed with ADHD more frequently. This is a situation that needs to be rectified. Of course, gender equity is *not* a good thing when it comes to psychiatric diagnoses (few people would wish both females and males to experience psychiatric disorders), but it is troublesome when one gender is summarily excluded, for no valid reason, from a diagnosis.

PERCEPTIONS TOWARD GIRLS WITH ADHD COMPARED TO BOYS WITH ADHD

Perceptions, even when they are completely wrong, are often powerful. They may directly affect how other individuals react toward a person with a specific diagnosis or symptoms, and they may also affect and reflect the level of acceptance by others. In some cases, there is a spillover of generally accepted and largely unconscious perceptions among the mental health community, which may explain the ambivalence that many physicians nurture about the validity of ADHD, as discussed in Chapter 5.

A 2004 survey regarding the perceptions that the general public, parents, teachers, and female adolescents with ADHD have toward young women with ADHD provided intriguing results (Quinn & Wigal, 2004). The researchers surveyed 1797 adults in the general public, 541 parents of children with ADHD, 550 teachers, and 346 children with ADHD ages 12–17.

The study revealed that most teachers (82%) and the majority of the general public (58%) believed that ADHD was more prevalent among boys than girls. Eighty-five percent of the teachers and 57% of the general public believed that girls with ADHD were unlikely to be diagnosed. The explanation for this finding may be that girls in general are deemed to be more obedient and less likely to act out, and as such, they often are not referred for evaluation. Even when girls do exhibit symptoms of ADHD, they are usually symptoms of the inattentive or combined subtypes rather than the primarily hyperactive form of ADHD that is more prevalent among males. (For more about patients less likely to be diagnosed with ADHD, see Chapter 4.)

The surveyed teachers also felt that certain types of problematic behaviors were more common in girls with ADHD than boys. Girls with ADHD were reported as more likely to be excessively talkative (73%) than were boys with ADHD (58%). Note that this perception may be an accurate one.

When the adolescents themselves were asked about their own perceptions of how ADHD affected them, girls were more likely to report that it was very difficult to get things done in general (57%), compared to boys with ADHD (39%). Girls also reported more difficulty focusing on schoolwork (77%) than boys (66%). In addition, girls were also more likely to report experiencing trouble getting along with their parents than boys (39% of the girls versus 26% of the boys).

The authors concluded: *Survey responses suggest that gender has important implications in the diagnosis and treatment of ADHD. Responses by ADHD patients demonstrate gender-specific differences in the personal experience of the condition* (Quinn & Wigal, 2004, p. 1). They also stated: *It was also widely perceived that ADHD presents differently in girls from in boys, and that this is a likely reason for missed or delayed diagnoses in girls. Symptoms such as inattentiveness, poor school performance, and depressive affect are seen as the hallmark signs of ADHD in girls, yet they elicit less attention from teachers and parents than characteristic ADHD symptoms seen in boys, such as disruptive behavior and 'acting out.'* (p. 6)

Much research concentrates on adolescent girls with ADHD; however, it seems likely that at least some findings could be generalized to adult women. For example, research indicates that adolescent girls with ADHD have a higher risk of depressive disorders and anxiety disorders than teenage boys with ADHD. There have been similar findings in adult women (Rucklidge & Tannock, 2001).

Females with ADHD are also more likely to have been diagnosed with a mood or anxiety disorder than males with ADHD. In one survey, 14% of adolescent girls with ADHD had received prior treatment with antidepressants, compared to 5% of males. A past diagnosis of depression, particularly if the patient showed little improvement, should be a red flag that further analysis of the patient is warranted (Quinn, 2005).

The publication of therapist Sari Solden's (1995) pioneering book on women and ADHD marked the beginning of a shift among many mental health professionals, who began to rethink the established view of ADHD as a problem limited to prepubescent males. Solden surmised that the condition did exist among females but that the symptoms were different, although no less debilitating. Contemporaneous to this rethinking emerged another idea; that maybe boys did *not* inevitably outgrow ADHD and consequently needed ongoing treatment. These two ideas eventually segued into the concept that adolescents and adults, including both males and females, could have persistent ADHD.

COMMON SYMPTOM CLUSTERS AND PRESENTATION

Only recently have clinicians begun to differentiate between the presentation of ADHD in males and females. The designation by the *DSM-IV* of ADHD into a predominately hyperactive-impulsive type and a predominately inattentive type, as well as a third combined type, inadvertently helped to define sex-based distinctions, although these types were not meant to be gender-based. The hyperactive male with ADHD, whose behavior is often described as "bouncing off walls," usually exhibits different behaviors from those seen in females, who more typically have the inattentive or combined form of the condition. Even hyperactive girls and women evince their symptoms differently from hyperactive males; he might be in perpetual motion whereas she is more often a rapid and excessive talker.

In general, the aggressive, "in your face" style of many males with ADHD is atypical for females with the disorder, who are more likely to be respectful and even demure with the mental health professional and other authority figures. Additionally, younger men with the hyperactive-impulsive type of ADHD are much more likely to be comorbid for oppositional defiant disorder or conduct disorder than females with ADHD (Weiss, Trokenberg Hechtman, & Weiss, 1999).

It is important for mental health professionals to realize that women with ADHD often cannot be evaluated in the same way as males with ADHD, just as women with depression may exhibit different symptoms from males with depression. For example, depressed women are more likely to exhibit internalizing behaviors, such as self-blaming or crying, whereas depressed males may exhibit increased aggressive and acting-out behaviors.

Similarly, girls and women with ADHD are also more likely to exhibit internalizing behaviors than males. Females with ADHD have a greater tendency to blame themselves for their symptoms—a behavioral reflex that is caused by, and contributes to, poor self-esteem. Oftentimes women with ADHD innately respond to their symptoms by becoming obsessive-compulsive. This affords them a measure of self-control that they otherwise do not feel they have. Table 7.1 compares males and females in terms of general symptoms and behaviors.

There are also differing presentations of ADHD symptoms in males and females. For example, the distracted male is likely to look around the room when being spoken to, whereas a female with ADHD may be able to look the person straight in the eye and seem attentive even when she is not listening at all. The hyperactive female may talk incessantly or twirl her hair, whereas the hyperactive male may jump up and pace. Table 7.2 lists gender differences in presentation of ADHD symptoms.

Considering the Case of Maggie

Maggie was diagnosed with ADHD inattentive type in her senior year of high school. She was earnest and well-liked; she had no hint of hyperactivity or oppositional behavior. By and large, she did well in school. Because she was an only child, her parents clearly projected their hopes onto her. Maggie's father was an educator and her mother, who also had ADHD, had been a poor student in high school. Both parents were supportive and even surprised by Maggie's academic and social accomplishments, yet Maggie felt burdened by and anxious about her parents' high expectations of her. Maggie's pressure was self-generated. She was apprehensive about disappointing others, especially her family.

TABLE 7.1
Gender Differences in General ADHD Symptoms and Behaviors

Symptom/Behavior	Females	Males
Onset of symptoms	Often occurs at or subsequent to puberty	Usually occurs well before puberty
Externalizing/ internalizing behaviors	Internalizing behaviors are more common	Externalizing behaviors are more common
Presence of oppositional defiant disorder or conduct disorder	More common than among girls without ADHD, but about half as common as with males with ADHD	Common
Presence of depressive or anxious disorders	More common among females with ADHD than among males with ADHD	Greater incidence than among males without ADHD, but much less common than among females with ADHD
Poor academic achievement	Common	May be less common than among females with ADHD
Shyness	Common	Not common
Feeling of shame because of symptoms	Common	Much less common than among females with ADHD
Hormonal fluctuations affect symptoms	Yes	No
Several or more traffic tickets or car accidents	May occur, but is seen less than with males with ADHD	Seen frequently
Many sexual partners (three or more in a 6-month period)	If behavior is present, it may be a symptom of ADHD	If present, less likely to be a symptom of ADHD than with females with ADHD

Substance abuse	May be a problem, but more common among males with ADHD	Very common
Hyperfocusing to overcompensate in performing school work	Common	Not common; males are more likely to hyperfocus on video games, hobbies, or enjoyable tasks
Peer relationships	Often has one or no friends	May have many friends, often with similar behavioral problems

Maggie's success came with a psychic cost. Always fearful that she would forget something important, she kept "to do" lists for everything. She developed routines for studying and cleaning her room and had rigid rituals for grooming. She enlisted her mother to help her maintain her "life's order," and she became irritable and blamed her mother whenever there were deviations from the routine. Lost lists were a disaster. Times of higher stress, such as when Maggie was completing her extracurricular yearbook assignment or preparing for college applications, consumed the entire family and resulted in more pronounced obsessive-compulsive behaviors.

When Maggie presented for help, several formulations were considered. One counselor had suggested that Maggie and her mother were "codependent." Another felt that Maggie was regressed and unwilling to assume adult responsibilities. Counseling was recommended.

After a few sessions, Maggie's doctor noted her high levels of anxiety and her inability to stay focused during their conversations. He diagnosed Maggie with ADHD inattentive type and started stimulant medications. Quickly the medications decreased her high levels of anxiety. Surprisingly, even her thumb-sucking and hair-pulling, self-soothing habits that she previously could not break, extinguished soon after medications were introduced.

Maggie's case underscores the fact that experts should not overly rely on the traditional template of ADHD symptoms. Reliance on the belief that

TABLE 7.2
Gender Differences in Presentation of ADHD Symptoms

Symptom	Females	Males
Not listening/ inattentiveness	Looking person in the eye, but not really listening	Looking away, apparently distracted
Hyperactivity/ fidgeting	Twirling hair, going through purse for no apparent reason, excessive talkativeness	Bouncing the knee up and down, moving about, pacing
Showing distress	Crying, looking sad	Seeking to leave session early; agitated
Impatience/ impulsivity in driving	Complaining to others (or self) about bad drivers but taking no other action	Cutting someone off on the road; possible road rage
Disorganization	Complaints about maintaining home as overwhelming; losing personal items	More likely to complain about work than about problems at home; losing items
Emotional empathy	Generally empathetic with others with regard to their problems	Often lacking in empathy for others outside his family (or sometimes even within the family)

ADHD is a condition of hyperactive and disorganized young boys who do poorly in school would have deprived Maggie of a helpful intervention.

ADHD Symptoms in Females and Their Onset

Disorganization is a hallmark feature of all types of ADHD. The lives of women with ADHD may be characterized by frequent job changes, rocky romantic relationships, and strained familial interactions with spouses, partners, and children. The therapist may find that these women present ostensibly to talk about tempestuous relationships, but the chaotic way these women handle relationships may be due to their undiagnosed ADHD.

Perhaps due to their impulsivity, females with ADHD are also more likely to have more sexual partners and earlier sexual experiences than non-ADHD girls (National Women's Health Resource Center, 2003). Female adolescents with ADHD are more likely than males with ADHD to engage in early sexual activity and disregard safe practices. Some researchers report that adolescent girls with ADHD are also more likely to have unplanned pregnancies than their peers (Arnold, 1996).

The onset of ADHD symptoms may not be detectable until later in life among females, despite the *DSM-IV* diagnostic criteria demanding that symptoms be evident prior to the age of 7. This mandate works against the diagnosis of girls and women (and other inattentive individuals), essentially by making the diagnostic bar unreasonably high. The issue may not be whether symptoms are detectable but rather *when* they develop. Some studies have shown that individuals with ADHD who are primarily inattentive experience a later onset of the disorder; for example, in one study, nearly half (43%) of individuals with the predominantly inattentive type of ADHD did not manifest any symptoms before the age of 7 (Applegate, Lahey, Hart, Biederman, Hynd, Barkley, et al., 1997).

Although little formal research has been performed on the onset of ADHD among females, puberty seems to be the time when symptoms surface in most patients. It is unclear if this later onset is a function of physiological changes, psychosocial stressors, or the greater expectations and responsibilities associated with sexual maturity. Nonetheless, the requirement that the symptoms be evident before age 7 should be dropped when ADHD diagnostic criteria are reconfigured in a later edition of the *DSM*. Age 14 appears to be a more realistic cutoff. This issue will be hotly debated before 2010, when *DSM-V* is scheduled to be published.

CONSIDERING THE IMPACT OF FEMALE HORMONES

Although adolescent girls and adult women are not solely products of their fluctuating hormones, many experts agree that hormonal changes can weaken or intensify ADHD symptoms. Hormonal fluctuations in females begin at puberty and continue until the woman experiences menopause. Some females experience the worst ADHD symptoms in the premenstrual phase of their cycle. For this reason, it is advisable to ask new patients where they are in their menstrual cycle when they first present to the clinician; for example, if the patient is premenstrual, she may seem more severely ill than if she appeared at another point in her cycle.

Some studies indicate that women with ADHD experience a worsening of their symptoms in the late luteal phase of their menstrual cycle. In these women, symptoms intensify several days before the onset of their period and relent when menstruation occurs. Symptoms remain stable through midcycle, but then reemerge at the next luteal phase (National Women's Health Resource Center, 2003).

Estrogen increases the levels of two key neurotransmitters, serotonin and dopamine, whereas a declining estrogen level is linked to decreased levels of these chemicals. This correlates with the luteal phase; women about to get their periods generally have lower levels of estrogen, which explains the greater incidence and intensity of their ADHD symptoms during this time. For women who demonstrate this pattern, the psychiatrist might consider prescribing a lower or higher dose of ADHD medication (depending on the type of medication used and whether it is a stimulant or not) for the week prior to menstruation. This technique has been used successfully in the treatment of depression that is exacerbated during menses. There is no general rule about whether the dose of stimulants should be increased or decreased, but the prescriber should be willing to adjust the dosage during the premenstrual period.

According to Quinn (2002), hormonal influences often are not considered by clinicians, and most treatment is based on "the experience of treating elementary school-aged boys." She added: "Hormonal fluctuations and its influence of estrogen on the brain are not even considered, much less addressed. No wonder many adolescent girls and adult women with AD/HD report only partial remission of symptoms. In addition, treatment approaches that work for boys with AD/HD may not work for girls or women" (p. 87).

Studies have shown that a declining estrogen level, as occurs in the premenstrual period, may increase the response to stimulants (Quinn, 2002). Note that it is not the absolute level of estrogen that is significant in an individual woman, but rather the decline of the woman's normal level that is relevant. Quinn advised that for women with worsened symptoms of ADHD during the monthly menstrual cycle, administration of estrogen may improve both memory and mood. In addition, combined therapy of a stimulant and an antidepressant may be needed by women who have worsened premenstrual symptoms of ADHD.

This was the case for Tracy, a 33-year-old attorney who noticed that she became very irritable and tearful in the week before her period. This did not happen during every cycle; however, in the past several years she had noted the problem occurred with increasing regularity. While a law student in Boston, Tracy was diagnosed with premenstrual dysphoric disorder (PMDD), the current nomenclature for what was earlier called premenstrual syndrome (PMS). Tracy could not tolerate birth-control medications, and serotonin reuptake inhibitor antidepressants did not noticeably improve her symptoms. When she was diagnosed with ADHD (which she learned about while defending a client who had the condition), stimulant medications were added to her antidepressant.

Within several months, Tracy was certain that the premenstrual worsening of her symptoms was less apparent. A year into treatment, she was elected to a key position in her professional organization. She reported that before her treatment for ADHD, "I would have never run for the office. I could never predict how I would feel during my period and I had to protect myself. I feel much more confident now that my moods will hold." Tracy remained realistic, however, adding: "I still have some bad days. Before my period, my breasts still get tender, I feel bloated, and my face always breaks out. Despite all that, I feel so much less anxious now."

Note that ADHD treatment does not address somatic symptoms, but patients note that their more stable mood and improved patience allows them to tolerate physical discomfort more easily. As with Tracy, women with ADHD who experience menstrually related worsening symptoms may benefit from both antidepressant and ADHD medications. A comprehensive evaluation of an ADHD woman includes assessing when in her cycle symptoms are most apparent. Further research will need to explore the relationship between ADHD and PMDD.

It needs to be stressed that a major hormonal impact is not present in all females with ADHD. One adolescent girl with ADHD may deal with her transformation gracefully, whereas a menopausal woman with ADHD might feel overwhelmed with her hot flashes and mood swings. Hormonal changes are only one piece of the complicated diagnostic puzzle.

DIAGNOSTIC ISSUES TO CONSIDER

The basic criteria for ADHD (discussed in Chapter 1) should be considered in making a diagnosis. However, further analysis is usually needed in diagnosing females. One helpful rating scale, the Women's AD/HD Self-Assessment Symptom Inventory (SASI), was specifically designed to help women self-evaluate for ADHD.

Developed by Kathleen Nadeau and Patricia Quinn, this gender-oriented scale includes self-test questions such as: "Other girls called me 'mean' or 'bossy'"; "I felt different from other girls"; "Other girls didn't like me, but I didn't understand why"; "It was hard for me to keep up with the conversation of a group of girls"; "I fought and argued with my friends"; "In conversation, I'd say something dumb, or couldn't think of anything to say"; and "I was very sensitive to teasing" (Nadeau & Quinn, 2002). Women are instructed to respond to each question on a scale of 0 to 3, with 0 meaning the situation almost never applies and 3 indicating that it happens frequently.

The SASI also addresses hormonal issues. Questions include: "I have PMS symptoms, including moodiness, irritability, and low frustration tolerance"; "My PMS symptoms have become worse over the years"; "My ADHD symptoms decreased during pregnancy"; "Right before my period, my ADHD symptoms become worse"; and "I did well in elementary school, but started having difficulty after puberty." Overall, this rating scale can be very useful in evaluating females with ADHD.

Why Are Symptoms Present Now?

Among the more common questions that ADHD therapists often field is: "Why now? Why was ADHD not diagnosed earlier?" The answer is often a multifaceted one. It might be, as with Maggie, that adaptive skills like obsessiveness and compulsivity enabled the patient to function for a while, but at a certain point she could no longer compensate for her deficits. Her adaptive skills failed her, whether because of increased demands from work, family, or other issues. Other explanations may be the onset of puberty, cyclical variations associated with menstruation, or the manifest demands that come with each particular stage of life. Sometimes a life crisis makes symptoms too difficult to handle, prompting women to finally seek help from a mental health professional.

There are several key issues that should be taken into account when considering a diagnosis of ADHD in girls and women. They include:

- In what life stage is the patient currently (puberty, childbearing years, menopause)?
- Is the patient pregnant?
- What problem behaviors has the patient noticed in herself?
- Does the patient seem shy, depressed, or anxious?
- If still in school, is the patient struggling with academic work?
- Is the patient experiencing a personal crisis?

LIFE STAGE

Each stage of a woman's life presents different challenges; women with ADHD are no different from other females in this regard. The pubescent girl's experience, dealing with body changes, acne, boyfriends, and changing class six times a day, is far different from the 22-year-old woman who is trying to manage her weight and establish a professional life. The 30-year-old seeking to become pregnant or struggling with infertility has vastly different burdens from those experienced by the 55-year-old heading toward menopause and coping with the life challenges of this stage. The overlaying of ADHD symptoms on normal life challenges makes these challenges extremely stressful.

Although challenges at any life stage can be difficult for females with ADHD, motherhood is often particularly difficult. All mothers have enormous responsibilities, and mothers with ADHD find these responsibilities uniquely challenging. Teachers expect them to help with organizing daily homework, coaches depend on prompt arrival for practice, and children have needs that vary daily. Many of these women struggle to meet their own needs, but even those who have found ways of accommodating long-standing symptoms become more aware of failings when their children's needs intensify. Not surprisingly, women with ADHD often present for evaluation as their children enter their school years.

When these mothers have children who also suffer from ADHD, memories of their own unpleasant past may be stirred up. Trish, a mother of two in her late thirties, was treated for ADHD and chronic depression with medications and counseling. Although her ADHD had only recently been diagnosed, in counseling she recounted that her symptoms were evident early on. By high school, she was doing poorly academically and felt socially ostracized. Her parents, devout Catholics, disapproved of her undisciplined ways, and their disappointment pushed Trish to reject them further.

From age 13 through her early twenties, Trish became involved in many sexual relationships—few meaningful, none lasting. The initial thrill of adventure and social acceptance soon soured, and her reputation and dignity were damaged by school gossip. Her childhood friends, frustrated with her poor decisions, left her one by one.

When her children were young, Trish was notoriously difficult to treat. Intentional overdoses were followed by psychiatric hospitalizations. She was repeatedly diagnosed with borderline personality disorder. Over time she was more accurately diagnosed with ADHD and she stabilized with atomoxetine (Strattera). Therapy allowed her to make sense of her past; her behaviors were determined to be a function of impulsivity and profound shame. For a while, Trish's reckless behavior attenuated. But as Trish got better, her children grew into adolescence and her daughter Casey became increasingly troubled.

Casey was now 16. In the past year she had been expelled from school twice, slit her wrists, and had an unplanned pregnancy. The father of the child was 22, and Casey was about to testify against him for charges including sexual assault. Casey had been hospitalized three times since age 14.

It was apparent that history had repeated itself and that Casey had inherited Trish's pernicious strain of hyperactive-impulsive ADHD. Trish became preoccupied with her daughter's self-destructive behavior and the parallel to her own younger life was painful. Her depression and despair mounted. "I see her and I see myself. I'm now so in touch with what I put my parents through." Medications and psychotherapy continued to help Trish, and instead of regressing as she had done in earlier years, she was able to participate in her daughter's care. Most recently, she had arranged for Casey's residential treatment in a noted psychiatric hospital.

PREGNANCY

Pregnancy demands special consideration. None of the ADHD medications is approved for pregnancy, and although there is little apprehension that they are harmful, many women and their doctors are not comfortable exposing the fetus to any risk. For many women with ADHD, the emotional high associated with a desired pregnancy provides a temporary partial reprieve from the impulsivity, distractibility, disorganization, and other symptoms that are associated with the disorder. Often these benefits, derived from the complex interaction of hormones and psychic energy, extend through the period of breastfeeding.

When seeing a new patient, it is vitally important for physicians to ask about the patient's last menstruation, because medications for ADHD have not been cleared for use in pregnancy and are generally to be avoided if possible. Some women decide that they will not take the risk of taking medications during pregnancy, but say that they cannot tolerate *not* taking medications during the period they are trying to conceive.

Melanie, age 37, had been on a stable dose of medications for ADHD combined type. She had married 3 years earlier, and she was excited at the prospect of starting a family. She spoke with her medical doctor about weaning off her nonessential medications. In therapy, we talked about her family planning.

"I'm also considering adoption," Melanie informed me, "because I know that I can't go off the ADHD medications. My husband just started a new job; we are reorganizing at work. I feel that if they put in a new computer system, I will never be able to learn it if I'm gone for a while. I just can't see being without my medications. If I got pregnant I would have to quit work and we can't afford that."

I replied, "Melanie, you are making a lifelong decision. Computer programs and office reorganizations come and go. If you don't decide to become a parent now, through birth or adoption, you may not have the opportunity in the future."

Melanie reiterated her apprehension about stopping her medications and surviving on a single income. Our conversation turned to other matters. I continued to see her periodically and uneventfully for the next several years. She enthusiastically updated me about her promotions and her intense professional satisfaction. Neither of us broached the subject of parenting.

Two years later, Melanie informed me that she was divorcing. "My husband could never get it together. He has had four jobs in 3 years and I don't see him making any progress. He never encouraged me to get pregnant or adopt or gave me the security that I could rely on him if I did." During the next 6 months, Melanie pursued her divorce and expressed great satisfaction when the legal process was completed.

A year later, Melanie informed me that she had been artificially inseminated and was pregnant. She had been off her ADHD medications since learning of her pregnancy. "I'm struggling at work—I'm not half as efficient and I have missed a couple of meetings—but my boss understands. She knows that once I deliver, I will be back on treatment and in full form. She has told me how valuable I have become to the company and assured me that they do not want to lose me."

Indeed this happened. Melanie delivered a healthy son at term and chose not to nurse. She restarted her medications and organized daycare for her child. "I've never felt better. I feel like I have it all. I love my work, I love being a mother, and I feel so good about how I am functioning. No one is making me feel badly about myself. I did not expect to start my family this way, but I am so glad I did."

SELF-IDENTIFIED PROBLEM BEHAVIORS

As with most patients, it is important for the clinician to identify the key problems that led the patient to the clinician's doorstep and to heed what she says. For example, a psychiatrist may identify a patient's shyness as a serious problem that needs treatment, but if the patient targets her main problem as constant forgetting and overall distractibility, these are the problems with which the clinician should provide assistance. If the clinician were to insist on helping the patient become more outgoing, the patient would be likely to suspend treatment out of frustration that she did not receive the help she asked for.

Of course, patients often do not *know* what their underlying problem really is; however, often they can identify the reasons that brought them to the clinician, at least in a general way and sometimes in a very specific way.

SHYNESS, DEPRESSION, AND ANXIETY

Clinicians need to consider ADHD in patients whose primary presentation is not distractibility or impulsivity. Girls with inattentive ADHD have characteristics that can be diametrically opposed to the common perception of ADHD. Rather than being loud and boisterous, they may be quiet and self-effacing. Rather than being extroverted and outgoing, they may be shy and withdrawn. In fact, shyness may be the natural consequence of a lifetime of fogginess and confusion. Of course, shyness and withdrawn behaviors alone are not sufficient to diagnose ADHD. However, the presence of these traits is not sufficient to *rule out* the diagnosis of ADHD, as many clinicians are prone to do.

Depression and anxiety are also common problems in females with ADHD. Often the female may be treated for depression and/or anxiety but *not* for her ADHD, which may be the driving force of both the depression and anxiety; hence, treatment will only achieve a piecemeal solution, since the main problem has not been addressed. Girls may become clinically depressed or anxious *because* they are unable to overcome their ADHD symptoms of disorganization, inattentiveness and distractibility, no matter how hard they try to do so. They may regard themselves as failures, while at the same time, they try desperately to find a way to overcome their ADHD symptoms, and continually fail to succeed.

ACADEMIC STRUGGLES

Girls with ADHD may struggle more with their schoolwork than boys with ADHD. According to a guide published by the American Academy of Pediatrics, "When looked at separately, girls with ADHD have been found to have noteworthy problems in academic achievement and grade retention, [and] an increased incidence of special education placement" (Reiff, 2004, p. 13).

However, average or even good academic achievement should not be a basis for ruling out ADHD, because some adolescent (and adult) females hyperfocus in order to complete their academic requirements. Hyperfocusing is the ability to concentrate intensely on a task to the exclusion of other stimuli. The hyperfocusing female may not notice hunger or hear the doorbell ring when she is concentrating on a task, and hours may pass before she returns to a full awareness of her surroundings. Hyperfocusing involves enormous amounts of time and energy. In order to achieve the grades that she feels she needs, the hyperfocused adolescent may unwittingly sacrifice her social life.

For the clinician this means asking even academically successful patients about other pursuits in order to assess whether the achievement is in lieu of balance in their lives.

PERSONAL CRISES

Many females seek the assistance of a therapist when they experience a "meltdown" type of personal crisis. Again, the existence of a crisis is in no way diagnostic for ADHD; however, the therapist should ask the woman if she is experiencing a significant life change, because her response will often provide information needed for the diagnosis.

For example, Sandra, age 33, had been a diligent assembly worker for several years when she was rewarded with a promotion to supervisor. Within weeks she developed panic and began to miss work. Because of her precipitous performance decline, Sandra was sent to her employee health program. There, the clinician learned that Sandra dreaded her new job. Her promotion had become a personal crisis. Instead of performing a few simple (albeit boring) repetitive tasks each day on the assembly line, now she was involved in hiring people, checking their work, and managing what seemed to her an enormous load of paperwork. She bemoaned, "I feel like I am a computer about to crash."

A careful psychiatric examination revealed that Sandra had always had trouble learning and multitasking. Her strength had been her tenacity. In school she succeeded by sheer repetition of her lessons. In her production job, she could hyperfocus and perform extraordinarily well. Her nephew had recently been diagnosed with ADHD and she suspected other family members had it as well. Medication and counseling were introduced successfully, but within a few months, Sandra and her counselor agreed that the tasks of being a supervisor were incongruent with her natural strengths. She asked to return to her original job. Sandra's company acquiesced and let her return but, to her amazement, continued to pay her at a supervisor's rate.

CONSIDERING JANE: TREATMENT FOR ADHD CAN BE LIBERATING

Some women have suffered from untreated ADHD for years, and when they are finally diagnosed and treated, their lives are markedly improved. Jane was 29 years old and had two small children, ages 3 and 5. She reported that she was always exhausted and felt like she couldn't get anything done. Jane was very distractible and also tended to hyperfocus; for example, she reported going into a "zoned-out" state when she drove, concentrating solely on where she was going. Her 5-year-old son often begged her to talk to him when they were in the car, but Jane said she could not talk to her son *and* drive safely.

Jane also reported being very disorganized and impulsive, buying items that she couldn't really afford on television shopping channels or the Internet. She had been upset about her weight gain since her pregnancies and was angry about her inability to exercise consistently or control her eating. She was completely disinterested in sex and unable to find any common ground on the subject with her husband.

Based on her symptoms, Jane was diagnosed with postpartum depression, but antidepressant medications did little to help her. A psychologist was consulted and a full battery of testing was performed. ADHD inattentive subtype was added to her diagnosis, and Jane's family doctor placed her on short-acting Ritalin.

The improvement was dramatic. Jane became more focused and energetic. She noticed that she was much more patient with her young children and found it much easier to be with them and entertain them. Her organizational skills improved, and she was able to compile a comprehensive "to do" list. She joked, "Not only did I not lose the list, but I was able to accomplish everything on it in a methodical way this morning."

When Jane's doctor suggested she transition to Focalin XR, a longer-acting ADHD medication, Jane resisted the recommendation; she did not want to change a winning formula. She also feared the 12-hour duration of action would cause insomnia. But ultimately she relented and tried the new preparation.

Within a few days, Jane recognized obvious benefits. As promised, the medication was far more convenient to take. After 12 hours the medication blood levels dropped and she did not experience insomnia. Jane also observed that she did not have frequent mood shifts during the day, which she had experienced on the short-acting medications.

The unexpected consequences of the long-acting medications were most valued. Focalin XR suppressed her appetite consistently throughout the day. In addition, the medication motivated Jane to exercise regularly. She lost 15 pounds in the first 2 months. Jane also noted that when on the medication she could focus more intensely on her sexuality. "Now when we have sex I can focus on feeling good and not being distracted by worry. It's been great for me and for my relationship with my husband."

QUESTIONS TO CONSIDER ASKING FEMALE
PATIENTS WITH PROBABLE ADHD

The clinician's understanding is only as good as the questions she asks. It is best to ask questions that will elicit something other than a monosyllabic "yes" or "no" response. Sometimes questions about how often or when behaviors occur may trigger short responses, but frequently they intrigue the patient enough that she will elaborate on her response.

Table 7.3 suggests some dos and don'ts with regard to interviewing questions. For example, don't ask the patient if she loses items frequently. Instead, ask her how many items she has lost in the past week or 2 weeks. In addition, ask about the circumstances surrounding the loss. These questions give the patient tacit permission to admit that she loses things. In describing the circumstances of the loss, she may say that, for example, she lost her car keys and was unable to meet a friend in another city for lunch, and she was really looking forward to this meeting. Her friend was annoyed with her. This underlines for her that she wants to make changes in her life.

Similarly, rather than asking a woman if she daydreams a lot, it is better to go for details. Ask her how often or when she daydreams. Does she "zone out" during daydreaming such that she momentarily loses track of her surroundings? If so, this is one indicator of ADHD.

TABLE 7.3
Interviewing Questions: Some Dos and Don'ts

Don't Ask	Do Ask
Do you lose a lot of items?	How many times in the past week have you lost your purse, car keys, or another important item? What was the consequence of the loss?
Do you sometimes blurt out comments you wish you had not said?	In what kind of situations do you find yourself blurting out what you are thinking to others before you realize it?
Do your symptoms affect your children?	Have you forgotten to pick up your child from school or another place for an hour or longer?
Are you forgetful?	Do you walk from one room to the next, immediately forgetting why you went into the other room? If so, about how often does that happen?
Does your partner say or probably think that you are "flakey" or unreliable?	How does your partner respond when you forget to do something that was important to him or her?
Do you sometimes get lost when you're going somewhere?	How many times have you forgotten where your car is in the parking lot? When you do, how do you react?
Could you be described as "daydreamy"?	How often do you daydream? When you do, do you lose all track of what is going on around you?
Can you concentrate on things that interest you?	Can you work for a much longer time period than others when it's an interesting task? If so, how many hours can you concentrate?
Do you get upset about being distractible or inattentive?	When do you get upset about forgetting things or not paying attention? How do you feel when this happens?

Another advantage of determining specific examples of ADHD symptoms in an individual is that when the patient is treated, the clinician can readdress the issue. After treatment, is the patient who was constantly misplacing important items now losing these items less frequently? Is she blurting out embarrassing comments less often? Identifying specific troublesome issues will offer qualitative and quantitative data to help the patient later determine whether her treatment was effective. It is also a way to increase medication compliance. If the patient notes that her symptoms have declined, she is more likely to adhere to the treatment plan.

SOCIETAL BLAMING OF WOMEN FALLS HARD ON WOMEN WITH ADHD

Societal expectations regarding the role of women, particularly mothers, have changed drastically in the last half century. Women are now expected to take on a widening range of responsibilities, including caretaking (of children, spouses, and elderly parents), housekeeping, and contributing to the household income. As Nadeau and Quinn (2002) aptly put it:

Working full-time outside the home, while being a hands-on mother and homemaker inside the home is no longer called being a superwoman, now, it's just called "life." After a long day at the office, so much is expected of contemporary mothers. No matter how tough her day has been at work, she still must be "up" and ready to fulfill her child's needs, whatever they may be. Carpooling, tutoring, attending athletic events, and helping with homework are all part of the daily mix.

In previous generations, homework was the child's work. There might have been punishments or admonishments if grades faltered, but few parents felt it was their nightly duty to help their children struggle through lengthy assignments. Today, many mothers feel they should monitor, supervise, and even participate in their child's homework, special projects, and test preparations night after night. (pp. 331–332)

To understand women with ADHD, the clinician needs to appreciate the cultural expectations they encounter. The assumption that women should anticipate the needs of others, maintain a neat and organized home, and aid their children with complex school projects may sharply conflict with the very symptoms that women with ADHD struggle with. Most women believe that these expectations have not diminished even as they have assumed increasing work responsibility and found greater overall opportunity.

"Women Are the Caretakers"

There is an underlying societal expectation that women will expertly manage their caregiving roles. When an elderly family member, a child, or another person needs help, often it is assumed that a woman will provide that help.

However, women with ADHD often do not come close to fulfilling these roles adequately. For example, Paige, a 43-year-old executive, reported: "My mother has been slipping and was just diagnosed with Alzheimer's disease. It's pretty clear she can't live alone and my brothers and I want to do the best for her, but everyone is turning to me as the only daughter to take her into my house. I just can't. I worked so hard to get to where I am. I travel and have an unpredictable schedule. I realize I have a crazy life because I want to have a crazy life. I love my mother but I would be miserable having her in my home. I don't think I am a good caregiver. I don't want to be a caregiver."

In counseling, Paige was able to understand that her disinclination to nurture was not at all unusual, nor did she have to apologize for it. With her impulsive ADHD came a general impatience with many things mundane, caregiving among them.

"Women Are Good Managers of the Home"

One area that is very problematic for women with ADHD (and is often an indicator of the disorder) is a very chaotic home life. Women with ADHD often become overwhelmed by housework, laundry, cleaning, and other routine tasks. Many ADHD women work outside the home and they often become overwhelmed with the demands of both work and home. They can learn to keep schedules and develop ways of managing their symptoms, but until they are treated, these women will be unable to create or follow any sort of plan.

"Women Keep Their Tempers"

Some women with ADHD are hyperactive and have a "short fuse." Medication and therapy may help considerably, but it is unlikely that these lively women can achieve the calm demeanor that appears to be an ideal. Clare was a case in point: "I say what I feel. I know that I shouldn't say anything at times. After my mother died I was raised by my father. He was so calm and I so admired this as the way civil people should behave. I just don't have it. I get mad easily and I scream when I shouldn't. The medications allow me to think before I rant, but sometimes my feelings can't be suppressed."

As noted earlier, many people with ADHD, especially when it is untreated, have a tendency to blurt out uncensored thoughts, no matter how embarrassing or hurtful they may be. In males such behavior may be laughed off as "plain talk." Among females, however, it is usually regarded as rude behavior that the woman should have known better than to exhibit. Such women can benefit greatly from receiving coaching and learning techniques to better control their emotions and their tempers. (For more about coaching see Chapter 10.)

"Women Are Understanding of Others"

It would be a kinder world if all people were considerate of others, but women with ADHD may have a difficult time fulfilling the expectation that women are generally empathic. Both adolescent girls and adult women with ADHD may be judgmental and intolerant. Perhaps this trait is learned, but girls and women with ADHD are more likely to misread their environment and miss social cues. As Birgit Amann (2005) observed, "Women with ADHD are more likely to see their world in stark contrasts. Black and white, good and bad. They sometimes miss the nuances and this can interfere with all aspects of their life."

This tendency may be a key reason why some women with ADHD suffer so much from unhappy (or nonexistent) peer relationships, as well as from trouble in their romantic relationships or a lack of romantic involvements altogether. Treatment and coaching can often help considerably with this problem.

Chapter 8

Challenging Patients, Difficult Treatment Choices

MOST INDIVIDUALS WITH ADHD want to be accurately diagnosed and treated so that they can improve their lives at school, work, and home. These patients are gratifying for professionals to treat, mainly because they often improve quickly in tangible, easily detectable ways.

Other patients are more challenging. They tap the therapist's energy, challenge his or her skills, and become a dominant subject of commiseration with colleagues. Every clinician has demanding patients—patients with substance use disorders, patients with issues surrounding sexuality, patients who engage in pathological gambling or shoplifting, patients who self-mutilate, or patients who struggle with self-destructive and borderline personality traits. Long-linked to depression, obsessive-compulsive disorder, and post-traumatic stress disorder, these behaviors may also appear in patients with ADHD. Impulsive almost by definition, they provide ADHD sufferers with a temporary sensation of focus and control.

In our clinic, where screening for ADHD is routine, some substance abusers and many patients with impulse dyscontrol are likely to screen positive. This observation has led us to question whether these behaviors are

179

manifestations of the impulsivity associated with ADHD. In our experience, conventional psychotherapy and antidepressant and anticompulsive medications offer minimal symptom amelioration; yet adding ADHD medications improves outcome. We conclude that ADHD lies at the core of many of these inexplicable but seemingly connected conditions.

ADHD creates clinical challenges, and so do the treatments. Clinicians battle medication noncompliance in their ADHD patients. At the same time, stimulant medications, the mainstay of ADHD treatment, are controlled substances and clinicians need to be concerned about drug diversion and abuse. The risks and the benefits of treatment need to be weighed daily.

CORE ADHD SYMPTOMS DRIVE COMPLEX BEHAVIOR

ADHD is a disorder first evident in the young. Core symptoms of impulsivity, distractibility, and hyperactivity fulminate into complicated behaviors as patients age. Patients with hyperactivity have an uncomfortable need to be in motion. As adults, they find methods to mollify the discomfort. Some choose positive behaviors like exercise. Others learn that alcohol or marijuana provides a calming effect. Impulsive children speak out of turn and are too self-involved to listen to others. Impulsive adults exhibit this behavior less productively; they are more likely to discover ways of instant gratification like gambling or shoplifting. Clinicians should not define adult patients by their most obvious adult symptom (e.g., this patient has substance use disorder; that patient is a shoplifter) without understanding these symptoms in the full context of ADHD.

ADHD AND SUBSTANCE ABUSE

Some ADHD patients have past or current substance use disorders (SUDs), whether the drug is alcohol, marijuana, cocaine, a prescribed pain reliever, another drug, or a combination thereof. Among these patients, the most commonly abused drugs are alcohol and marijuana. In those who develop a SUD, adults with ADHD have an earlier age of onset (average of 19 years) compared to adults without ADHD (22 years; Wilens, 2004c). Adults with untreated ADHD are at twice the risk for developing a SUD compared to adults without ADHD (52% versus 27%; Biederman et al., 1995).

Vicky presented to our clinic ostensibly to seek help with her marriage. She was married for the second time to Larry, a successful retired GM executive. Vicky was very reserved during our first few meetings until Larry came into a scheduled session. He started talking before I could even take my seat. "Something needs to be done. I can't go on living with her. She drinks every night and spends most of the day in bed, knocked out with her pain patch. I am constantly lying to our friends. They call, she's drunk, and I have to tell them she is in the shower so she won't embarrass herself."

Vicky had been through several treatment centers but had maintained sobriety for only short periods. Her husband's outburst finally prompted her to open up. "I just get so nervous and fearful. I'd rather just feel stoned. It's easier. I am afraid to keep drinking and using and I'm afraid not to have it as a crutch."

A diagnostic workup revealed that Vicky did meet criteria for ADHD combined type. Treatment was started and immediately she reported feeling calmer and more focused. Initially she stopped drinking altogether and she discontinued her opiate pain patch. She relapsed to drinking in the evenings, but once the ADHD medications were changed to cover evening hours, even this urge diminished.

Stimulants May Be Protective Against Substance Use Disorders

Vicky's case is an example of how untreated ADHD symptoms may drive substance abusing behaviors. In her particular situation, ADHD treatment was instrumental in promoting sobriety. Issues surrounding treatment for ADHD substance abusers are controversial. Some doctors (and many parents) worry that treating ADHD children and adolescents with stimulants will model inappropriate behavior; they fear that children will learn that "drugs" are an acceptable way of modifying behavior, and this will increase their proclivity to use substances later in life.

Some physicians avoid stimulants in patients with past substance abuse, even if the problem occurred years earlier and there is no current use, lest there be a kindling affect that reignites the problem. In a telephone survey of 250 physicians who treated ADHD, few differentiated between patients with a history of substance use and those with a currently active SUD. Most (97%) said that they would prescribe a nonstimulant over a stimulant to these patients, whether the SUD was current or in the past (Verispan Research, October 2003).

Some parts of the debate are clearer. As noted earlier, when substance abuse occurs among unmedicated ADHD patients, it presents at younger ages than among their substance-abusing peers without ADHD. Furthermore, if abuse does occur, it is more severe in the unmedicated ADHD patient (Barkley, Fischer, Smallish, & Fletcher, 2003; Biederman, Wilens, Mick, Faraone, Weber, Curtis, et al., 1997; Fischer & Barkley, 2003; McCabe, Teter, & Boyd, 2004). Available studies have demonstrated that treating children and adolescents with ADHD with stimulants actually reduces their risk for developing SUD in later years (Wilens, 2004c).

It is ideal to identify and treat ADHD in childhood or early adolescence if possible, before a SUD develops. Moreover, in the newly ADHD diagnosed adolescent or young adult who has not yet developed a SUD, ADHD medications may still offer protection against the later SUD development. Treatment for ADHD with stimulants before adolescence does not "immunize" patients against all risks for substance abuse, but it does appear to cut the risk in half (Korn, 2004). This is an encouraging finding for therapists struggling with these challenging patients.

Research has also shown that in patients with past substance abuse disorders, stimulants do *not* prompt the patient to revert to past behaviors (Schubiner, 2005; Wilens, 2004b). Simply put, prescribing a stimulant to a recovered patient with a past substance use disorder is not, as many doctors fear, tantamount to encouraging a recovered alcoholic to drink. By improving focus and concentration, the stimulants may protect against, rather than hasten, a potential relapse. In general, the consensus is that doctors can confidently treat these patients with stimulants if at least 6 months have elapsed since the last substance usage.

Another concern among some clinicians, parents, and patients is that treating substance abusing ADHD patients with stimulants (themselves controlled medications) is simply "trading" one set of problems with another. To address this concern, it is important to review the elements of substance-related disorders. In substance abuse, the drug use interferes with normal functioning at work and home. For example, an individual who has "abused" cannot make it to work on Monday following a weekend of excess.

Individuals who are substance-dependent (or "addicted," to use the more common term) require the substance to function. They develop tolerance over time and need greater amounts to achieve the desired effect. The classic example of tolerance is nicotine dependency; almost inevitably the longer one smokes, the more nicotine is needed. Young adults almost always consume more cigarettes than they did as adolescents.

Substance-dependent patients experience physical withdrawal symptoms if they suddenly lose access to their drug of choice. When intake is decreased, mild withdrawal symptoms emerge. When substances like opiates are abruptly discontinued, a painful clinical condition called *opiate withdrawal syndrome* develops quickly and often demands medical attention. Opiate addicts will literally lie, cheat, and steal to avoid a disruption in their supply. Substance-dependent individuals (think: alcoholics) pursue the substance at the expense of other normal activities. Finally, dependent individuals see their quality of life deteriorate; they perform less well on the job and in their relationships.

Stimulant-treated patients with ADHD rarely fit this description. After establishing the proper daily dose of stimulant in the first several months of treatment, most of these patients do not require escalating doses over time. If their stimulant supply is interrupted, they miss the benefits but do not experience physical withdrawal or go to extremes to replace the medication. Finally, with treatment, ADHD patients find that the quality of their life improves; they become better-educated, drive more safely, find higher levels of employment, and seek fewer divorces. As with Vicky, they may derive the added benefit of decreasing their use of harmful substances.

A Profile of Adolescents and Young Adults at Risk for Diverting or Misusing Medication

In 2006, Wilens and his colleagues reported on their findings on the characteristics of adolescents and young adults who were most likely to abuse stimulant medications in the *Journal of the American Academy of Child & Adolescent Psychiatry* (Wilens, Gignac, Swezey, Monuteaux & Biederman). The researchers studied 98 patients taking psychotropic medications, including 55 subjects with ADHD and 43 subjects taking psychiatric medications for another purpose. The average age of the ADHD group was 20.8 years and the average age of the non-ADHD group was 23 years. About two-thirds of the subjects were males.

Most of the subjects in the ADHD group were taking stimulants (96%) as well as other medications, such as selective serotonin reuptake inhibitor or tricyclic antidepressants. In the non-ADHD group, 10% were taking stimulants. Most of the subjects in the non-ADHD group (80%) were taking selective serotonin reuptake inhibitors.

The researchers found that 11% of the ADHD group reported having sold their medication, while none of the non-ADHD group had sold their drugs. In addition, 22% of the ADHD group reported misusing their medication, compared to 5% of the non-ADHD group. Ten percent of the ADHD group reported getting high on their medication, compared to 5% of the non-ADHD group. Some subjects reported using their medication along with alcohol or drugs: 31% of the ADHD group and 25% of the non-ADHD group. Five percent of the ADHD group and none of the non-ADHD group said that they had experienced adverse effects of using their medication with alcohol or drugs. As a result, the majority of both groups were using their medications as prescribed, although the ADHD group clearly had a higher rate of problems.

The researchers analyzed further and found that all of the medications that were either diverted to others or that were misused by the patients themselves were immediate-release stimulants. This finding supported the belief among the researchers that among groups at risk for diversion or misuse, extended-release stimulants or non-stimulants are preferable to immediate-release stimulants.

The researchers also found that 80% of those who diverted or misused their drugs were comorbid for either conduct disorder or a substance use disorder. Said the researchers, "Clinicians need to be particularly vigilant in discussing and monitoring adolescents and young adults with ADHD and CD or SUD for the appropriate use of their medications. Such monitoring may include questioning, specifically about appropriate use or misuse of the medication, as well as potential diversion of the medicine, and observing that pill counts are accurate" (Wilens, Gignac, Swezey, Monuteaux & Biederman, page 412).

A Few Valid Questions About Stimulants and Substance Use

Although stimulants have been shown to be effective in decreasing substance abuse behaviors, clinicians are wise to remain educated about the medications and their possible (albeit unlikely) abuse (J. B. Ashtin Group, 2005). Difficult treatment decisions can only be made when the clinician is comfortable with the following issues:

- The relative abuse potential of ADHD medications
- The role of ADHD treatment in recreational drug users
- The potential harmfulness of stimulants

ARE SOME STIMULANTS MORE ADDICTIVE THAN OTHERS?

Although certain stimulants have a reputation for greater abuse than others, research has not confirmed this. Methylphenidate and amphetamines offer little physiological reinforcement. Patients do not report feeling "high" after taking the pill. Stimulants are far less appealing to abusers than opiates, alcohol, cocaine, or street drugs. Many kids who snort stimulants do so only one time, as they do not experience a sense of well-being or euphoria. If snorted, the substance often irritates their nasal mucosa, and if injected, it causes irritation to the blood vessels. Little about the experience leads them to want to repeat the effort.

The National Institute on Drug Abuse and numerous studies have demonstrated that people with ADHD who take stimulants as directed rarely become addicted. However, short-acting stimulants are powdered, and some physicians, despite the studies, fear that kids will grind up and snort the pills.

The introduction of long-acting stimulant preparations (Concerta, Focalin XR, and Adderall XR) has calmed apprehension. Concerta, the least abusable long-acting methylphenidate, utilizes the Oros system, a technology that delivers methylphenidate over 12 hours, via a virtually indestructible capsule. Only a very motivated chemist could dissolve Concerta, reduce it, dry it, and snort it. Strattera, the only approved nonstimulant, has no abuse potential, and it is emerging as the most comfortable choice for doctors caring for ADHD patients with a history of substance abuse.

RECREATIONAL USE OF STIMULANTS

Recreational users experiment with drugs of abuse, but they are not regular users. Often ADHD individuals fall into this recreational use category because they can be adventurous and are willing to try illicit substances like methamphetamine or Ecstasy.

The key issue for clinicians, though, is that most ADHD patients do not misuse their stimulant medication. For this reason, stimulants remain a credible option. Arguably, their usage will decrease the patient's fearlessness and subsequently their frequency of recreational use. For patients' safety, the clinician should emphasize that stimulants should not be taken with illegal drugs (especially with other stimulants like cocaine), even occasionally, because of potential drug interactions.

ARE STIMULANTS HARMFUL OVER THE LONG RUN?

Because most physicians who treat ADHD become comfortable prescribing stimulants, they may accentuate treatment attributes in an attempt to improve compliance. Physicians have reason to be confident. Stimulants are time-tested and very safe.

Groups ideologically opposed to treating ADHD exploit the fear that stimulants are dangerous. Even though these groups have little credibility, it is important for the clinician not to be dismissive of these concerns. When misused, stimulants can be detrimental even when patients have a valid diagnosis of ADHD. Patients may take excessive doses or they may use the drug inappropriately. Snorting powdered stimulants can be a route of abuse. It is advisable for the parents of adolescents to count their pills periodically to ensure that the child is not over- or underusing the medication.

In one published case, a 15-year-old boy with ADHD developed severe psychiatric symptoms of paranoia, depression, and suicidal thinking after taking intranasal doses of 60 mg of sustained-release methylphenidate for about 2 weeks (Morton & Stockton 2000). Other patients have abused methylphenidate to the point of toxicity and have developed delirium, panic, and aggression. Amphetamine intoxication can also result in behavioral unpredictability, and in extreme cases some patients develop hallucinations or other psychotic symptoms (Morton & Stockton, 2000). Yet it is important to emphasize that these are uncommon circumstances. When evaluating untoward outcomes, always consider that the patient might have other psychiatric diagnoses, such as bipolar disorder or schizophrenia, in addition to ADHD. (For more about comorbidities see Chapter 2.)

Considering Nonstimulants and Therapy

When physicians do not want to prescribe Schedule II drugs for ADHD to an individual with an ongoing SUD, there are varieties of excellent nonstimulant choices that are available. Chapter 9 explores atomoxetine (Strattera) and modafinil (Provigil). Of the two, only atomoxetine is specifically approved for the treatment of ADHD in adolescents and adults. It has no abuse potential. There are also off-label choices such as bupropion (Wellbutrin), venlafaxine (Effexor XR), and various other antidepressants. Patients with ADHD and SUD also may benefit from cognitive-behavioral treatment. Twelve step programs and supportive counseling can also be effective.

ADHD AND SEXUAL ISSUES

Struggles with sexuality are commonplace in the therapist's office, and individuals with ADHD present disproportionately. It is important to understand these issues in the context of the condition. Problems may range at either extreme—some patients with ADHD are hypersexual, exhausting their partners, whereas others complain of a lack of desire. Some have trouble starting relationships, whereas others cannot remain monogamous. Promiscuous sexual behavior, commonly seen in adolescents with ADHD, can cause remorse well into adulthood. Many individuals and their partners feel quite frustrated and turn to the therapist for help. Although ADHD represents only one component of a person's sexuality, it is an area that merits discussion.

Past Abuse

When patients with ADHD complain about issues of sexuality and intimacy, the therapist should consider a childhood history of physical or sexual abuse. Children with ADHD are more likely to have been raised by parents with ADHD, and they are also more likely to be the product of divorced families. In addition, their relatives are at greater risk for substance abuse. Children with ADHD can have impaired self-esteem and feel the need to please others. They can be less perceptive than others to dangers in their environment. They might be overly trusting of older children and adults. Taken alone, each of these elements may not make the child at greater risk, but taken cumulatively they do. While no firm data validates this contention, the therapist should have an elevated level of concern.

Impulsivity and Sexual Behavior

Impulsivity, a core ADHD characteristic, pervades sexual behavior. For example, a person *without* ADHD may decide impulsively to have sex in the kitchen with his partner at home on his lunch break on a slow day; the person *with* ADHD might make this choice even if it was not a slow day and he was scheduled to make a major presentation at work at 1 P.M., requiring him to look and behave impeccably. Having sex now would be more important to the person with ADHD—to hell with allowing enough time to get ready for the presentation and be on time. In contrast, the person without ADHD could control his impulse, regretfully deciding to pursue the sexual opportunity on another day. For the person with untreated ADHD, there is *only* now; hence, his reaction. For the person who does not have ADHD, the future offers opportunities in addition to the here and now.

Using Sex to Sublimate Excessive Energy or Hyperactivity

Hyperactive individuals with ADHD may find sex to be a good method to dissipate their excessive energy. In their youth, they may view sexual partners as objects to be used and discarded; in established relationships, their partners may feel that the sexual activity is perfunctory and devoid of any emotional connection.

ADHD medications can have contradictory effects on sexuality. Effective treatment may help the individual either increase or throttle back on sexual desire. Janey, the spouse of a hypersexual patient, thanked her husband's psychiatrist for prescribing stimulants. Without treatment, he demanded sex once or twice a day. "If I wasn't into it at the time, he would become so moody that I would just give in. It wasn't worth putting up with his meanness," she said. With medications, his sex drive was more akin with her own, vastly improving their relationship.

Carol, an occupational therapist, appreciated the focusing effects of the medications. "I've always been very sexual, more than any man I've been with, but now that I am treated, I feel like I can connect emotionally with my husband. I feel like I am *there*. I am slowed down just a little. I still really need orgasms, but it's less mechanical now."

Inattentive symptoms can be particularly troublesome for women with ADHD. Although stimulants do not have a direct aphrodisiac effect, obtaining an ability to concentrate on the intimate moment that is occurring in the present, rather than on planning the next event and worrying about the next obligation, clearly improves orgasmic potential.

Bad Decisions

Individuals with ADHD who are highly impulsive need to develop ways to balance sexual opportunity with propriety. Sometimes they make the wrong decision. It is not uncommon for ADHD specialists to have treated patients who have been criminally prosecuted for sexual acts that resulted from impulsive, not cruelly intentioned, behavior.

For years, Max's hyperactivity and impulsive symptoms had been treated with Ritalin. Max's parents knew that his grade-school class-clown antics were better controlled when he was compliant. However, he resisted the medications, taking them irregularly and rarely in the evenings or during vacation. Max grew gracefully into an attractive adolescent and maintained the magnetism that always drew him into the center of his social group. By his late teens, Max had a sexual smorgasbord always available to him. Max had a voracious appetite for sex and adventure, and his male friends could not contain their admiration for his triumphs. Among the girls in his own community, his reputation was more circumspect.

In the summer before his senior year, Max started dating Jesse, a 16-year-old, at his high school. He met her parents and spent time with her family. All was well until November, when Max met Perry, a senior at the private school across town. For months, Max was involved with both girls, neither knowing of the other's existence.

In many ways, Max enjoyed the situation and took it lightheartedly. But within a couple of weeks, rumors emerged and Jesse confronted Max. Sensing his lack of contrition, she ended the relationship. Max left the relationship emotionally unwounded and oblivious to Jesse's hurt. He continued to date Perry.

Over Christmas break, Max met Jesse at a friend's party. They talked civilly and drank a small amount of beer. Max immediately sensed that Jesse was ambivalent about him and felt that he could charm her as he had done before. He led her to the cabana in the backyard and they started kissing. When the sexual activity began to move beyond kissing, Jesse protested, but Max continued to intercourse. He rationalized it himself by saying, "No doesn't really mean no. It's Jesse after all. She expects me to take the lead." The encounter ended when Jesse's sister, also at the party, found them and called for help.

Two days later, Max was arrested and charged with criminal sexual behavior. He spent the night in jail. He had just turned 18 and was charged as an adult. Over the next 6 weeks, Max was suspended from the football team, asked to withdraw his scholarship application, and ostracized by many of his friends. His parents retained an attorney for $10,000. Max's mother had just completed a round of chemotherapy for breast cancer and their home became somber.

Max's trial began in the fall, when all his friends were starting college. The prosecuting attorney alleged that Max's behavior recklessly put Jesse in harm's way and the rape was planned. During testimony, Max conceded that Jesse verbally resisted during the encounter but that he did not take her protestation seriously. "I felt it was part of the game." The court learned that Max had had several sexual partners in high school, although none ever lodged a complaint about him.

Max had a paltry defense. His attorney argued that Max was imperfect but not a criminal. He had a long history of ADHD hyperactive-impulsive type and he often acted before he thought. On the night of the incident Max had not taken his ADHD medication. His psychological testing did not reveal significant character pathology. He had never faced criminal charges before, but he periodically clashed with teachers and had served four separate detentions during high school. Nonetheless, the attorney explained that Max had no intention of hurting Jesse. He felt she was acquiescent and on some levels she signaled Max to proceed.

The judge and jury were not moved. Max was convicted and sentenced to 4 years in prison. His mother died of cancer before he was released. Jesse seemingly did well in therapy.

Max's experience is cautionary. A court of his peers deemed his actions criminal and doled out his sentence. Judging and punishing is the job of the criminal justice system. Mental health professionals, however, have a different mission. We need to understand Max, not just judge his behavior. Therapists need not assuage responsibility, and adults with ADHD are ultimately accountable for their behavior, but grasping the full meaning of impulsivity in the context of ADHD allows for a more meaningful analysis of this tragedy.

Working on ADHD-Related Sexual Problems in Therapy

Sexual issues associated with ADHD can often resolve with time, but a combination of psychotherapy and medication may hasten recovery. Most importantly, therapists need to validate their patients' experiences. Understanding life through the prism of the ADHD experience helps clinicians understand their patients' relationship turmoils, promiscuity, and hypersexuality. Expressing this empathy might also provide a foundation to tackle delicate past abuse issues.

All of the approved ADHD medications are used to reduce impulsive actions, and psychotherapy and coaching serve to harmonize troubled relationships. As a rule, the serotonin reuptake inhibiting antidepressants significantly decrease libido. This can be a desirable effect in hypersexual men with ADHD who have concurrent mood or anxiety symptoms. Sex Addicts Anonymous, a 12-step self-help group, is a useful nonmedical therapy.

Although clinicians should not judge a patient's sexual partner or decide how many sexual partners is too many, precautionary advice remains good form. For patients engaging in nonmonogamous sexual activity, the therapist should emphasize the protective necessity of condoms. Adolescents can never hear strongly enough that "no" really does mean no. Still, the highest priority for the mental health professional in dealing with these critical issues is to provide a safe and uncritical therapeutic milieu.

ADHD AND GAMBLING

Some studies indicate that people with ADHD, mood disorders, or anxiety disorders are more likely to become involved in gambling activities, largely because they lack effective impulse control (Potenza, Kosten, & Rounsaville, 2001). Men with ADHD are at greater risk for pathological gambling than women, but women are not immune.

Few medication studies have been conducted with gambling, hoarding, and other addictive behaviors. Most studies presuppose that these patients are either hypomanic or have obsessive-compulsive disorder. In one study, 70% of gamblers who took fluvoxamine, an SSRI indicated for obsessive-compulsive disorder, improved (Hollander, DeCaria, Mari, Wong, Mosovich, Grossman, & Begaz, 1998). Several studies support the use of mood stabilizing medications like lithium carbonate or valproate acid (Depakote) for pathological gambling (Pallanti, Quercioli, Soud, & Hollander, 2002). Naltrexone, a drug used to treat opiate overdoses and alcoholism, can help select patients (Grant, Kushner, & Kim, 2002).

SHOPPING, SHOPLIFTING, HOARDING, AND SURFING THE INTERNET

Patients with ADHD may exhibit addictive behaviors beyond (or in addition to) substance abuse and gambling. Some patients with ADHD take solace in retail shopping and become financially overextended. "To me, it's like hunting," said Patricia, a member of a therapy group. "I love the whole ritual of shopping more than what I actually buy. Sometimes I bring the stuff home and I just put it in my closet. I either return it or never look at it again." Patricia's crisis started soon after her credit card companies pushed up their minimum monthly payment requirements. "I just can't keep it up any longer. I've been able to use household money for the credit payments, but if I tell my husband what I've done again, he'll explode. We just got out of the hole from the last time."

Another group member, Kyle, a successful real estate broker, faced a greater threat: his fifth shoplifting arrest. "I've already spent a year in jail. If I get convicted again, I will lose everything—my job, my pension. My wife and kids will be so humiliated." Awaiting trial and hoping to obtain a forensic psychiatric testimony to explain his condition to the court, Kyle admitted to shoplifting on the morning of his doctor's appointment.

Charles and Lynn presented for counseling because of marital tension. Initially passive, Lynn gained more faith in the therapy during the second session and declared that "she had reached her limit." She explained that Charles had a fascination with metal automotive molds used to make car parts. Initially he collected only the dyes, but in recent years, he bought and hoarded all things metal. He could not throw anything away, and shafts and gears overran their house. In the past 6 months, the hoarding had intensified to the extent that she could no longer walk though the hallways or physically turn around in her bedroom. Charles conceded, "I never know what auto part I may need down the road, so I decide not to decide. I keep them all."

Patricia, Kyle, and Charles all had ADHD. Patricia, perhaps the least severely afflicted, responded well to Concerta. She noticed that on the medication, she did not feel preoccupied with shopping. "I don't feel as frenzied. But I have learned that if I don't take the medication, some of the old impulsive behavior can return." She entered marital therapy with her husband and together they paid off their debt and agreed jointly to limit her line of credit to minimize further problems.

Kyle asserted that his ADHD medications decreased his shoplifting bouts. "Before I shoplift, I get in this hazy zone, when I feel very disconnected to other things that are going on. On the stimulants, I do not dissociate as easily and I don't get in the zone." He was also relieved that on medications he no longer had the interest to endlessly surf the Internet looking for pornography or engage in time-wasting interactive "chatting."

In court, he fared less well. A state examiner found him to be competent to face trial and the trial judge imposed a 6-month prison term. His ADHD medications were discontinued during his incarceration.

In contrast, Charles did very well. He had previously been diagnosed with obsessive-compulsive disorder and treated with high doses of Prozac and Luvox. Taken alone, neither helped much. Once his ADHD was diagnosed, Adderall XR was added to his antidepressants. Concurrently, Charles's wife hired a professional organizer to help the couple tackle the cleanup. Charles related, "On Adderall I woke up. I felt more motivated to do things. I felt more confident that I could throw things out. And I felt more comfortable making decisions." Lynn added, "With the medications he was able to act on what the organizer instructed. We are doing so much better."

SELF-INJURIOUS BEHAVIORS

Therapists often struggle with patients who intermittently harm themselves. A small percentage of self-mutilators are overly psychotic. Schizophrenic patients are occasionally known to self amputate fingers or even limbs but this behavior is directly associated with overt delusional thinking.

In contrast to psychotic patients, "cutters" are not evidently bizarre. They use razors or knives to inflict tiny cuts in their arms or legs. The cutting is superficial and the individuals usually deny that death or injury is their goal. Uniformly their intent is to use physical pain to mute their emotional distress. Most cutting is impulsive and is triggered by a transient feeling of frustration over a life circumstance. Given the relationship between impulsivity and ADHD, the therapist should suspect cutters have the condition.

Risk Factors for Self-Injurious Behaviors

Some studies have found that being white and female, with a history of sexual abuse and poor impulse control, are risk factors that are associated with self-injurious behaviors among adolescent patients hospitalized in a psychiatric facility. In addition, researchers have found that individuals who cut themselves were 3.5 times more likely to engage in some forms of risky sexual behavior (Brown, Houck, Hadley, & Lescano, 2005).

Alisa, a thin, boyish-looking 26-year-old, typified the nonpsychotic self-injurious patient. When feeling psychologically overwhelmed, Alisa superficially cut her forearms with a razor blade. On several occasions she hammered her fingers intentionally. During a particularly bad episode she burned her forearms with a cigarette.

Alisa had received mental health treatment for many years and had been diagnosed with chronic depression. She had been adopted into a loving family after spending her early years in foster care. The details of the foster care were murky, but Alisa believed that an older boy had molested her when she was 6. Alisa did poorly in school, particularly after an injury sustained during an auto accident, which prevented her from participating in sports—the only true connection she had to her classmates. In 7th grade she started smoking, and by 11th grade she regularly used marijuana. She was unsure of her sexual orientation, although she surmised she was lesbian. She had not been in a long-term relationship, nor had she sustained meaningful employment. Based on this history and an extensive workup, we recognized that in addition to her depression, Alisa had a history of undiagnosed ADHD.

CRISIS WARNING INDICATORS

Self-harming actions can be difficult to distinguish from overt suicidal behavior. Psychotic patients may report, "My body is being invaded by an alien force, I need to cut my arm to rid myself of these forces." Truly depressed patients experience profound and persistent hopelessness that so distorts their thoughts that being on the receiving end of a gunshot is comforting rather than terrifying. In these situations, the therapist will find the safe harbor of an inpatient psychiatric unit necessary to protect these motivated patients from self-harm.

But therapists should not confuse cutting with willful suicidal behavior. With the nonpsychotic self-harming patient, therapists should develop an emergency plan in advance, should the self-injury go too far and become life-threatening. Cutters usually deny a plan for suicide, but when they end up in an emergency room with bleeding from a self-imposed injury, most clinicians are disinclined to accept this reassurance. They often require brief psychiatric hospitalization to protect patients from extending their injuries.

In crisis, frequent physician contact is required. All wounds should be examined. Infection and arterial bleeding are infrequent but are serious complications of self-cutting. Known cutters (often evidenced by the presence of healed scars) can be medically treated and released back to the outpatient setting.

ALISA'S PREVIOUS TREATMENT

Alisa's self-mutilation had been ongoing and her arms and legs carried many scars in varying degrees of healing. Because of her chronicity, Alisa frustrated her previous therapists and she was thought to be resistant to psychotherapeutic interventions. Behavioral contracts in which she promised not to self-injure prove unsustainable and ineffective. Alisa was diagnosed with borderline personality disorder, a diagnosis that many therapists see as synonymous with a hopeless situation. Her community mental health program placed her in dialectical behavioral therapy, a cognitive approach that is the current psychotherapy of choice (Linehan, 1993).

From a medication perspective, self-mutilating behaviors are considered variants of obsessive-compulsive disorder. For this reason, Alisa was placed on serotonin reuptake inhibitors (SSRIs), which are the conventional drugs of first choice (Fong, 2003). If SSRIs are ineffective, or the patient appears dissociative, physicians can employ antipsychotics or mood stabilizing medications. Benzodiazepines are useful for short-term anxiety relief in this population. At various times, Alisa had been on all these types of medication.

THERAPEUTIC INTERVENTIONS FOR ALISA

The major intervention made with Alisa was gaining her trust by demonstrating consistency and projecting confidence. Her cutting behavior was deconstructed and identified as an impulsive gesture. It was noted that Alisa was more likely to injure herself after an introspective session of psychotherapy or a life event that triggered a memory of previous abuse. We told her that our evaluation found her to have ADHD. With some trepidation, Alisa agreed to try Focalin XR. She became less impulsive and the frequency of her cutting diminished. She was still susceptible at certain periods of the day, particularly in the evening, so the medication was sculpted to "cover her" at these more vulnerable times. Alisa and her therapist noted that she had better mood stability. She was able to expand her hours to full-time at the downtown bookstore and she was successfully managing a healthy relationship. Two years into her therapy, her doctor and therapist recalled how rocky and hopeless things seemed at first and how much better they were now.

DIFFICULT TREATMENT OPTIONS

Part of the apprehension clinicians have about diagnosing ADHD has to do with the available treatments. Although it is not common, some patients do engage in drug diversion, stimulant abuse, and devious methods to obtain medications. These section discusses these issues and offers strategies and guidelines for assessing risk. Accurate diagnosis and expert management of side effects are only helpful if the patient is taking medication as prescribed. The chapter concludes by addressing the complicated issue of ADHD medication compliance.

Adolescents and Drug Diversion

Although drug diversion is not limited to adolescents and young adults, this group's increased tendency to divert drugs of any kind makes them a population that bears scrutiny. Stimulants improve focus and wakefulness in all brains, ADHD and non-ADHD alike. Adolescents buzz about these virtues and in some schools, particularly college campuses, a market has developed for amphetamines and methylphenidate. Generally, the student's intention is to enhance studying, and most of these abusers limit their use of the stimulant to a few days. Longer-term use of stimulants in the non-ADHD person leads to side effects like agitation and appetite suppression. Stimulant-seeking adolescents without ADHD obtain the medications through a number of sources, from their peers to illicit orders over the Internet.

In the 2004 "Monitoring the Future" survey, an annual study of drug use among adolescents and young adults nationwide, 2.5% of eighth graders abused methylphenidate. That percentage increased to 3.4% of 10th graders and 5.1% of students in grade 12. These statistics suggest that the risk of abuse should be considered.

Clinicians should forewarn their ADHD patients that others might approach them for their medication. Most patients have no diversionary intentions when they initially receive a stimulant prescription, but they may surrender the drug if money is offered to them. For others, the currency is social acceptance. Occasionally clinicians hear reports of students threatened for their medication.

Several student surveys quantified the pressure that adolescents treated for ADHD encounter. A study of middle- and high-school students revealed that peers who wanted to buy or trade the drugs approached a quarter of those taking stimulants for their ADHD. Girls taking stimulants for ADHD were more likely to be approached (29.6%) than were medicated boys (20.6%), and white students were more likely to be approached (27.4%) than African-American students (16.0%) (McCabe, Teter, & Boyd, 2004).

Of high-school students, nearly half (46.4%) of the ADHD students reported being approached by peers seeking stimulants. Interestingly, students not planning to attend college were asked for their medications twice as often (32.4%) as students who planned to further their education (17.9%).

These findings provided information on students approached by others seeking drugs but did not report on the percentages of students who actually relinquished their medications. Poulin (2001) found that 14.7% of students taking prescribed stimulants reported they had given away their medications whereas 7.3% said that they had sold their medication. Males were more likely than females to sell their stimulants. In addition, during the last 12 months of the study, more than 7% of the students reported that their medication had been forcibly taken or stolen in the past year (Poulin, 2001).

Physicians who prescribe stimulants should frankly discuss the health and legal risks of giving away or selling a scheduled drug. With new state and federal laws, the penalties for selling drugs in a "drug-free zone" (usually on school grounds or children's playgrounds), are significantly greater than penalties for drug-selling elsewhere. Adolescents should be aware that law enforcement agencies and the courts will be intolerant of such behavior. In addition, teens should be told that giving stimulants to others could cause them to need emergency room help or could even cause their deaths. To avoid these situations, clinicians should proactively counsel their patients to be discrete about revealing that they have a supply of stimulants.

CONSIDERING OTHER FAMILY MEMBERS

When prescribing a stimulant drug, it is important for physicians to consider which other family members might have access to the medication. Ideally, inquiries about past or present substance abuse among all family members or anyone who lives in the home should be assessed before stimulants are prescribed.

The most common reason for family members to seek the stimulant is that they themselves have ADHD, often undiagnosed. Nefarious motivations are also possible. An older brother with a history of drug-dealing or an eating-disordered sister who wonders if amphetamines might suppress her appetite could be potential abusers of the teenager's stimulant. Sitting in the medicine cabinet, the drug may be too tantalizing for others in the family to resist.

ASSESSING RISK

It is not possible for the clinician to know what is in the hearts and minds of the patients or their family members; however, a few pointed questions can help screen for potential risks. Clinicians may ask:

• Have you or any of your friends ever shared their medications with others? (The more frequently that peers share drugs amongst themselves, the greater the risk for drug diversion to occur if a stimulant is prescribed.)
• Have you or anyone in the family developed a tolerance to a drug, meaning that more was needed to achieve the same effect?

- When you become upset, what do you do to calm yourself? What do other family members do? (This will help you determine if there are unhealthy coping patterns such as substance abuse, overeating, violent behavior, and so forth.)
- Have you or anyone in the family been arrested? (If it was a crime re-lated to drugs, giving the patient a potentially divertible stimulant should give the prescriber pause.)

Adults Who Abuse or Sell Drugs

Despite some physician's fears, most patients with ADHD do not seek stimulants in order to obtain a euphoric "high." Frequently, patients openly question why the stimulant is controlled and insist that they do not derive any physiological or psychological reinforcement from taking it. It can be difficult, however, to distinguish drug-seeking patients from patients with ADHD, because their behaviors may be similar. However, there are some indications of drug-seeking.

LONG-ACTING METHYLPHENIDATE MAY HAVE LOWER ABUSE POTENTIAL
THAN SHORT-ACTING FORMS

A study by Spencer, Biederman, Ciccone, Madras, Dougherty, Bonab, Livni, Parasrampuria, & Fischman (2006) found that patients taking Con-certa, a long-acting stimulant, experienced a significantly lower rate of euphoria than did subjects taking a short-acting form of methylphenidate. In this study of 12 adults who did not have ADHD, the researchers used positron emission tomography (PET) scans to study the rate of the drug delivery to the brain. They compared this data to hourly reports from sub-jects on how they felt over a 10-hour period. According to the researchers, "the findings suggest that the abuse potential of oral methylphenidate is strongly influenced by the rate of delivery and not solely by the magnitude of plasma concentration or brain transporter occupancy. These results advance understanding of the underlying central effects of methylpheni-date in humans and identify a potentially less abusable methylphenidate formulation" (p. 387). In other words, longer-acting stimulants may have

otential, which is backed up by the Wilens study reported
chapter.

Drug-Seeking and Drug-Diverting Adults

ake exam, stimulant-seeking patients usually focus the con-
particular medication; they are not interested in discussing
else. Their ADHD history may be suspect, and the clinician may
be left feeling the patient is far more interested in the outcome than the
process.

Patients with untreated ADHD may also seem fixated on obtaining a
particular scheduled medication that they have heard is helpful. In contrast to the abuser, however, these patients appear more earnest and desperate. They are open to discussing their agenda and willing to entertain
alternative suggestions. Clinicians do not leave the interaction feeling manipulated. Although making the distinction between these two groups can
be difficult, it becomes easier with experience.

Stimulant-seeking adults are more likely to manipulate the mental
health care system than adolescents are. Commonly employed tactics,
usually used by individuals seeking narcotic pain medications (i.e., oxycodone or meperidine), include:

- Doctor-shopping
- Forging prescriptions
- Stealing drugs from others
- Buying from Internet pharmacies

DOCTOR-SHOPPING

Some individuals present themselves to two or more physicians, complaining of symptoms they know are likely to lead to the prescription of the
drugs they want. In the case of stimulants, patients may complain of symptoms of inattentiveness, hyperactivity, and distractibility, which would lead
many physicians to the diagnosis of ADHD.

Cautious doctors, however, ensure that the deliberate diagnostic steps
described in Chapter 1, are followed, including taking a careful history, re-

questing that the patient's primary-care doctor order laboratory tests to rule out other conditions, and obtaining rating scales from outside sources. An informal policy of not dispensing medications before the second visit slows the process to an appropriate pace. This practice also protects the clinic from developing a reputation for easily prescribing stimulants.

FORGING PRESCRIPTIONS

Patients who are drug-seekers may receive legitimate prescriptions that they subsequently alter, whether it is to change an order for 30 pills to 90 pills or some other form of alteration. It is best for physicians to write out the quantity of tablets prescribed and photo- or carbon-copy the original. In the future, electronic medical records should eliminate this problem, but until then the office staff should protect the physician's DEA number and guard against leaving errant prescription pads lying about in plain view. Offices should cultivate relationships with local pharmacies to enhance cooperation in dealing with the small number of unscrupulous patients.

STEALING DRUGS FROM OTHERS

Medications can be stolen even by acquaintances. Perpetrators visit a friend's or relative's home, scope out the medicine cabinets, and pocket any drugs of interest. Physicians can do nothing about this other than to warn patients that their medications can be a desired commodity. Advise patients to limit the number of people who know they are being treated and to keep the medications in a secure place.

BUYING FROM INTERNET PHARMACIES

There are hundreds of Internet "pharmacies" from which individuals can order virtually any drug they want, up to and including scheduled drugs. Some adolescents "borrow" their parent's credit card to purchase Internet drugs. Usually the primary users of this service are adults who order these drugs in their own name, using their credit cards.

Physicians should advise their patients against obtaining medications from unverified sources. Most of the clearinghouses operate outside the United States, often in Mexico and Thailand. Because the Food and Drug Administration has no jurisdiction or oversight, the purity and safety of these drugs is suspect. Several years ago, an unregulated Asian company produced contaminated L-tryptophan as a mild sleep aid and sold the product in American health food stores. Some consumers developed serious blood abnormalities. Many injuries occurred before the contamination was identified and linked to the product. Many months later, public health officials banned the product from the market. This example may be used to deter patients from making illegal purchases of drugs over the Internet.

MEDICATION COMPLIANCE: A COMMON PROBLEM

Many physicians become frustrated when their patients do not take their medications as prescribed. Medication noncompliance is a problem with all types of patients, but it is particularly notable among patients with ADHD.

One analysis of the medication patterns of more than 14,000 ADHD patients found that 84% of children and 88% of adults complied with their medication regimen for less than 2 months. In other words, only 12% of adults and 16% of children took the medications as their doctors ordered for two months or more. Children were compliant with their initial ADHD medication for an average of 34 days and adults for 50 days (Perwien, Hall, Swenson, & Swindle, 2004).

ADHD patients may fail to take their medication for a number of reasons:

- They forget to take the medication.
- The patient is a rebellious adolescent.
- They lose the medication.
- They give away the medication.
- They expect immediate results.
- They say the medication does not help (even though others say their behavior is markedly improved).
- They think they are "cured" and no longer need the medication.
- Others discourage them from taking stimulants or other ADHD medications and they fear disclosure.

They Forget to Take the Medication

The most common reason for not complying with a medication regimen is that patients with ADHD simply forget to take it. Perhaps the physician has not helped the patient to tie taking the drug to other daily activities, such as meals or brushing one's teeth. Or perhaps the patient forgets despite such recommendations. In these cases, doctors should work with patients to try to find ways to help them remember, such as placing the medication on the bathroom sink so they see it in the morning when they are getting ready for school or work.

Physicians also need to emphasize to patients that they cannot obtain results without taking action, and taking their medication is an important and simple action that they need to do.

The Patient Is a Rebellious Adolescent

Adolescents may rebel against their parents by refusing to take their medications, much as they resist cleaning their room. To deal with adolescent rebellion, the therapist should tell both parties that the parent will be in charge of the medication initially, but if the adolescent proves to be responsible, he or she should take over. Parents resistant to this idea can be persuaded by the argument that if the adolescent feels empowered, compliance will improve.

This problem is compounded if the parents are forgetting to prompt their teenager to take the medications. Consider that the parent may have untreated ADHD. Among other benefits, treating the parent will improve the child's compliance.

They Lose the Medication

Clinicians are alarmed when patients report losing their stimulant prescription and instinctively question whether the excuse is legitimate or a devious effort on the patient's part to get more medication. The answer is that either case could be true. Generally drug-seekers demonstrate a pattern of frequent excuses whereas disorganized ADHD patients might lose their medication, but not often.

Some experts advise writing prescriptions more than twice monthly for patients who have a problem with compliance. The physician may write "ADHD" on the prescription so the pharmacist will understand the reason for the frequency. Unfortunately, this strategy is time-consuming and runs counter to the increasingly common practice of 90-day mail-order refills and 30-day HMO refills, but it can be effective in select situations.

They Give Away the Medication

The problem of patients' giving away medications was addressed earlier in this chapter. Again, preventative measures work best: Inform patients (especially adolescents) that providing others with drugs can have disastrous consequences. Patients should be encouraged to avoid disclosing their treatment to friends and classmates.

They Expect Immediate Results

Patients with ADHD may be extremely impatient and expect the medication to work within a few days. If they do not feel significantly improved within days, they may give up on the medication altogether.

These patients, consciously or unconsciously, regard ADHD medication in much the same way that they view an over-the-counter medication for a headache or diarrhea. That is, if they have a headache, they take a headache remedy and feel better in an hour or two. It is important to emphasize to patients that some ADHD drugs start to work quickly, sometimes within 60 minutes, whereas others (typically atomoxetine) may take weeks before there is any discernible improvement.

They Say the Medication Does Not Help

Sometimes patients report that they feel no different with medication treatment, despite comments from family and friends about their changed behavior. Thus, they see no reason to continue taking the drug. They reason that if they do not feel any differently, how could the drug possibly be working?

The therapist should inquire about how other people reacted to them when they were taking the medication. Did their spouses compliment them more often? Did friends indicate that they were more attentive in conversations? Were they more productive at work? By raising these questions, the patient may be able to reflect on the objective rather than the subjective experience.

They Think They Are "Cured" and No Longer Need the Medication

Patients can become noncompliant even after they see improvements with the medication. They take it for a while, get better, and decide that they are cured. This is a common error among patients treated for chronic psychiatric or nonpsychiatric conditions, and it is a frequent battle waged by doctors of all specialties.

ADHD patients may think that the medication somehow "reset" them back to normal, like restarting a malfunctioning computer can sometimes magically fix it. These patients often forget that their symptoms caused them a great deal of trouble in the past, and they are quick to dismiss the importance of the medication. Likening ADHD medications to eyeglasses is a productive metaphor. Your vision (or ADHD) only improves when you wear the glasses (or swallow the tablet first thing in the morning). Once the eyeglasses are removed or the medications wear off, the visual or emotional blurriness returns.

Devaluing the role of medications is more common in patients with ADHD than in other patients. Initially medication results can be dramatic, but patients can accommodate very quickly to their enhanced level of functioning. They can easily forget about their compromised pretreatment functioning and consequently lose the belief that the medication was a primary vehicle of change.

This places the prescriber in a tenuous position. Patients typically do not want to credit medications for their life changes. Instead, they will say, "I am doing better because of changes that I have made." The doctor needs to acknowledge improvements, whatever the cause, but may believe that the patient is minimizing the role that the medications made in their recovery. Sometimes patients need to figure these things out for themselves, and the doctor might encourage a drug hiatus. Many patients gain renewed appreciation for their medications in their absence. This process can take many months. If the patient chooses to return to medications weeks, months, or years later, the clinician should be supportive. It is more therapeutic for the doctor to say, "I would have done the same thing if I were unsure of the value of the medication," than it is to say "I told you so."

> *Others Discourage Them From Taking Stimulants or Other*
> *ADHD Medications and They Fear Disclosure*

Some people are fervently opposed to all psychiatric medications and may be specifically opposed to ADHD medications. For example, in 2005, the actor Tom Cruise, a member of the Church of Scientology, used national network time to vilify the use of Ritalin, negate the validity of ADHD, and liken the work of psychiatry to Nazism. (He also belittled actress Brooke Shields for taking antidepressants to treat postpartum depression.) For years, the Church of Scientology and similar groups have issued alarming statements warning of dire outcomes that may result from ADHD medications. Such groups advocate dietary changes, church attendance and tithing, (promising ten percent of their income to the church) and alternative "treatments" (such as mild electrical skin stimulation) that have no demonstrable evidence of any true benefit. To these groups, anything is better than taking psychiatric medications.

It is best that physicians warn patients that they may encounter articles and websites highly critical of all psychiatric drugs, ADHD medications in particular. A frank discussion about this social phenomenon can have a lasting impact on patients. For example, clinicians can explain that public and scientific thinking constantly evolves. Many years ago, "bleeding" patients was considered helpful; now, of course, it isn't. Germ theory, the concept that invisible microbes could cause infection, initially seemed sensational, but now it is among the first concepts young children learn when they are trained to wash their hands after toileting. The theory that the brain controls all behavior and that, like with other organs, the brain's malfunctions can be remediated with medications will continue to gain acceptance.

Because of the many biases ADHD patients will encounter, therapists may wish to advise that although there is no shame in taking medications, they need not share the information with others, at least until they become comfortable with the process. There are some exceptions to this; some individuals will not even start treatment until important people in their life affirm the decision. In other situations, such as random workplace drug testing, sharing the information may be essential. Amphetamines will show up on routine screening; methylphenidate, because of a different chemical composition, does not.

Telling the employer's medical department in advance about stimulant drug use for ADHD may subject the patient to some negative bias, but is preferable to trying to explain the situation after a positive drug finding occurs. Similarly, adolescents on ADHD medications may need to inform the school nurse, as many schools ban all medications from being carried on the student's person and punish those who violate policy. As a result, the school nurse administers all medications given during the school day. Medication compliance may improve if the worry of accidental disclosure is not an option.

III

MEDICAL AND PSYCHOLOGICAL ASPECTS OF ADHD TREATMENT

Chapter 9

ADHD Medications

Medications play an essential role in the treatment of adolescents and adults with ADHD. They can effect dramatic changes, allowing individuals to concentrate and focus, sometimes for the first time ever. The benefits often lead to marked improvements in school and work performance, as well as enhanced interpersonal relationships. A person who suddenly can attend to what is said and then follow through on what needs to be done becomes easier to work with and live with. There is an increased recognition that medications for ADHD can help individuals previously not treated: Between 2000 and 2004, the number of prescriptions doubled in young adults, eclipsing the growth rate in children. An estimated 2.5 million children and 1.5 million adults now take ADHD medications.

WHAT DO ADHD MEDICATIONS ACTUALLY DO?

ADHD medications have been shown to be helpful in many ADHD domains. A recent study of 45 adolescents with ADHD demonstrated the therapeutic effects of methylphenidate (Evans, Pelham, Smith, Bukstein,

Gnagy, Greiner, et al., 2001). Over 6 weeks, 45 students (40 males and 5 females) were given daily doses of either placebo or 10 mg, 20 mg, or 30 mg of the drug. The adolescents were randomized so that each received one of the four options. The researchers found significant overall symptom reduction with the methylphenidate, with the largest improvements seen from the placebo to the 10 mg dose and smaller incremental improvements from 10 mg to 20 mg.

Medications helped the adolescents with their work productivity; for example, 53.2% of the adolescents given placebo did a history worksheet correctly. When they received 10 mg/day of methylphenidate, 70.2% did the worksheet correctly. This increased to 79.8% at 20 mg/day. The improvements plateaued at 30 mg/day, demonstrating that a point of diminishing returns may occur at higher doses.

Methylphenidate also proved helpful in controlling some of the adolescents' maladaptive behavior. Using standardized scales, 5.2% of the adolescents were disruptive on placebo. On 10 mg, this dropped to 3.9% and to 2.5% on a 30 mg/day dose.

Higher doses of methylphenidate were associated with improved homework completion. On placebo, 33% of the adolescents finished their homework. With 10 mg/day, this increased to 37.7%; with 20 mg/day, to 39.3%; and with 30 mg/day to 42.5%.

This study is typical of a large body of research showing that methylphenidate improves focusing and concentration and enables adolescents and adults with ADHD to complete their work (Bellak, 1979). Similar populations have had dramatic treatment effects on Adderall XR. When treated, patients with ADHD with significant behavior symptoms were found to drop from impaired to normal ranges (Biederman, Lopez, Boellner, & Chandler, 2002).

Of course, patients should be steered away from thinking that medications have magical properties that will resolve all their core ADHD symptoms as well as any comorbid conditions. Medications can help patients with ADHD considerably, but they cannot resolve all difficulties. Consequently, the clinician must provide an encouraging yet realistic view of the medications—positive enough that the patient will be motivated to comply with the regimen but not so effusive that the patient is devastated if the medication effects are disappointing. Ideally, coaching or psychotherapy is prescribed concurrent to the medications.

There is no one perfect drug to treat ADHD. Not all hyperactive patients respond to one medication class and inattentive patients to another. There is not a preferred agent for adolescents, women, or ADHD patients with depression. Treating ADHD is a lifelong proposition; there are a large number of available medications and medication combinations, and clinicians find that each patient needs an individualized approach.

Before receiving their prescription, patients should be encouraged to give the medication a fair trial—at least 2 weeks for stimulants and 6 weeks for non-stimulants—unless the side effects are truly intolerable. Often patients' confidence in medication directly affects their compliance with the drug regimen, although some ADHD symptoms, such as forgetfulness and procrastination, may play a role in noncompliance.

This chapter discusses the major stimulant and non-stimulant medications used to treat ADHD, as well as their benefits, side effects, and overall safety. The primary stimulants prescribed to patients with ADHD fall into two categories: forms of methylphenidate (e.g., Ritalin and Concerta) and types of amphetamines (e.g., Adderall and Dexedrine).

Non-stimulant ADHD medications have become increasingly popular. Atomoxetine hydrochloride (Strattera) was the first nonstimulant to receive Food and Drug Administration (FDA) approval for the treatment of ADHD, but others such as bupropion (Wellbutrin), tricyclic antidepressants, and alpha 2 agonists are commonly used off label. Modafinil (Provigil) has long had the FDA indication for narcolepsy and other sleep disorders, but it is also known to be useful for some patients with ADHD.

UNDERSTANDING, THE ADHD BRAIN

Research has shown that ADHD brains look and function differently than non-ADHD brains, although few experts believe that brain imaging can be used for diagnosis. Researchers have identified structural abnormalities in the frontal lobe and key subcortical regions. Functional imaging, a more advanced technique that observes brain structure and metabolism, has shown that the dorsal anterior cingulate, the structure dividing the brain's two hemispheres, is less easily activated in ADHD patients compared to controls. It is also evident that the brain neurochemicals dopamine and norepinephrine are deficient. The exact relationship between the observed structural brain abnormalities and the imbalances in neurochemical production is unclear, but with medications it is established that increasing dopamine levels improves attention and decreases hyperactivity in patients with ADHD. In the same population, increasing brain norepinephrine demonstrably controls impulsivity and dampens excessive "noise" in the brain. This helps the brain filter external stimuli more effectively.

Because physicians cannot reformat the brain or change its basic structure, the goal of ADHD treatment has been to find techniques that modulate dopamine and norepinephrine levels. Most of the available ADHD medications, in the form of methylphenidate, amphetamine, or atomoxetine, target these dopamine and norepinephrine deficiencies.

The Effect of Stimulants

Stimulant medications act on the central nervous system and potently affect levels of dopamine. They do this by blocking the dopamine transporter (DAT), a complex protein on the surface of brain neurons that normally clears dopamine from the interneuron space, or synapse. By blocking this mechanism, stimulants retard the breaking down of dopamine, making the effects of the neurotransmitter more persistent. These medications control the transport of norepinephrine in a similar manner (Volkow, Wang, Fowler, & Ding, 2005).

Brain imaging studies of subjects with and without ADHD reveal that an enhanced level of neurotransmitters available in the hippocampus of the brain allows the patient with ADHD to remain on task by overriding the signals of the amygdala, another brain region. According to Stahl (2005), the stimulant's enhancement of norepinephrine and dopamine in the dorsolateral prefrontal cortex may improve concentration, attention, executive function, and wakefulness. In addition, increased levels of dopamine in the basal ganglia may ameliorate symptoms of hyperactivity, whereas in the hypothalamus and the medial prefrontal cortex this effect may address fatigue and depression.

The Effects of Non-Stimulants

As noted earlier, atomoxetine (Strattera) is currently the only non-stimulant approved by the FDA for treatment of ADHD. In contrast to the stimulants, atomoxetine is primarily a norepinephrine reuptake inhibitor. By blocking the reuptake of norepinephrine, atomoxetine allows the ADHD brain to filter unimportant extraneous stimuli more effectively. In social conversation, the treated patient can focus on what is being said rather than getting distracted by passing street noise. Atomoxetine also boosts dopamine, but this effect is limited to the prefrontal cortex, a far more limited area of brain distribution than is seen with the stimulants.

Other non-stimulants include modafinil (Provigil), buproprion (Wellbutrin), tricyclic antidepressants, and certain antihypertensive drugs such as clonidine (Catapres) and guanfacine (Tenex). Each of the non-stimulant medications has a different mechanism of action. In general, non-stimulants have a less direct effect on dopamine compared to stimulants, and they have little risk of abuse. Accordingly, some physicians have migrated to non-stimulants, particularly for ADHD patients with a history of drug or alcohol abuse. The mechanism of the drug's action depends on the category of drug (types of antidepressants, alpha 2 agonists, and so forth) and sometimes it is easier to see their benefits than understand how they work.

CHOOSING BETWEEN STIMULANTS AND NONSTIMULANTS

When ADHD treatment is considered, the clinician must decide whether to prescribe a stimulant or non-stimulant medication. Stimulant medications, primarily methylphenidate and amphetamines in various forms, have been the treatment mainstay for decades. Amphetamines were first identified as treatment for hyperactivity in the 1930s. Methylphenidate has been used for more than five decades. Stimulants are highly effective and currently no class of ADHD medication demonstrates as impressive an effect size (*effect size* is a statistical term used to assess treatment benefit in clinical studies). According to some reports, the first stimulant selected for an ADHD patient is effective 70% of the time (Stoner, Dubisar, & Strong, 2003).

Stimulants work within the first few doses. When orally ingested, they are rapidly absorbed into the central nervous system, and they have the seemingly paradoxical effect of increasing attention and exerting a calming effect in patients with ADHD. Stimulant medications directly affect brain dopamine levels, the neurotransmitter regulating pain and pleasure, but most patients with ADHD do not report obvious changes in how they experience these senses.

Theoretically, overactivation of dopamine circuits can cause euphoria, an exaggerated sense of well-being, and potentially even psychosis. For these reasons, the Drug Enforcement Administration (DEA) considers stimulants to have abuse potential, and it has placed restrictions and controls over these medications that go beyond those imposed by the FDA.

Simply put, there are five distinct drug schedules. Selected drugs with abuse potential are each placed in a schedule that categorizes its level of governmental oversight. For instance, Schedule I includes illegal drugs such as heroin and marijuana. (The DEA does not recognize any medical efficacy for marijuana, despite some state laws.) Schedule II prescribed drugs include some pain medications, such as oxycodone, and the stimulants. Schedule III medications include some pain medications, such as hydrocodone, as well as some drugs in the barbiturate class. Benzodiazepines, the prototypical antianxiety medications, have Schedule IV designation, as do prescribed sleep remedies.

Stimulant prescriptions will only be filled with a written and signed prescription of a licensed physician. They are not refillable; consequently, a new hard copy of the prescription must be given to the patient monthly. As of 2004, the DEA forbade physicians from giving their patients advance-dated prescriptions of scheduled drugs. The policy change was primarily meant to cover Schedule II pain medications; however, in deference to this regulation, physicians prescribing stimulants should not postdate prescriptions. Instead, they should affix the date the prescription was written but specify elsewhere on the form in which succeeding month the medication can be filled.

The reputation for abuse of stimulants dissuades many doctors from prescribing them. Pharmacists may take a hostile view as well. Thomas, a downtown business owner diagnosed with ADHD, spoke with his doctor about the difficulty he experienced getting his stimulant prescription filled: "What's the deal? When I go to the pharmacy, they make me feel like a criminal. I have to go to the suburbs to get my script filled. I've been taking these medications for years. I feel normal, not high, when I take them. I pay more in income tax than most people make in a year, but each time the clerk makes me feel like a criminal."

Physicians may choose to prescribe non-stimulants for a variety of reasons, including a patient's poor past response to stimulants or a concern that the patient will misuse or become dependent on the stimulant. Non-stimulant medications pose no threat for misuse. Non-stimulants are also longer-acting than current stimulant medications and usually need to be taken only once per day.

On the downside, clinicians with extensive experience in treating with stimulants may not yet have the same level of confidence in non-stimulants (especially atomoxetine and modafinil) that they have in stimulants. When compared to stimulants in clinical trials, non-stimulants do have a lower effect size (Faraone, 2003).

STIMULANTS

The two primary types of stimulants used to treat ADHD are methylphenidate and amphetamine (Table 9.1). Both regulate brain levels of dopamine and norepinephrine through fundamentally similar mechanisms of action in the brain. The most common types of methylphenidate are Ritalin, Ritalin SR, Concerta, Metadate CD, Ritalin LA and D-methylphenidate (Focalin, Focalin XR). Amphetamines are available as single salts (Dexedrine, dextroamphetamine, Dexedrine spansules, Dextrostat) and mixed salts (Adderall and Adderall XR). Select patients who did not respond to conventional stimulants used Pemoline (Cylert) in the past; however, the drug was withdrawn in 2005 due to concerns about liver toxicity.

TABLE 9.1
Stimulant Medications Used to Treat ADHD

Generic Name	Brand Name	Usual Starting Dose/Typical Daily Dose Range*
Mixed amphetamine salts	Adderall	5–10 mg every 4–5 hours (10–120 mg)
	Adderall XR	10 mg/morning (10–120 mg)
Dextroamphetamine	Dexedrine	5 mg every 4–6 hours (10–100 mg)
	Dexedrine spansules	5–15 mg every 6–8 hours (5–100 mg)
	Dextrostat	5–10 mg every 4–6 hours (5–80 mg)
Long-acting methylphenidate	Ritalin SR	20 mg/morning (10–140 mg)
	Ritalin LA	20 mg/morning (20–120 mg)
	Concerta	18 mg/morning (18–144 mg)
	Metadate CD	10–20 mg/morning (10–120 mg)
Short-acting methylphenidate	Generic MPH	10 mg every 4 hours (20–140 mg)
	Methylin	10 mg every 4 hours (20–140 mg)
	Ritalin	10 mg every 4 hours (20–140 mg)
Transdermal system skin patch (MTS)	Daytrana (skin patch)	10 mg patch/morning (10–30 mg) [9 hour wear time]
D-methylphenidate	Focalin	5 mg every 4–6 hours (10–80 mg)
	Focalin XR	5–10 mg/morning (10–80 mg)

*May exceed FDA label recommendations.

Methylphenidate

Historically, methylphenidate (MPH) has been the most popular stimulant used to treat ADHD. Methylphenidate blocks the reuptake and increases the amount of dopamine (and to a lesser extent, the amount of norepinephrine) released in the brain. Brand names of MPH include Ritalin, Ritalin SR, Ritalin LA, Concerta, and Metadate ER and Metadate CD. Dextromethylphenidate, a chemical variant of MPH, is available under the brand names of Focalin and Focalin XR. Methylphenidate is also available in a generic form. Patients may be prescribed short- or long-acting forms of the stimulant, depending on their individual needs.

SHORT-ACTING METHYLPHENIDATE

Immediate-release MPH (Ritalin, Methylin) is available in 5-, 10-, and 20-mg tablets. These short-acting forms take effect within 30 to 60 minutes, and each dose lasts from 2.5 to 5 hours. Adolescents and adults are usually prescribed 20 to 80 mg per day, at doses given from two to four times daily. Short-acting preparations are inexpensive and available in generic form.

Low cost is not the only virtue of short-acting MPH. Patients can develop a love-hate relationship with their Ritalin: They recognize that the medication helps them with daily functioning but they dislike the sensation of being medicated. Reports of feeling emotionally blunted while on the medication are common, as Nicholas observed: "When I take Ritalin I study well, but I feel disconnected from my friends. I'm too quiet and not funny. It's almost like I'm 'emotionally cocooned.' I can tolerate this when I'm in a lecture, but I don't like long-acting Ritalin because I don't want to feel so serious all day long."

LONG-ACTING METHYLPHENIDATE

Extended-release MPH preparations such as Concerta, Ritalin LA, Metadate CD, and Focalin XR have been widely adopted in the past several years. These medications take effect within an hour and last from 8 to 12 hours, depending on the product and the patient's unique metabolism. In most cases, long-acting preparations can be given once a day. For adolescents, this means no embarrassing midday visits to the school nurse; adults do not need to compromise their privacy by excusing themselves from a business meeting. In contrast to the choppy blood levels of short-acting stimulants, long-acting preparations offer smoothness and consistency. This effect decreases rebound, the dramatic return of symptoms that occurs when short-acting medication wears off.

Ritalin SR and Metadate ER, now technologically surpassed, were the first sustained-release preparations. In these formulations, active MPH is embedded in a wax matrix. Six to eight hours after ingestion, the wax matrix slowly dissolves in the gut, prompting the release of MPH. This older technology is widely available, inexpensive, and generically produced. However, most physicians find wax-matrix technology to be an unreliable method of delivering medication. Heavy meals interfere with consistent absorption. Patients report that some days the medication works well whereas on other days, the poor absorption convinces them that they have swallowed blanks.

Ritalin LA and Metadate CD offer better delivery methods. These longer-acting capsules are composed of two different-sized MPH beads. When swallowed, the smaller beads are immediately released into the gut. About 4 hours later, the larger beads burst lower in the intestine, delivering a second bolus of drug. Unlike drugs using the wax-matrix system, these products rarely are subject to inconsistent absorption.

The Swiss company Novartis makes Ritalin LA in 20-, 30-, and 40-mg capsules. The immediate- and delayed-release beads are equal in proportion. A patient taking the usual starting dose of Ritalin LA (20 mg every morning) is replicating the effect of taking 10 mg of short-acting MPH immediately and another 10 mg 4 hours later. In adults, the dose is titrated upward from 40 to 80 mg per day.

In contrast, Metadate CD was designed so that 30% of the dosage is released immediately, with the balance released 4 hours later. The first peak of Metadate CD occurs within about an hour and a half, and the second peak occurs in about 4.5 hours. Depending on the individual, the effects of the drug last between 7 and 9 hours.

Concerta is the most common extended-release form of MPH. Concerta employs Oros technology, a sophisticated delivery system that exploits the osmotic pressure of the intestine to force MPH through a small opening on the tip of the capsule. Concerta was developed to deliver MPH continuously in increasing concentrations throughout the day. This drug is manufactured in 18-, 27-, 36-, and 54-mg strengths. Patients are usually started at 18 mg, and the dosages may be given in the morning. The first peak of the drug occurs within an hour or two of taking the pill and the effects last up to 12 hours. The outer casing of Concerta has the unusual property of being delivered unchanged in the stool even though the MPH inside has been fully released.

WHICH LONG-ACTING METHYLPHENIDATE TO CHOOSE?

Concerta, lasting 10 to 12 hours, is the longest-acting oral MPH agent. In general, the effects of Ritalin LA and Metadate CD are an hour or two briefer. Concerta's reputation for being long-acting partially explains its dominance in the market. However, for adolescents and adults with dawn-to-dusk responsibilities, even 12 hours of treatment may be insufficient. In these situations, clinicians tack on a late-afternoon dose of short-acting MPH to the Concerta to offer an additional 3 to 4 hours of coverage. Another approach is to give medications with an 8-hour duration of action (Metadate CD and Ritalin LA) in the morning and again 8 hours later. Using Metadate CD or Ritalin LA twice daily also obviates the need for two co-payments as occurs when Concerta is prescribed with short-acting MPH.

CHEMICAL VARIATIONS OF METHYLPHENIDATE

Like many compounds, MPH is composed of two molecules that are mirror images of each other. D-methylphenidate is the biologically active isomer; R-methylphenidate does not have clinical benefit and may even contribute to side effects. Novartis manufactures Focalin, a pure D-methylphenidate medication. As it does not contain any of the inert isomer, Focalin is twice as potent as MPH. Focalin is a short-acting medication, but some patients report that it lasts somewhat longer than ordinary MPH. The effect of the drug peaks 1 to 4 hours after administration.

Focalin XR, the extended-release version, was released in 2005. Using the same delivery system as Ritalin LA, albeit with a different molecule, Focalin XR delivers half of the dosage immediately and the other half 4 hours later. Focalin XR is available in 5-, 10-, and 20-mg tablets. Its duration of action, somewhere between 10 and 12 hours, parallels Concerta. This long-acting MPH product has been approved for children and adolescents with ADHD, but it is the only agent in this category to have a specific FDA indication for adults.

TRANSDERMAL SYSTEM

In 2006, a new transdermal delivery system of MPH was approved. Manufactured by Shire and Noven Pharmaceuticals, the methylphenidate transdermal system (MTS) is marketed under the brand name Daytrana. It is recommended that the skin patch be applied to the hip each morning. The MPH is quickly absorbed into the blood stream, and unlike oral medications that traverse the gastrointestinal tract, the MTS bypasses the first pass effect of the liver. This means that low MPH doses will reach higher blood levels than equivalent oral doses. As livers differ in how efficiently they filter medications, the required doses of oral medications vary considerably between individuals. The patch may lead to more uniform MPH dosing.

A small percentage of patients develop mild irritation to the adhesive, but this sensitivity is usually transient. Daytrana utilizes a novel DOT Matrix™ system whereby the MPH is highly concentrated into the patch. Unlike older transdermal systems, Daytrana is flat and compact and can be worn unobtrusively under clothing.

In children, the patch causes more insomnia and weight loss than Concerta, but somewhat greater efficacy at similar doses. Daytrana's initial approval is for children ages 6–12, nonetheless its greatest benefit may be for adolescents and adults who require a longer duration of coverage. Once the patch is removed, the clinical benefits last another three hours. Theoretically, a patient who demands 16 hours of coverage may wear the patch for 13 hours and benefit from the residual effect. If consumers adjust to the concept of a patch, Daytrana could capture a significant portion of the ADHD market. It appears that a transdermal amphetamine system is more complicated technically and will not be imminently available.

Amphetamines

Although it is not fully understood why, some patients with ADHD prefer amphetamines to MPH. In the brain, amphetamines block the reuptake and cause the release of both free and stored norepinephrine and dopamine from nerve cells. These related mechanisms have the effect of increasing the concentration of both neurotransmitters in the synapse. Previous generations of doctors prescribed amphetamines for obesity, but as the appetite-reducing effects are not sustained, this approach has been abandoned. Amphetamines still are used for sleep disturbances and some brain injuries. Like MPH, amphetamines are available in both short-acting and long-acting forms in varying doses and preparations.

Dextroamphetamine has been available for many years. It is generically available and rather inexpensive. The key brand names of dextroamphetamine are Dexedrine, Dexedrine spansules, and Dextrostat. The immediate-release form of Dexedrine comes in doses of 5- and 10-mg tablets. Most adolescents and adults are started at 5 mg, either once or twice per day, and the drug may be increased by 5 mg per dose each week. The medication should be taken with meals, as it can cause mild gastrointestinal distress. Decreased appetite is a common adverse effect. Dextrostat, another form of the short-acting dextroamphetamine, is also available in 5- and 10-mg tablets. Both Dexedrine and Dextrostat usually act within 20 to 30 minutes and the effects of the drug last from 3 to 6 hours (Braun, Dulit, Adler, Berlant, Dixon, Fornari, et al., 2004).

Dexedrine spansules offer an extended release form of dextroamphetamine in 5-, 10-, and 15-mg capsules taken once daily. Patients are generally started at 15 mg taken two times daily. The drug usually peaks within 1 to 4 hours after being swallowed. Because spansules have such a variable onset of action, they are viewed as undependable and have given way to the mixed amphetamine salts.

Adderall, a mixed amphetamine salt (MAS), combines amphetamine and an associated isomer with dextroamphetamine and dextroamphetamine aspartate. Adderall is short-acting and is available in many different dosage strengths. Generic versions are manufactured, although many consumers feel the generics are inferior to the Shire brand product.

The starting dosage of Adderall for adolescents and adults is 10 mg, given every 4 to 5 hours (up to 3 doses per day). The dosage may be adjusted in increments of 5 or 10 mg per dose, with 1-week intervals between the increases. Once taken, the drug takes effect within about 60 minutes, and its effects last about 5 to 8 hours.

Adderall XR, the long-acting form of this drug, has become widely popular. Adderall XR is an extended-release capsule produced in strengths of 5, 10, 15, 20, 25, and 30 mg. The starting dose is usually 10 mg/day, and it may be increased weekly by 10 mg. Fully grown patients should return a month after initiation at 30 mg/day. The maximum recommended daily dosage is 30 mg/day, but in clinical practice that guideline is considered archaic and arbitrary. With careful monitoring, doses two to three times that level are sometimes necessary.

The Adderall XR capsule contains two different sized amphetamine-containing beads in equal proportion. The smaller beads release the medication soon after the capsule is swallowed and the larger beads burst about four hours later. A new Shire product in late development contains a third bead that will activate about eight hours after the first bead. This will extend the duration of the tablet to at least 16 hours. Some patients will surely experience insomnia but for many adult patients with ADHD, this new delivery system will enhance convenience and reduce the unpleasant nature of stimulant rebound.

Possible Rebound Effects

Stimulants may have rebound effects. Rebound occurs when the medication blood levels rapidly decline and patients demonstrate moodiness and irritability and complain of depression and headaches. The rebound effect complicates the clinician's assessment of a patient's treatment response, as it is difficult to distinguish between the rebound phenomenon and the patient's underlying ADHD symptoms. As rebound is more likely to occur with short-acting stimulants, they should be avoided if possible. The use of long-acting stimulant preparations or atomoxetine minimizes this confounding problem.

Side Effects

The common side effects of stimulants—weight loss, headaches, stomach distress, and insomnia—are usually transient. In some thin patients, weight loss is concerning, but these adverse effects can be mitigated by frequent small meals and taking the medication with meals. Very few adults treated with ADHD medications have any long-term difficulties sustaining normal weight and good nutritional status. Patients usually welcome the suggestion of taking a daily multivitamin.

The waters are murkier surrounding stimulant treatment and growth. A recent analysis of 29 previous studies revealed that a majority of adults treated with methylphenidate as children grew to their expected heights. A subgroup of the population studied, those who experienced nausea when first given methylphenidate, had small height retardation as adults (Poulton, 2005). Bear in mind that these findings are limited to adults who were treated with methylphenidate as children. This represents a fraction of ADHD adults; the majority of adults seeking ADHD treatment have never been exposed to previous treatment.

Precautions Before Starting Stimulants

A complete medical history should be gathered before stimulants are prescribed for an individual with ADHD. Particular attention should be paid to heart health. Stimulants increase blood pressure minimally, but some cardiologists believe that even a small blood pressure rise increases cardiac risk in patients with preexisting hypertension.

A recent report analyzed more than 300 people who died while taking stimulant medications (Carey, 2006). In 25 of the cases (19 children and 6 adults) the deaths appear related to stimulant medications. Patients with hypertrophic obstructive cardiomyopathy, a congenital structural abnormality of the heart chambers, may be at greater risk of sudden death when taking stimulants. As a result of this finding, Shire changed its package label to discourage Adderall usage in this population.

Out of concern, Canadian health officials briefly took Adderall off the market. This controversy erupted in a February 2006 report from a subcommittee of the Food and Drug Administration that recommended that a black-box warning be included in the labeling of all stimulant medications. In March 2006, the FDA rejected this recommendation, but they did not issue guidelines directing physicians on how to manage healthy stimulant-treated patients. Obtaining an ECG, an inexpensive record of the heart's electrical conduction, on each patient may be prudent, but this adds to the expense of ADHD treatment. It is unclear if routine monitoring protects patients. In general, though, patients with essential hypertension should have their blood pressure stabilized prior to starting stimulants. If the patient has a preexisting heart condition, such as a congenital abnormality or muscle damage from a heart attack, the prescriber should coordinate care with the patient's cardiologist.

Some physicians are extremely and vocally opposed to the use of stimulants as treatment for ADHD. These physicians believe that stimulants are over-used in the United States, and they advocate for a "black box" warning cautioning patients against potential drug risks (Nissen, 2006). However, other physicians argue that stimulants are protective against substance abuse, car crashes, and academic failures, and they are concerned that a black box warning would unduly concern patients with ADHD and their families, to the extent that they might forego using stimulants (Anders & Sharfstein, 2006).

It should not be forgotten that for many years stimulants have proven safe and highly effective at treating ADHD. Although physicians must be mindful that stimulants should be used cautiously in individuals with cardiac disease, the vast majority of patients do well with these medications.

Additionally, patients with narrow angle glaucoma should avoid stimulants, as should patients with Tourette's syndrome or a history of tics. Stimulants have traditionally been associated with the worsening of tics, although this is not universally accepted. Still, in this population, the nonstimulants have become a very popular alternative.

Actions to Take Before Stimulants Are Prescribed

Before receiving their prescription, patients should be encouraged to give the medication a fair trial—at least 2 weeks for stimulants and 6 weeks for nonstimulants—unless the side effects are truly intolerable. Often the patient's confidence in medication directly affects his or her compliance with the drug regimen, although some ADHD symptoms, such as forgetfulness and procrastination, also may play a role in noncompliance.

Patients who are taking monamine oxidase inhibiting antidepressants (MAOIs) like Nardil or Parnate should be washed out of the MAOI for at least 14 days before starting stimulants, as the drug interaction can cause a large increase in blood pressure. Fortunately, these older-class MAOIs are no longer commonly used. Selegiline (Emsam), more recently introduced, is a safer version of the MAOIs. It is a more selective monoamine oxidase inhibitor and is administered through a skin patch. Its safety with concomitant use of stimulants is not established.

Bias Against Stimulants: Common but Counterproductive

Sometimes bias against stimulants by non-ADHD specialists can interrupt care. There may be times when ADHD clinicians must help patients make difficult treatment choices. Phillip, a 54-year-old engineer, had a long history of diabetes, cardiomyopathy (weakening of the heart muscle), and ADHD. He had become increasingly weak, but before he could qualify for a heart transplant, his transplant surgeon contacted me and expressed concern that the stimulants might have caused or at least complicated Phil's heart disease. I suggested that this assertion was not scientifically supported; Phil's heart disease preceded stimulant exposure and he had a number of other risk factors—family history, diabetes, and obesity—that were more likely responsible. Still, the transplant team stood firm in their decision to keep him off "all nonessential medications." Phil and I acquiesced and discontinued his stimulant so as not to jeopardize his chances for this life-saving procedure.

Phillip waited 16 months for his transplant and did so entirely without his Adderall. Finally, a match did arrive and he was successfully transplanted. He visited me about 4 weeks after surgery and he appeared blasé. Eight weeks later he was physically stronger but appeared quite depressed. "I feel no joy having gone through all this," he reported. Two months later, Phil's surgeon contacted me, concerned that Phil was not taking his antirejection medications consistently. We agreed to restart his stimulant medications.

Upon resuming stimulants, overnight, Phil felt better. "I feel motivated and productive," he reported. He was able to comply with his doctor's order, stay on his post-transplant diet, and feel great pleasure in having survived the procedure. Several years later, there is no indication that the stimulants have caused any injury to the new heart.

A Safer Stimulant?

An exciting development in ADHD pharmacology is the Shire/ New River compound currently called NRP104. This commercially unnamed compound is an amphetamine prodrug, an orally administered therapy that has no psychotropic activity until the tablet is swallowed and the body's gastrointestinal enzymes severe the bond between the amphetamine and an attached amino acid.

Drug seekers can abuse traditional amphetamines by nasal snorting or direct intravenous injection. A medication activated exclusively through the GI tract eliminates the most pernicious type of medication abuse. Furthermore, there is some evidence that the compound will be safer in overdose than currently available amphetamines.

Several questions remain. Will the single amphetamine be as effective in treating ADHD symptoms as the mixed amphetamine salts used in the Adderall products? Will the FDA relax the designation of NRP104 to a less regulated level than Schedule II? If the FDA approves the product, and it proves efficacious in large studies, the implications of having a less easily abused, and hence less controversial, amphetamine–based ADHD product are considerable. The drug may combine the safety advantages of non-stimulants with the favorable efficacy profile of stimulants.

NON-STIMULANTS

Currently only one non-stimulant medication has won FDA approval for ADHD treatment. Atomoxetine (Stratterra) was released in 2002 by Eli Lilly and was approved for the treatment of ADHD in children and adults. Cephalon was surprised to learn in 2006 that its non-stimulant, modafinil (Sparlon) was rejected by the FDA over a single report that the medication caused a child to develop the serious systemic skin rash Steven's Johnson Syndrome. The FDA action essentially quashed any further development of modafinil, although many clinicians will continue to use it in monotherapy or with other ADHD medications.

Sometimes antidepressants or alpha 2 agonists are used to treat hyperactive and impulsive ADHD symptoms. In general, they are utilized more frequently in childhood ADHD, although some clinicians have found a role for these agents in older patients. Shire is seeking approval of long acting guanfacine. This non-stimulant will likely undergo review in 2007.

Antidepressants have a mixed profile. Selective serotonin reuptake inhibitors are less effective than tricyclic antidepressants and bupropion that exert their therapeutic properties through their effects on norephinephrine.

Non-stimulant medications have become popular in ADHD treatment. As they are less dopaminergic than stimulants, they do not offer a sense of well-being. Accordingly, some physicians have embraced the nonstimulants for their patient with a history of drug or alcohol abuse.

Non-stimulants are generally available as samples and unlike stimulants, orders can be called into a pharmacy and a hard copy of the prescription is not needed for each refill. Given all the variables that go into choosing a medication, including safety, tolerability and efficacy, non-stimulants have appealing properties that have won them a significant portion of the ADHD market. See Table 9.2 for information on non-stimulants.

Atomoxetine

Atomoxetine (Strattera) is a norepinephrine reuptake inhibitor. It works by increasing the forward transmission of norepinephrine between nerve cells and is the only NRI currently available approved for ADHD. The effects of atomoxetine on dopamine are more limited in the brain than those of the stimulants. All three classes of medication increase dopamine levels in the prefrontal cortex, but unlike MPH and amphetamines, atomoxetine does not increase dopamine in the nucleus accumbens or the striatum. Clinically, this translates into the finding that atomoxetine has beneficial effects on ADHD symptoms (by modulating dopamine in the prefrontal cortex) without causing euphoria (a result of increased dopamine levels in the nucleus accumbens). By sparing the striatum of increased dopamine concentrations, the likelihood of causing tics (a striatal effect) is also reduced.

Atomoxetine is a long-acting agent, and it is available in strengths of 10, 18, 25, 40, and 60 mg. In young adolescents, the dosing of atomoxetine is weight-based. Clinicians should start at 0.5 mg/kg/day for the

TABLE 9.2
Non-stimulant Medications Commonly Used in ADHD Treatment

Generic Name	Brand Name	Usual Starting Dose/ Typical Daily Dose Range
ADHD Medications		
Atomoxetine*	Strattera	40 mg/day (40–140 mg)
Modafinil	Provigil	200 mg/day (100–400 mg)
Antidepressants		
fluoxetine	Prozac	20 mg once per day (20–120 mg)
sertraline	Zoloft	50 mg once per day (50–200 mg)
citalopram	Celexa	20 mg once per day (20–80 mg)
escitalopram	Lexapro	10 mg once per day (10–40 mg)
paroxetine	Paxil	10 mg/day (10–40 mg)
	Paxil CR	12.5–25 mg/day (12.5–37.5 mg)
fluvoxamine	Luvox	50 mg once per day (100–300 mg)
venlafaxine	Effexor	50–75 mg two to three times daily (100–375 mg)
	Effexor XR	37.5–75 mg once per day (75–225 mg)
duloxetine	Cymbalta	30–60 mg once per day (30–120 mg)
bupropion	Wellbutrin IR	37.5 mg once per day (75–300 mg)
	Wellbutrin SR	100 mg once per day (100–400 mg)
	Wellbutrin XL	150 mg once per day (150–450 mg)
mirtazapine	Remeron	15 mg at bedtime (15–45 mg)
	Remeron SolTab	15 mg at bedtime (15–45 mg)
desipramine	Norpramine	75 mg once per day
imipramine	Tofranil	75 mg once per day (200–300 mg)
Alpha 2 Agonists		
clonidine	Catapres	0.1 mg twice a day
guanfacine	Tenex	1 mg/day

*Only agent specifically FDA approved.

first week and reach a target dose of 1.2 to 1.4 mg/kg/day. In fully grown adolescents and adults, the recommendation is 40 mg/day for the first week and 80 mg/day after that. Only rarely is there a need to exceed 120 mg/day.

Unlike the stimulants, which have a noticeable impact within several doses, atomoxetine builds up in the system over time, and its maximum efficacy may not be realized for a month. It can be worth the wait. The drug does not have a rebound effect, as do some stimulants, and it can elevate mood (Weiss & Weiss, 2004). In fact, atomoxetine was originally developed as an antidepressant before it was studied as an ADHD treatment (Stein, 2004).

ADHD commonly presents with anxiety symptoms and these symptoms increase in prevalence with age. Thirty percent of teens and more than 35% of adults with ADHD have panic disorder, generalized anxiety disorder, or obsessive-compulsive disorder. A recent study of young people with ADHD and anxiety showed that compared to placebo, atomoxetine improved patients' life participation score. Treated individuals had improved social interaction, improved school performance, and a greater ability to express themselves and regulate their behavior. This benefit is seen with adults as well. Thus, atomoxetine is emerging as a first choice for ADHD patients who are comorbid for anxiety disorders (Lilly Research Laboratories, 2006).

POSSIBLE SIDE EFFECTS

Atomoxetine may have a sedating effect, which is a good reason to initially prescribe the medication in the evening. Some patients experience mild increases in blood pressure. Pulse fluctuations have been reported and should be monitored. The most problematic side effects are usually gastrointestinal symptoms; these symptoms generally abate within the first week of treatment. Atomoxetine should be given with meals to avoid nausea. Fewer patients experience appetite loss with this drug compared to stimulants, but this is commonly reported. Eight percent of men who take atomoxetine may have diminished libido or erectile dysfunction. A similar number have urinary retention or hesitation.

Patients with pre-existing heart disease or structural cardiac abnormalities should avoid atomoxetine as it has been linked to a small number of sudden deaths in children and adolescents. Although serious heart problems like cardiomyopathy and heart rhythm disturbances carry an independent risk of health complications, the noradrenergic effects of atomoxetine may add to this risk. Adult patients with hypertension or hypotension should also avoid atomoxetine as should patients with liver disease, as atomoxetine is metabolized by the liver.

Patients who develop jaundice on atomoxetine should discontinue the drug and not restart it at a later time. If there are any signs of liver dysfunction, such as pruritus, darkened urine, or right-upper quadrant tenderness (or jaundice), liver enzyme function tests should be ordered, and if any abnormalities are revealed, the drug should be discontinued. Well over 2 million patients have used the medication; only two cases of liver injury linked to Strattera have been reported. Both patients fully recovered with medical help. The FDA has noted this phenomenon, but because it is so rare and random, routine liver functions are not considered helpful in detecting new cases.

In some rare cases atomoxetine can cause an allergic reaction, such as a severe rash. Should this side effect occur, the physician should be contacted immediately and the drug discontinued. When taken with atomoxetine, the antidepressant medications fluoxetine (Prozac) and paroxetine (Paxil) increase serum levels, resulting in an increase in the amounts of atomoxetine in the blood. In these cases, the clinician should slowly increase the atomoxetine to avoid side effects. In daily practice, few clinicians encounter true clinical difficulties combining atomoxetine with either of these selective serotonin reuptake inhibitors. Atomoxetine may be casually related to the emergence of mania. In short term studies of children and adolescents, 0.2% of subjects developed hallucinations and delusions. If this occurs, the clinician should discontinue Strattera and examine the patient carefully for a history of bipolar disorder.

SUICIDE RISK WITH ATOMOXETINE

More than 2 years after atomoxetine was released, the FDA warned that it had been associated with increased suicidal thoughts in latency-age children. In a study conducted by Eli Lilly (2005), 5 out of 1357 subjects treated with atomoxetine (compared to 0 out of 851 not treated with atomoxetine) were retrospectively found to have violent words or actions ascribed to them by clinicians during their clinical trial. None of the five children actually harmed themselves; there was one nonfatal overdose (Lilly Research Laboratories, 2005). These findings have not been replicated in adults.

Modafinil

While modafinil will not receive formal FDA approval for ADHD, it is a widely used agent in the ADHD armamentarium. Although the mechanism by which it exerts its effect on the brain is unclear, it is known that modafinil works differently than the stimulants and atomoxetine. It is not evenly distributed throughout the brain, but is thought to be most active in the anterior hypothalamus. As it does not have a significant impact on the brain's dopamine-rich pleasure areas, modafinil is not a controlled substance (Malcolm, Book, Moak, DeVane & Czepowicz, 2002).

Modafinil marketed as Provigil is a wakefulness-enhancing medication currently used to counteract fatigue for narcolepsy, obstructive sleep apnea, and sleep problems associated with alternating work shifts. For these conditions, the Provigil dosage is between 100 and 400 mg/day. Most patients start on 200 mg/day.

Recent studies examined modafinil for ADHD treatment. When Sparlon (the proposed name for the new product) was derailed for approval due to safety concerns, the studies used the medication in doses higher than typically used for wakefulness promotion. Published data supports impaired cognition and decreased impulsivity in adults with ADHD. Even at the required higher doses, modafinil was well tolerated, although some patients complain early in treatment of headache (Turner, Clark, Dawson, Robbins, & Sahakian, 2004).

Bupropion

Bupropion is an atypical antidepressant that affects the transmission of both norepinephrine and dopamine. Some research has demonstrated its effectiveness in adolescent patients with ADHD. However, the drug has not won FDA approval for ADHD treatment and its use for the condition is off-label.

The forms of bupropion used to treat ADHD are Wellbutrin IR, Wellbutrin SR, and Wellbutrin XL. In one small study of 15 ADHD patients ages 7–17 years old, researchers compared the efficacy of MPH and bupropion and found them both to be equally effective at treating core symptoms (Barrickman, et al., 1995).

Wellbutrin IR is a 3-time-daily short-acting formulation; Wellbutrin SR (twice daily) and Wellbutrin XL (once daily) have respectively longer effect durations. Immediate-release bupropion increases the risk of seizures (especially at higher dosages) and consequently patients who are either prone to or at risk for seizures should avoid this medication. Some patients develop dermatologic reactions to bupropion.

Unlike the selective serotonin reuptake inhibitors (SSRIs), bupropion generally does not cause weight gain or sexual dysfunction. It is often used alone or in tandem with an SSRI to treat depression. Occasionally it is added to an SSRI to counteract the symptoms of diminished libido and alterations in orgasmic response that result from altering serotonin levels. Bupropion is also effective in treating patients with cocaine dependency (Levin, Evans, McDowell, Brooks, & Nunes, 2002). Marketed as Zyban, the medication also is used to dampen the symptoms of nicotine withdrawal during smoking cessation therapy.

Wellbutrin IR tablets come in strengths of 75 and 100 mg, and the starting dose is usually 37.5, which means that the 75-mg pill must be split in two (patients need to be advised of this requirement). The drug may be increased at intervals of 3 days to 2–3 doses per day, with a maximum of 150 mg given at one time and a maximum dose of 450 mg/day. The effects of Wellbutrin IR last from 4 to 6 hours.

Wellbutrin SR comes in 100-, 150-, and 200-mg strengths. The usual starting dose is 100 mg, and the medication should be increased to twice daily, at no more than 200 mg per dose (or a maximum of 400 mg/day). The effects of Wellbutrin SR generally last from 10 to 14 hours.

Wellbutrin XL lasts longer than Wellbutrin SR, and is truly a one-time daily medication. It comes in tablets of 150 and 300 mg. The starting dose is 150 mg given once per day, and the maximum dose is 300 mg daily.

Other Antidepressants

Some tricyclic antidepressants (TCAs) have been shown to be effective at treating adolescents and adults with ADHD. Some of the earlier ADHD studies assessed imipramine (Tofranil) and desipramine (Norpramin) at starting doses of 75 mg/day. Symptomatic improvement was found at dosages of 100–300 mg, once or twice per day. Other TCAs used to treat ADHD include amitriptyline (Elavil) and nortriptyline at daily doses of 50–200 mg. Tricyclics can cause constipation, dry mouth, and weight gain, as well as changes in vital signs and electrocardiogram rhythms. They are not safe in overdose and desipramine has been linked to sudden death. As a result, TCAs have been largely abandoned for ADHD treatment (Wilens, Faraone, & Biederman, 2004).

Antidepressants from the selective serotonin reuptake inhibitor (SSRI) class alone are not effective for core ADHD symptoms. By decreasing a patient's anxiety without addressing the core symptoms of inattention and distractibility, SSRIs may be counterproductive and actually worsen the overall clinical situation. Patients who worry about their poor concentration or inability to stay organized may compensate for their deficits by doubling their basic efforts; void of this anxiety, the individual may lose the drive to perform better. However, when ADHD patients present with comorbid anxiety and depression, SSRIs can be effective in tandem with ADHD medications, as the ADHD medications treat the symptoms of inattention and distractibility while the SSRIs treat the anxiety and depression.

Other commonly prescribed serotonergic antidepressants are citalopram (Celexa), escitalopram (Lexapro), fluvoxamine (Luvox), paroxetine (Paxil, Paxil CR), sertraline (Zoloft), and mirtazapine (Remeron and Remeron SolTab).

Venlafaxine (Effexor and Effexor XR) and the newest antidepressant, duloxetine (Cymbalta), are dual reuptake inhibitors of serotonin and norepinephrine. Both are potent antidepressants. Because of their effects on norepinephrine, both drugs have been considered prime agents to study for efficacy in ADHD, although at this point little controlled data exist, particularly in regard to duloxetine.

SUICIDE RISK WITH ANTIDEPRESSANTS

As it did with atomoxetine, the FDA has issued a black-box warning that antidepressant medications may increase the risk of suicidal thoughts, and patients and their families should be advised of this. In an analysis of thousands of young individuals treated for depressive disorders, suicidal thoughts were more commonly detected in the group treated with antidepressants than in the group treated with placebo (Food and Drug Administration, 2004). It is important to note that no child studied actually committed suicide. The depressed patients studied were not specifically evaluated for ADHD, but other studies show that the risk for suicide is increased if patients have ADHD, bipolar disorder, a family history of bipolar disorder, or if they or someone else in the family has attempted suicide.

How we should interpret this data is unclear. Perhaps antidepressants (and atomoxetine) activate depressed individuals, giving them greater energy to consider self-harm. As of now, the FDA warnings apply only to children and adolescents, but review of adult data is underway. Most clinicians believe that the increased risk appears to be quite minimal. Unfortunately, however, although the warnings were designed to protect, they are having the direct consequence of scaring some clinicians and families away from treating these common psychiatric conditions.

ALPHA 2 AGONISTS

Alpha 2 agonists, such as clonidine (Catapres) and guanfacine (Tenex) are antihypertensive drugs that can address symptoms of hyperactivity and aggression in select patients. They do not have FDA indication for ADHD and are more commonly prescribed in children than in adolescents and adults with ADHD.

Clonidine is available in tablets with dosages of 0.1, 0.2, and 0.3 mg. The starting dose is 0.1 mg twice a day and the maximum daily dose is 2.4 mg. The tablet takes effect in about 30 to 60 minutes, and its effects last from 3 to 6 hours. Clonidine skin patches are also available, and they correspond to dosages of 0.1, 0.2, and 0.3 mg per patch. Each skin patch lasts 4–5 days. Patients who are taking antidepressants may notice a decreased effect if clonidine is added. Clonidine is sedating, particularly if taken with alcohol, narcotics, or benzodiazepines.

Guanfacine is available in tablets of 1, 2, and 3 mg. In general, the starting dose is 1 mg taken in the evening. The drug may be increased by 0.5 mg every 7 days and may be given from 2 to 4 times daily. The range of daily dosage should not exceed 4 mg. It is generically available and lasts from 6 to 12 hours. Currently this drug is not frequently used in cases of adult ADHD, but newer delivery systems are being explored and the medication will receive greater scrutiny as a potential agent in childhood and adult ADHD.

COMBINATIONS OF MEDICATIONS

As with many other medical and psychiatric problems, one medication is often insufficient to control the patient's symptoms, and consequently, many patients need two or more drugs to achieve their best response. For example, depressed ADHD patients may need a stimulant and an antidepressant. ADHD patients with profound fatigue may require both a stimulant and modafinil. Those with insomnia may require the addition of a sedative-hypnotic. Alpha 2 agonist medications are combined with ADHD medications for management of behavioral outbursts and sleep induction, particularly in younger adolescents. Combining medications is fundamental to the treatment of ADHD comorbidities. Chapter 2 addresses these issues in greater depth.

SLEEP REMEDIES

Some patients taking stimulants will complain of stimulant-induced insomnia. In these cases, the medication should not be taken after 4 P.M. Paradoxically, other ADHD patients actually sleep better with medications given late in the day. Dodson (2005) studied twice-daily dosing of Adderall in ADHD patients with insomnia. Dodson found that a number of patients reported enhanced sleep onset and a greater ability to "turn their brain off" at night. He asserted that insomnia results from restlessness and may be best understood as a nighttime manifestation of daytime hyperactivity. When insomnia is severe and unremitting, however, the physician may supplement the stimulant with a sleeping remedy.

Some antidepressants, like mirtazapine (Remeron) and trazadone (Desyrel), have sedative effects. They also have side effects: Mirtazapine is associated with weight gain and oversedation; trazadone can cause blood pressure changes and, on rare occasions, priapism, a persistent erection that requires urgent surgical attention (Lippmann, 2001). Benzodiazepines such as diazepam (Valium) and temazepam (Restoril) have long been used in treating insomnia including the insomnia related to ADHD, but their abuse potential is of concern (Ringdahl, Pereira, & Delzell, 2004).

Like benzodiazepines, nonbenzodiazepine sedative hypnotics are considered Shedule IV medications, but they have a reduced abuse potential. This makes them a more attractive choice to some doctors. Zaleplon (Sonata), a short-acting agent, is helpful with inducing sleep. For some patients, middle-of-the-night awakening is a problem, and longer-acting medications are employed. Zolpidem (Ambien, Ambien CR) has been a proven standard in this class for years. Eszoplicone (Lunesta) is newer to the market but has the distinction of FDA approval for long-term use. (See Table 9.3 for a listing of sleep remedies). Melatonin, a natural hormone secreted by the pineal gland in response to darkness, is a regulator of the sleep-wake cycle. Melatonin is available without prescription and is used for sleep induction, but many physicians are concerned about the quality and consistency of preparations found in over-the-counter preparations. Ramelton (Rozarem) is a melatonin receptor agonist that is far more potent than melatonin and has virtually no abuse liability. As such,

TABLE 9.3
Commonly Used Sleep Remedies

Generic Name	Brand Name	Usual Starting Dose/ Typical Daily Dose Range
eszoplicone	Lunesta	2–3 mg at bedtime
ramelton	Rozarem	8 mg at bedtime
trazodone	Desyrel	50 mg at bedtime (50–300 mg)
zaleplon	Sonata	10–20 mg at bedtime
zolpidem	Ambien	5–10 mg at bedtime
	Ambien CR	6.25–12.5 mg at bedtime

it less regulated than standard hypnotics but currently does require a prescription. The standard dose is 8 mg an hour before desired sleep (Bansell, 2005).

DOSING AND RELATED ISSUES

Even when a physician feels confident with the medication selection, often there are concerns about the dosage and how best to reach the optimal benefit. This section summarizes practical tips and common issues with regard to dosages, particularly for stimulants.

- Introduce one medication at a time, if possible
- Prescribe a sufficient dose and convert doses appropriately
- Brand-name products may outperform generics
- Beware of dosage creep
- Consider the rebound effect of short-acting agents
- Don't forget about extra evening doses, as needed
- When to consider drug holidays

Introduce One Medication at a Time, If Possible

As discussed in Chapter 2, the majority of adolescent and adult patients with ADHD have comorbidities. In these cases, it is best to prescribe a medication for the most distressing problems first. This strategy ensures that the worst symptoms will be ameliorated first, and it allows the clinician later to determine if that medication helped the patient. If the physician prescribes multiple medications at the same time, it can be difficult to impossible to assess which were effective. If it appears essential to immediately prescribe more than one medication, limit the treatment to two medications at a time.

Prescribe a Sufficient Dose and Convert Doses Appropriately

Many physicians have a tendency to be stingy with stimulant dosing, particularly with methylphenidate. The goal, however, should be to give the patient adequate dosing to control symptoms. If switching a patient from amphetamine to methylphenidate, keep in mind that 1 mg of amphetamine roughly equals 2.5–3 mg of methylphenidate.

Brand-Name Products May Outperform Generics

Just as some people are happy with any form of cola whereas others eschew all but the "real thing," some patients have a preferential response to brand-name medications whereas others find generics sufficient. Generics have become increasingly popular, partially because insurance companies incentivize patients to select them by offering lower co-pays. For a generic medication to enter the market, it must mimic the bioavailability properties of the brand-name medication within plus or minus 20%. Some patients cannot tolerate this variation. If a patient has an unexplained decline in performance, the clinician should inquire if there has been some change in the medication brand. If the patient is unsure, request that he or she bring in the actual tablet.

Beware of Dosage Creep

Occasionally dosages can creep up over time, particularly with stimulants. As stated earlier, clinicians must realize that dosages in excess of recommended amounts may be needed; however, when patients require ever-increasing stimulant doses, the physician should consider possible medication misuse. Ask patients who is actually taking the medication and whether they are diverting some of the supply. See Table 9.1 for information on starting dosages and dose ranges of common stimulants.

Many patients start slow and initially tolerate only low doses of stimulants, but as they become more comfortable, they seek dose increases to advance their benefit. Typically, most patients plateau at the end of 3 to 4 months of regular adjustments. If dose escalation continues after 3 months, despite receiving generous amounts, the clinician should consider the development of comorbidity. For example, patients who have both ADHD and depression but are treated only for their ADHD often require high doses of stimulants. Once the depression is identified and independently treated, the stimulant dose comes down.

Consider the Rebound Effect of Short-Acting Agents

As discussed earlier, some patients have a rebound effect with stimulants. This is more common with short-acting stimulants but may occur with long-acting medications as well. At the end of a dose of stimulant (short- or long-acting), patients may report that their symptoms intensify. They notice that they are forgetful, irritable, and extremely tired. In this case, if the patient is on a short-acting medication, he or she should be switched to a long-acting medication. If the patient is on a long-acting medication, a short-acting stimulant should be added an hour before the usual onset of the symptom to extend the duration effect.

Don't Forget About Extra Evening Doses, As Needed

Most long-acting ADHD medications are promoted for once-daily dosing, and for many patients, this is sufficient. However, there may be a number of reasons to give a second dose of medication. For example, patients may report that their morning Concerta dose lasts until midday, but as it wears off they become unfocused and irritable. Adding a short-acting Ritalin tablet at 4 P.M. may counteract this effect. Some patients actually are calmer and able to sleep better when they are on a stimulant. This group can benefit from twice-daily dosing of long-acting stimulants.

When to Consider "Drug Holidays"

In the past, physicians recommended "drug holidays" for children during weekends, holidays, and summer vacations. The practice was predicated on the belief that long-term exposure to stimulants might retard growth and that a drug hiatus would enable catch-up. However, drug holidays are no longer in vogue, because for patients who unequivocally respond to treatment, the risks of not being on medication exceed the possible benefits of a hiatus.

For fully grown adolescents and adults, growth retardation is a nonissue. For many patients, untreated ADHD symptoms adversely affect their home, work, and social life. Physician-endorsed drug holidays send the unfortunate message that ADHD need only be treated during the school or workday.

Stimulant medications decrease the occurrence of impulsive and potentially devastating behaviors like temper tantrums and road rage. For these reasons, it is not reasonable to medicate only on a part-time basis.

On the other hand, a drug holiday may make sense for an ambivalent teenager or adult who is unsure of the medication's benefit. Ross, age 15, had been on Adderall for 3 years. His grades and behavior had improved during the treatment period. Ross's parents believed that the medication was fundamental to his improvement; Ross felt that the medications played a marginal role. Faced with this conflict, the clinician suggested a semester off the medication. Halfway through the semester, Ross realized that his performance had suffered and he returned to treatment, this time more invested in it.

Similarly, Simon, a 40-year-old postman treated for ADHD and depression, questioned his need to remain on ADHD medications after 6 months of treatment. His physician, convinced that the medication was helping, encouraged him to continue. The following month, Simon raised the same concerns, this time more passionately. Realizing that Simon was uncomfortable, this time the physician gave Simon instructions on how to stop his stimulant. In this case, stopping the stimulant went smoothly and Simon remained on antidepressants alone. His story illustrates the fact that adult patients should stay on treatment only if they see personal benefit—not to please anyone else, including their doctor.

OFFICE PROCEDURES

Outpatient practices should develop policies regarding stimulant prescriptions. In some states, triplicate forms are required: One copy stays with the doctor, the second copy stays with the pharmacist, and the third copy is sent by the pharmacist to the state regulatory agency for accountability. Even in states without the triplicate program, it is advisable that offices keep copies of all prescriptions. Newer electronic medical-record programs record and store all authorized medications, and some even allow Internet transmission of prescriptions to pharmacies. Highly regulated medications still might require a hard copy, but this seems likely to change with advances in Internet security.

Some physicians will allow only the identified patient to pick up the prescription from the office, whereas others will release the prescription to a trusted family member. Mailing the script out on a monthly basis (after a request has been made by phone or e-mail) is another option. In general, considering the convenience of the patient increases compliance and therapeutic success. Still, the office staff should be suspicious of frequently lost prescriptions, requests for early refills, and a trend of adolescent children routinely picking up the prescription for their parents.

Increasingly, insurance plans offer 3-month mail-order refills with a co-payment competitive with the local pharmacy. For patients on long-term ADHD medications, this allows four co-pays per year instead of twelve. As co-pays can be as high as $50, physicians feel pressured to acquiesce, and most do. These programs, although economical, usually decrease the amount of control that medical offices have over medication supply. If there are irregularities in the way patients take their medications, the office has fewer opportunities to intercede.

Regarding how frequently ADHD patients should be seen, no standard rule exists. Early on, monthly visits are appropriate so that benefits and adverse effects can be assessed and dosing can be fine-tuned. Once treatment is stabilized, quarterly medication reviews are optimal. Ideally the visits coincide with refills, although this synchronization usually is difficult to sustain. Some stable patients can be seen twice yearly. Face-to-face contact is preferable, but for college students or patients who have recently moved, telephone consultation is an option.

COMMON MEDICATION ERRORS AND HOW TO AVOID THEM

Some examples of common medication errors include the following:

- Not asking patients if they understand the regimen
- Failing to tie medication to daily activities
- Not helping patients organize their medications
- Failing to warn patients not to overdose
- Underdosing
- Not allowing sufficient time for the drug to take effect

Not Asking Patients If They Understand the Medication Regimen

The clinician should be sure that patients and their families understand the treatment plan. Sometimes clinicians provide information too quickly, and anxiety or cognitive difficulties interfere with the patient's full comprehension. It is also important to remember that some patients, not wishing to seem stupid or uncooperative, will say that they understand the treatment plan even when they don't.

Medication directions should be written out legibly and copies should be saved on the patient's chart. Patients can then refer to the instructions after the appointment, and if they lose the paper, the medical office has a copy. This practice obviates the clinician's need to reconstruct a detailed conversation from memory. When possible, product information brochures should be given. Although they are provided by the manufacturers, they are generally balanced and offer information about benefits and adverse effects associated with the medication. In addition, most ADHD products have a website. It is a safe bet that adding ".com" to the product name will bring the patient worthwhile information and important links.

At return visits, doctors should routinely ask their patients to report what medications they are taking and how often. Do not accept "I'm taking them like before," or "You know what I am taking—after all, you prescribed them to me." This is only slightly more accurate than "I'm taking the yellow pill and the pink capsule." Asking patients to keep a spreadsheet or a handwritten 3 × 5 card of all their medications will increase the accuracy and efficiency of communication between doctor and patient.

After explaining the drug regimen, including the intended effects and possible adverse effects, it is good practice to ask the patient to explain the instructions back, as if the patient were the doctor. This technique is a simple way of minimizing misunderstandings, as the following conversation with Jay, an anxious gentleman in his early forties, illustrates.

Doctor: You should take this medication when you wake up and then again 8 hours later. Take it in the morning and again before you leave work in the late afternoon.

Jay: But does it have any side effects?

Doctor: I promise to cover that. But first, tell me back how to take the medication.

Jay: I guess swallow it. Is that what you mean?

Doctor: When should you take the medication?

Jay: At breakfast?

Doctor: That's half right. You also need to take it before leaving work in the late afternoon. It's a twice-a-day medication. Here is a copy of the information on how you should take the medication.

Note that it may take several tries before distractible patients get the answer "right," but this is worth the effort because it will increase compliance. The clinician should try to avoid any sign of impatience or annoyance if the patient does not grasp the instruction. Nonmedical therapists should also emphasize medication compliance and ensure that the patient clearly understands the doctor's orders. Often the therapist can act as a liaison between the patient and the prescribing doctor.

Failing to Tie Medication to Daily Activities

More than most patients, individuals with ADHD struggle with medication compliance, especially when they are taking more than one medication or one medication multiple times a day. Routines are important to establish, and they work best when patients learn to associate taking their medications with certain daily activities like awakening or mealtimes.

Stimulant medications can accelerate this important transition from sleep to wakefulness. Patients with inattentive ADHD often have difficulty awakening; sometimes by the time the patient is fully alert, a good part of the day has passed. In these situations, patients should be instructed to place the stimulant medication and a glass of water at their bedside each evening and to set their alarm for 30 minutes prior to the desired awakening time. If the medication is swallowed when the alarm sounds, the patient is rewarded with another half hour of sleep. This gives the medication more time to enter the bloodstream and hasten the process of waking. A potential pitfall of taking stimulant medication so early is that the patient's breakfast appetite will be suppressed. For underweight patients this can be problematic.

Most ADHD patients benefit from consistent schedules. Clinicians should encourage daily routines such as running or yoga every morning or walking the dog every evening. ADHD patients should be advised to keep their weekend schedule generally consistent with weekdays; getting up at noon on Saturday and Sunday makes the 7 A.M. Monday morning wake up seem brutal.

Timing of medications is simpler with long-acting medications; almost always they should be taken upon awakening. Medications that last 6 to 8 hours may require a second dose. Atomoxetine is the longest-acting ADHD medication, and after a couple weeks of daily use a steady state is achieved. This continuous effect may explain why some atomoxetine-treated patients report that getting started in the morning is noticeably easier.

Not Helping Patients Organize Their Medications

With many disease states, like hypertension, diabetes, or depression, failure to take medications is usually not noticeable in the short run. For many ADHD patients, however, missing medications yields immediate symptoms. Absent a dose, many patients feel uneasy, unfocused, and fatigued. The quick return of these symptoms becomes a built-in reminder to take the next dose. Still, when a medication needs to be taken once or twice daily, year in and year out, consistent compliance can be problematic. Patients can forget whether they took their medication or not, and once they lose track, most do not have the patience to deduce where they went wrong.

It is helpful to advise patients to invest in a plastic pillbox so they can easily see if the dose has been taken. They should restock the box weekly. This is particularly helpful when the patient is on short-acting ADHD agents that need to be taken several times daily. Patients may initially resist this technique—nobody wants to emulate his or her grandparent's medication habits—but for some it is a valuable way to manage this ongoing concern.

Failing to Warn Patients Not to Overdose

Although many individuals with ADHD have lived a lifetime without treatment, once they are diagnosed, they have a desperate need to feel better immediately. Sometimes doctors fail to sense their patient's urgency and fail to imagine the measures they can take to speed up the rapidity of their response.

Impulsive adolescents and adults with ADHD may conclude that if one pill is not making them feel better within a few days, then doubling or tripling their dose will expedite their recovery. Fortunately, most ADHD medications have wide dose ranges and severe consequences of overdosing occur rarely and only at many times the prescribed dose. Still, some patients will push the margins and justify taking too many tablets. Doctors should instruct patients away from dosing experimentation for many reasons, including that patients will run through their pills too quickly, the doctor will not have a realistic idea of dose response, and this unilateral practice will jeopardize the therapeutic relationship. Doctors want controlled substances taken their way or no way. Therapists should inform patients that ADHD medications affect the brain and behavior, that they should follow medication regimens as accurately as possible, and that all changes should be done in concert with the physician.

Underdosing

To minimize side effects and ensure compliance, it is standard practice to start patients on a low dose of a medication and titrate upwards slowly. The pitfall of this cautious practice is stopping short of an efficacious dosage, whether due to pressure from the patient, concern about safety, or the clinician's ambivalence about treatment. In general, prescribers of ADHD medications are conservative; many do not want to exceed prescribing limits. However, clinicians should be cognizant that although the package insert identifies maximum doses, all ADHD medications can be used in doses that exceed the FDA guidelines.

For example, the maximum dosage recommendation of methylphenidate is 60 mg/day; amphetamines are limited to 30 mg/day. These recommendation limits were developed years ago, well before adult needs were known. Some patients may require twice this amount, and most tolerate these higher doses quite well. The stated maximum doses of atomoxetine are 1.4 mg/kg/day for children, but doses up to 2 mg/kg/day are routinely used. In adults, the recommended 100 mg/day dose limit is often surpassed by 40%.

Not Allowing Sufficient Time for the Drug to Take Effect

Doctors should also avoid switching to another medication too quickly, without first trying adequate doses of the original medication. Switching too frequently can have a demoralizing effect on some patients.

In other cases, patients may pressure their doctor to prematurely switch the medication. Many patients with ADHD are desperate to obtain immediate relief. If the medication does not "work" within a few days or a week, they may become disenchanted. Urging patience to patients can be taxing, but acceding to them by switching prematurely to another drug may have unintended consequences. Many of these patients are distressed, but they are usually not emotionally hemorrhaging; realistically, the clinician has time to refine the dosage.

Patients may take some time to adjust to a stimulant. Six weeks into treatment they may benefit from a full dosage, but early on, they may be unable to handle a fraction of their ultimate dose. Atomoxetine can take a full month to take effect. Abandoning a medication too quickly may result in the permanent loss of the agent, as patients and doctors tend not to revisit discarded agents.

COMMON FEARS PATIENTS HAVE ABOUT MEDICATION

Many people are ambivalent about psychiatric medications, particularly as the popular media routinely laments that too many American children and adolescents are being "drugged." In addition to the media onslaught, each patient brings his or her own bias about the legitimacy of ADHD diagnosis. Many encounter a hostile reception from friends or family members about their decision to seek treatment. Patients will surely have many concerns and fears that clinicians need to address realistically. Following are some of the most common:

- Fear of addiction
- Fear of personality changes
- Fear of losing creativity
- Fear of extreme side effects

Fear of Addiction

Although some patients abuse stimulants, particularly those with active substance abuse disorders, the vast majority of compliant patients do not become dependent. Patients with ADHD may have used drugs or alcohol in the past in an unconscious attempt to self-medicate their symptoms. Still, some physicians refuse to prescribe any scheduled drugs to patients with a past substance abuse problem.

Patients and clinicians struggling with this issue may be heartened by studies that have shown that after 4 years of stimulant treatment, adolescents with ADHD were significantly less likely to abuse substances than were unmedicated ADHD adolescents (Biederman, Wilens, Mick, Faraone, Weber, Curtis, et al., 1997; Biederman, 2003a). (Chapter 6 addresses this issue). For those who remain unconvinced by this statistic, nonstimulant medications like atomoxetine and modafinil, which have no abuse potential, are excellent choices.

Fear of Personality Changes

Like adolescents who believe taking ADHD medication will cause them to become robotic, some adults fear that taking any psychiatric medication is tantamount to a chemical lobotomy. It is important to explain to these patients that the goal of medication is to improve their symptoms and to enable their true personalities to unfold. ADHD medications decrease impulsive behaviors, allowing patients to think before they speak or act. They do not transform charismatic individuals into dull and uninteresting people; active individuals will not devolve into plodders. Wit and energy do not disintegrate. That said, patients should be reassured that if the medications do have any untoward effect on personality, simply stopping the medication will resolve the issue.

Fear of Losing Creativity

Patients may also fear that medications will somehow control their minds and constrict their creativity. Usually the opposite is true. ADHD medications do not interfere with the development of creative ideas; rather, they allow ADHD patients to execute their ideas.

Natalie's experience was emblematic of artistic patients on treatment. "I was very frustrated before. I would have great ideas, but I could not translate the thoughts into art. Now my visions meet canvas and my thoughts meet paper."

Tony, the director of a social service agency, reported, "When I got medication, I was able to implement an employee-review system that I should have introduced years earlier. I am now much more innovative." The goal of ADHD treatment remains to increase the control and execution that patients have over their life.

Fear of Extreme Side Effects

Some patients worry that they may become ill from the side effects of a medication. They may have read on the Internet or in a magazine that a particular drug causes severe side effects. (These warnings are often posted by groups who are opposed to all psychiatric medications.) In addition, patients may read the package insert provided with the prescription and immediately worry that they will develop the listed side effects.

Although clinicians should not minimize potential side effects, it is prudent to tell patients that very few people experience all of the drug's identified side effects. For example, one stimulant drug lists abdominal pain, fever, and vomiting as potential concerns, but in practice patients rarely encounter these side effects and almost never at the same time in the same patient.

The doctor may also wish to mention that even medications such as aspirin or acetaminophen can cause health risks, and that if ADHD medications are used carefully and appropriately, most patients will not have adverse effects from them.

A FINAL WARNING: INCREASED SELF-AWARENESS MAY HEIGHTEN AWARENESS OF DEFICITS

For most patients, medication allows for increased self-awareness. Although this is generally beneficial therapeutically, some patients may become more tuned into their original deficits. With treatment, patients objectively may be sharper, but they may also become more cognizant and less forgiving of their baseline forgetfulness. Other patients report that they are more talkative on medications when they actually are in better control of their conversation.

Treated ADHD adults can become overly distressed by the impact residual symptoms have on their life. Whenever possible, seek to quantify the concerns. Patients complaining of memory problems should be asked how many times their memory has failed in the past week. Assuming the medication is effective, the response is likely to be within the normal range. If so, the patient should be assured that even individuals without ADHD sometimes forget their keys or talk too much. The clinician should also reinforce that with increased self-awareness, therapy or coaching becomes more effective, and that perfection is not the entire objective.

Chapter 10

Psychotherapy, Coaching, and Other Techniques

ALMOST ALL PEOPLE TACITLY or explicitly exploit their strengths. Surgeons acknowledge their dexterity; singers, their voice quality. Individuals with ADHD must also identify their strengths while at the same time coming to terms with their weaknesses. Sometimes a person's strength is in avoiding a weakness, even if this involves compromise—for example, a dyslexic's avoiding a literature class despite loving drama. Some patients are more successful than others with this adaptation, but ADHD therapists should be aware of the importance of helping patients work through these delicate issues. A successful adaptation means exploiting strengths and avoiding weaknesses, but mostly it involves being honest with oneself about dreams and limitations.

Although medications can result in dramatic symptomatic improvement in many patients with ADHD, physicians should not assume—nor should they let their patients assume—that drugs alone can resolve the broad array of problems that usually accompany ADHD. Alone, even the most efficacious medication, given at the optimal doses and for adequate periods, cannot help patients overcome certain persistent behavioral problems that are present with ADHD. In many cases, adding psychotherapy to the medications is essential. This chapter explores two forms of therapy that have been proven as most effective with ADHD: cognitive-behavioral therapy (CBT) and coaching.

Most patients with ADHD have suffered for years from their core symptoms of impulsivity, inattentiveness, and hyperactivity. The consequences of these symptoms, such as poor self-esteem and a dearth of self-confidence, are directly related to untreated ADHD. Self-blaming and anxious rumination over past failures result from a lifetime of disappointing others. Bad habits, like hoarding useless junk, arise when individuals are not self-assured enough to make even the simplest executive decision about what should be kept and what should be discarded. The goal of therapy is for the therapist to identify these behaviors, help patients realize the patterns of these behaviors, and work with patients to find ways to rectify them.

Norma, a 53-year-old woman whose ADHD had been treated for a year with Adderall XR, noticed that with treatment she was less likely to blurt out hurtful remarks when she was frustrated. Her family welcomed her improved impulse control, but she lamented that her relationships with her adult children had not substantially improved. The people that mattered the most to her still held her at arm's length.

In therapy, Norma came to understand that before she was medicated, shouting was her reflexive response when she was irritated. As medications decreased her impulsivity and allowed her a moment to think before shouting, Norma expected her relationships to flourish. After two sessions of family therapy, her children conceded her improvements over the past year but concluded that collectively they had lingering, unresolved anger. Adderall XR made Norma less testy, but long ago, the children had become conditioned to her unpredictability.

Fortunately, the children sincerely wanted their family to heal, and with her therapist, Norma developed a concrete treatment plan. She tried to exercise as a way of sublimating her inner tension. She avoided social gatherings that heightened her anxiety and put her at risk for making critical comments, and most importantly, she apologized for the residual behavior that still occurred and that she could not control. Over time, and with regular reinforcement of the treatment plan provided in therapy, Norma regained some of her children's confidence.

An adult treated for ADHD is similar to a heavy person who suddenly loses a tremendous amount of weight. Despite the new exterior, the person's self-concept remains fat and unworthy. Others may openly admire the transformation, but after a lifetime of hostile reactions, the person retains old insecurities and is unable to shake this reflexive self-loathing. Therapists for these types of patients assume the assignment of not only helping the patients restructure their cognitive distortions about weight and attractiveness, but also give them permission to move on.

ADHD medications offer a similar opportunity for adult metamorphosis. Objectively, patients quickly can recognize improvement of their symptoms, but they may continue to feel like the same kid who could do nothing right. "I am so happy that I have these medications," said Sherry, a 33-year-old bank manager. "I just wish I had them 20 years ago. I'm angry at my parents for not getting me help when I was 10." The therapist must recognize the emotional impact associated with righting lifelong symptoms and how, as in Sherry's situation, the diagnosis redefines family issues (e.g., anger at parents for not acting earlier).

COGNITIVE-BEHAVIORAL THERAPY

Cognitive-behavioral therapy (CBT) is a form of psychotherapy that assists patients by teaching them how to identify their irrational thoughts and the emotions that accompany these cognitions. Patients learn how to challenge these internalized self-defeating beliefs and replace them with more positive and logical reasoning. A benefit of CBT is that these more positive thoughts usually generate an improved mood.

This may sound simple, but in practice, it is not. Cognitive-behavioral therapy is a thinking-on-your-feet type of interactive therapy in which the therapist works within the basic framework of the patient's own views and core values to liberate patients from their negative and unrealistic self-views. It requires time for the therapist to understand how patients perceive life events, and patience to help them address problematic misperceptions. The grit of the process is demonstrating to patients how reframing their automatic thoughts can lead to rational behavioral changes. Cognitive-behavioral therapy does not mean years of psychoanalysis (which would probably be untenable for an ADHD patient), but it is not a quick-fix in which one or two sessions can produce a major turnaround, either. Unlike traditional psychotherapy, CBT focuses on current situations and spends less time on past conflicts.

It is important to note that CBT does not attempt to turn patients into perpetually happy Pollyannas who never experience a negative thought. Instead, CBT concentrates on helping patients understand the reality of their situation and their potential responses, as well as acknowledge the areas that require them to make further effort and change.

Which ADHD Traits Can Cognitive-Behavioral Therapy Help Treat?

Different ADHD patients have different problems, but many share common issues. Many fail to perceive their own strengths and constantly compare themselves to those who do not have ADHD struggles. They may blame themselves for everything that goes wrong in their lives. Cognitive-Behavioral Therapy is not mindless cheerleading; it must be rooted in honesty of the true score. Therapists cannot put on a happy face when the team is three touchdowns behind, but by addressing the patient's cognitive distortions, they can optimistically develop a comeback plan.

OVERGENERALIZING THE NEGATIVE

Russell Barkley (2004) noted that patients with ADHD advance their negative self-concepts to an extreme, overemphasizing their problem areas and generalizing their deficits to their entire lives. In so doing, they fail to recognize areas of competence or value the strengths that they possess. The therapist using CBT can help patients learn to identify not only their weaknesses but also their attributes. The following conversation with Jenny, a middle-aged woman who has returned to college, illustrates this point.

Doctor: Jenny, why are you giving up on the semester?
Jenny: When you diagnosed me with ADHD, I realized how distractible and bored I get every day.
Doctor: Everyone in your family believes you are doing better with treatment.

Jenny: Maybe, but when I sit in class, I just think how much easier other students have it. Then I get mad at myself for thinking about other people when I should be listening to the professor. It's like I have two cycles. I am either resentful or I am kicking myself for getting lost in thought. I don't have what it takes to be a student.

Doctor: I can see how you are thinking, but you may need to rethink your premise. You already are accomplished. You raised a family and managed the museum gift store for years before you were diagnosed with ADHD. Treatment will only make you more effective. You are obviously smart, and putting words to these complicated thoughts is evidence of how well your brain works. You may have to work a little harder than other students, but that doesn't mean you can't be successful with this new task.

COMPARING THEMSELVES TO PEERS WHO DO NOT HAVE ADHD

Another common trait among patients with ADHD is that they may base their own self-worth on how they believe they stack up in comparison to other individuals, particularly those who do *not* have ADHD. Patients with ADHD may also idealize the achievements of others, not recognizing that even in the absence of ADHD, everyone has some type of cross to bear.

Ari, 32, had been diagnosed with ADHD at age 28. In therapy, he reported that most of his high school friends had graduated from college. Ari worked full-time mixing paint colors in a chemical factory. He referred to himself as a chemical engineer, a title his wife characterized, in demeaning tones, as "wishful" and misleading. She reported that his mundane job was primarily clerical, and she predicted that robotic technology would soon replace him.

Ari seethed as younger workers completed their education and quickly surpassed him. Promotions and pay increases were rare for Ari. He struggled to complete evening college classes; he had received only six credits in the past 18 months. Graduation looked increasingly remote. Ari concluded that his stagnation was due solely to his lack of a degree. To him, the situation was black or white, either/or: If a person graduated from college, he was a success. If he did not, he was an abject failure.

Cognitive-Behavioral Therapy can be used in two primary ways with adults like Ari who have ADHD. First, the therapist should help Ari develop broad strategies to overcome his deficits. (This is not the same as coaching, which is far more practical and detail-oriented, as discussed later in this chapter.) Second, the therapist should challenge Ari's automatic thinking styles, which may have resulted from his lifelong ADHD experience. Problems with attentiveness, impulsivity, and disorganization may have led to past underachievement and to resultant dysfunctional beliefs. Constantly replaying the deficits in the patient's mind will surely result in anxiety or depression (Safren, Sprich, Chulvick, & Otto, 2004).

At the same time, Ari's CBT therapist needs to display sympathy and honesty. Ari's core belief that worth comes solely from a prestigious job should be respected, but also challenged. His job propels the larger operation, and no organization can function without a dedicated command structure. Restructuring the importance of his designated job is important.

Second, Ari's longstanding ADHD undoubtedly has contributed to his frustration with school. Here, the therapist should emphasize that Ari's school experience would have been more successful with early ADHD treatment. However, even the best medication treatment does not ensure school completion. It is far easier to finish school before having a job and a growing family. The therapist should remind Ari that he did not have this advantage.

Third, Ari should be reminded that at age 32, it is not too late to complete his degree, but having a degree should not be the only measure of success. Ari must recognize that his lack of promotions may not be due to the lack of a college degree. Rather, his employer may object to Ari's lack of candor (such as calling himself a "chemical engineer"), his jealousy of coworkers, and his general inflexibility. Ari can hope to change these shortcomings only if he is made aware of them. For the therapist, supporting the patient demands being honest with him.

No matter how flawed, each person has identifiable strengths. Children receive frequent praise—"Boy can you run fast!" "My gosh, you are so pretty!" "I can't believe how tall you've become!"—and these commendations motivate them and mine their personal best. Age does not make praise less necessary, yet most adults receive scant praise for living their lives. The therapist should commend Ari for working hard each day to support his family and should acknowledge his superior attendance record. His interest in self-improvement exceeds the standard. The therapist should capture this need and be mindful that encouragement is part of the therapeutic process.

Sometimes therapists must recognize that patients' attributes are less about what they *are* doing and more about what they are *not* doing. For example, substance abusers may have given up alcohol. Compulsive shoppers may have reigned in their impulses by going on a strict budgetary diet. These are commendable achievements that should be regularly praised in therapy sessions. Some patients think that they are undeserving of any praise; they fear that somehow, if they are too generous to themselves, they will unravel and return to their undesired behaviors. The CBT therapist can help ADHD patients accept praise by modeling the process.

Cognitive-Behavioral Therapy can help patients reframe their thoughts about their goals while at the same time teaching them that there are *always* others who are seemingly doing better than they are, just as there are many others who are struggling. In short, CBT can help ADHD patients stop relentlessly comparing themselves to all others. Better yet, they may begin to create their own individual plan of success, devoid of debilitating cognitive distortions.

BLAMING THEMSELVES FOR EVERYTHING THAT GOES WRONG

Patients with ADHD often tend to blame themselves for everything that goes wrong, sometimes rather grandiosely and even when the problem is not of their doing. Women may be more susceptible to overreaching the scope of their responsibility, perhaps because they so often are caretakers. When patients constantly take the position that everything is their fault, the therapist may need to use extremes to break them out of this mode of thinking. For example, the therapist may ask, "Is the war in Iraq your fault?" The patient will say no. The therapist might then say, "Is world poverty your fault?" The patient will again say no. The therapist may then reply, "Apparently not all problems everywhere are caused by you, and maybe some of the problems you're fixated on now are not your fault either." Working with the therapist, patients can learn how to distinguish between what they have control over (and should take responsibility for) and what circumstances are beyond their control.

From the objective perch of the therapist, CBT can provide a reality check on the situation. The key is to help patients discover how to differentiate between the things that they may have caused and those that were caused by others. For example, the mother of a struggling ADHD adolescent may need to work through her decision, made many years earlier, to reject treatment for the child, but the therapist must insist that she not bear responsibility for her adolescent's current poor life decisions.

Sandy, age 51, received a final notice from the power company and reported that she had berated herself all day for not having paid the bill. "As usual, I feel so stupid and disorganized." She told her therapist that she thought she *had* paid it after the first notice, but reasoned she may have overlooked it and dismissed a second notice as well. To make matters worse, she knew that her pattern was to procrastinate; she would not find the initiative to track down the answer to the question. This predicament may seem mundane but it loomed large to Sandy, partly because she was fearful that her lights would be turned off and partly because she felt that it was another illustration of her overall ineptness. Sandy encountered shame over disorganization and guilt over procrastination daily, and this thinking perpetuated a great deal of her anger and self-defeating emotions. With minor thematic variations, these feelings are common among ADHD patients.

In such a case, the therapist should equip Sandy with a "how to" checklist starting with the most obvious.

"Is there is any chance that you might have paid the bill? Just because you have ADHD does not mean you are always wrong."

Perhaps Sandy did pay the bill; perhaps she did not. The therapist should help her identify that her anxiety is compounded by not knowing if a payment was made. At the same time, the therapist should offer her logical techniques to problem-solve. Advise her to examine her check register to see if she has a carbon copy of the check, consult her most recent bank statement, talk to the bank personnel—all are actions that can quickly answer the question one way or the other.

If it is determined that Sandy did not pay the bill, the therapist must assert that self-chastisement is not productive. Instruct her to pay the bill on the Internet or go to the company office and pay it in person. Tell her that she will not be the first person the staff has ever encountered who was late paying a bill. Help her restructure her thoughts from "I'm stupid because I forgot to pay that bill" to "I forgot to pay the bill and made a mistake. I'll pay it now and I will try to not make this mistake again." A CBT therapist can empower patients like Sandy to understand their maladaptive thinking and behavior in general terms, but this should not be done at the expense of solving the problems at hand.

Identifying Other Common Irrational, Negative Beliefs

For many adolescents and adults with ADHD, negative beliefs they have held about themselves have been internalized and tacitly accepted for so long that they are deeply engrained in the patient's self-identity. By identifying and challenging these core beliefs, CBT can help individuals discover and disown these ideas, replacing them with a more positive schema.

Some common beliefs among individuals with ADHD are:

- I'm stupid (stupidity is also attributed to virtually every symptom of ADHD).
- I'm lazy (often confused with distractibility and procrastination).
- I don't try hard enough.
- I can't do anything right (often confused with disorganization and distractibility).
- Nobody has confidence that I can get the job done.

I'M STUPID

This viewpoint is so common among patients with ADHD that one of the most popular consumer books about adult ADHD is titled *You Mean I'm Not Lazy, Stupid or Crazy* (Kelly & Ramundo, 1996). In truth, many patients with ADHD have average or above-average intelligence and many are highly creative. Nonetheless, humiliations such as firings, traffic tickets, and school failure are recurrent themes in their lives and many remain convinced of their ineptitude.

The CBT therapist helps patients disconnect from the implicit assumption of their own incompetence and infuses the idea that ADHD can (and does) afflict accomplished people. Letting patients know that the waiting rooms is full of Ph.D.s, CPAs, and CEOs with the same problems, often on the same medications, can be normalizing, inspiring, and of great comfort.

I'M LAZY

The highly distractible and procrastinating patient with ADHD may seem lazy to others because it takes the person so long to perform routine tasks—if the tasks are completed at all. But rarely is laziness the problem. Many people with ADHD are high-energy individuals who start many projects but burn out before they finish them. This is distractibility, not laziness. However, if patients often hear that they are lazy, they may begin to believe it. This self-recrimination needs to be actively challenged by the therapist.

I DON'T TRY HARD ENOUGH

Many patients with ADHD have been told that if only they would *try* harder, they would be able to achieve so much more. The implication is that it is the patient's fault for not exerting enough effort. In fact, patients may be spending a great deal of time and worry trying to perform tasks that others can perform more efficiently. However, others are not distracted by butterflies flitting about outside the window, a loud noise from another room, or any of the numerous distractions that those with ADHD are transfixed by. Therapists must help patients challenge the idea that they are not trying hard and point out that this perception, although erroneous, is very common.

Occasionally, however, patients with ADHD really do not try as hard as they might, in part because of a fear of failing or being told they did something wrong yet again. Patients need to learn to say to themselves, "I am going to try this. I may not be able to do it exactly right, but I will do my best and it is worth it to try it and see how it comes out.

I CAN'T DO ANYTHING RIGHT

Some patients are fearful of making changes because they assume that whatever they do, it will automatically be the wrong thing. In these situations, the therapist needs to help patients discover some things that they have done right. Some patients may need prompting. For example, the therapist might remark that the patient came to the appointment on time, which was a "right" kind of behavior. This may seem trivial (although not to most therapists), but in the menu of all possible actions that could have been taken, such as not showing up at all or showing up late, the patient took the actions needed to arrive on time. This was good.

Once some good choices have been identified, however small, the path to more significant changes becomes clearer. The therapist should affirm that life is complicated and that everyone, with and without ADHD, sometimes is faced with problematic choices.

NOBODY HAS CONFIDENCE THAT I CAN GET THE JOB DONE

In some cases, patients may correctly perceive that others have lost confidence in them because of their poor follow-through. The therapist must emphasize to these patients that they are *not* doomed to failure forever and that every day brings new opportunities to resurrect their public image. Correcting this distortion offers hope and motivates patients to exhibit the trophies of achievement, to themselves and others, as a means of redemption. The therapist can use CBT to help patients make this vital transformation. For example:

Doctor: Tell me about your week.
Patient: We had a work retreat. I helped organize it.
Doctor: How did it go?
Patient: Things need to get better next year.
Doctor: How so?
Patient: Well, my supervisor said that the conference room was too small and it had to be better next year.
Doctor: That sounds like the retreat went well enough for them to plan another one for next year. It also sounds like they want to make it bigger. Was your supervisor pleased?
Patient: I guess so. I heard her boss praise her about the meeting. She seemed excited.
Doctor: You seem to remember only the critique. Perhaps you need to hear the positive comments as well. Maybe you expected your bosses to be disappointed with your work?

Even when others comment on a job well done, the patient may deflect the compliment by making self-effacing remarks such as "Oh, yes, once in a while I get something right." Or the patient may give others the credit: "Heidi deserves the praise—she had all the good ideas." Through careful listening, the therapist can detect and correct these cognitive traps.

Using Cognitive-Behavioral Therapy Interventions

Patients with ADHD may be so certain that they will fail at some tasks that they fear or refuse to try at all. For example, Sheila, a 47-year-old woman treated for ADHD with Ritalin for several years, recently had been fired as a sales representative for a college-textbook supplier. During her 6 years at the job, Sheila had established a book of stable clients. When a competitor acquired her company, suddenly Sheila was responsible for many new products. Other workers caught on quickly to the new systems, but Sheila had trouble adjusting. Her supervisor tried to tutor her, but this was to no avail; Sheila was hopelessly lost. Within a couple of months she was terminated. No severance package was offered per the company's policy, and Sheila was immediately escorted out of the building, accompanied by a security guard.

Several days later, Sheila, extremely humiliated, made an appointment with her therapist. Since the firing, she had been virtually paralyzed, unwilling to talk with her husband or friends and unable to apply for another position. She did not know how to start a new job search and was fearful that even if she found a new position requiring similar skills, she would ultimately meet the same fate and be fired yet again.

Sheila's therapist approached the problem efficiently. In the first session, she offered unwavering listening skills and complete sympathy. She advised Sheila to consult an employment attorney to be assured that her employment rights were protected. She sent Sheila to a medication specialist, as she believed that newer ADHD medications would serve her better. (The doctor agreed and substituted Strattera for the Ritalin.)

As they considered Sheila's future, the therapist sought to identify and exploit Sheila's strengths and recognize and avoid her weaknesses. She used software-based psychological testing to survey Sheila's likes and aptitudes. The program generated a list of "good fit" job categories. Sheila was intrigued that the testing confirmed her instinct that sales were not her forté, and that instead, she had the skill set needed for teaching. The community college had a certificate program for teaching English as a second language and Sheila was encouraged to enroll.

Finally, the therapist used CBT techniques to deconstruct Sheila's cognitive distortions. Getting fired did not negate all her work accomplishments. Being escorted out of an office is a standard security procedure not specifically intended as a humiliation. Once the therapist challenged Sheila's wrongheaded belief that one setback ensured lifelong failures, Sheila was able to move on. She found a position tutoring East-Asian immigrants. The job paid less than her previous job had, but she was infinitely happier.

Finding a Cognitive-Behavioral Therapist

Cognitive-Behavioral Therapy is a widely disseminated technique, and it should not be difficult to locate a well-trained therapist. It is optimal if the therapist has experience working with ADHD patients, as a comprehensive understanding of the condition is fundamental to successful treatment. Patients should meet with a potential therapist at least once to determine if a proper chemistry can flourish before starting a therapeutic relationship. Patients may ask their physicians for recommendations, and various websites, such as that of the Academy of Cognitive Therapy (www.academyofct.org), provide lists of therapists experienced in CBT.

OTHER PSYCHOLOGICAL STRATEGIES

Therapists may find other psychological strategies that are particularly helpful for patients with ADHD. For example, rather than fighting the ADHD symptoms, some therapists try to manage or use the symptoms in a productive way. Triolo (1999) described one such paradoxical strategy: The patient is instructed to have four or five different work stations, either at home or at work, that the patient can move between.

For instance, bills to be paid could be placed in one area, paperwork from the office in another, a woodworking project in another, and so on. While paying the bills, as the mind starts to wander off and feelings of boredom emerge, the patient is instructed to switch to a new station and begin work there. In turn, as boredom and a lack of attention are experienced again, another switch is made. The idea is to take a symptom of ADHD that is normally perceived as being negative and make it work more constructively. One patient noted that the problem may not have been so much the fact that she wandered off task as much as she had no place else to go but to drift away aimlessly once she did lose concentration. The fact that she had a concrete place to go to helped her become more productive. (p. 154)

EXPLAIN THE DIFFERENCES IN THERAPISTS TO PATIENTS

Many patients are very confused by the differences between mental health professionals, and it is important to provide at least a cursory explanation of these differences. Patients should know that psychiatrists are physicians who graduate from medical school and spend the first part of their training alongside internists, neurologists, and pediatricians. After this basic grounding, psychiatrists spend the next 3 to 4 years specializing in behavioral medicine. As medical doctors, they are licensed by the state to prescribe medications. Some psychiatrists provide psychotherapy, but many now apportion their time to make psychiatric diagnosis, manage medications, and supervise nonmedical therapists. Unlike psychiatrists, psychologists are not medically trained and do not prescribe medications. Limited licensed psychologists have a master's degree. Only a psychologist with a Ph.D. can become fully licensed. Psychologists specialize in testing and psychotherapy and are licensed by the state in which they practice. Social workers and family therapists have master's degrees and provide the majority of outpatient care. Psychiatric nurse practitioners with advanced training can prescribe psychiatric medications usually (but not always) under the auspices of a psychiatrist. In some states, this supervision is not required and they can practice independently. Nurse practitioners are not allowed to prescribe controlled substances like stimulants, which makes it difficult for them to independently support an ADHD practice.

ADHD therapists use a variety of modalities to treat their patients. However, despite the diversity of educational backgrounds, most rely upon CBT or other forms of time-limited "talk therapy." Traditional psychoanalysis does not play a role in ADHD treatment.

COACHING

Coaching is another form of therapy uniquely suited to ADHD patients. A good coach can help clients effectively manage their daily symptoms. (The term *client* is preferred over *patient*, which derives from the medical model.) Many ADHD coaches suffer from the condition themselves, and thus they can identify with the struggles of a person with ADHD. These coaches have developed their own adaptive strategies and can provide practical advice as well as empathy and understanding. Coaching appeals to patients with ADHD because it is highly interactive and centers on practical problems of daily living such as being on time, remembering to perform key tasks, keeping track of frequently lost items, and paying attention.

The primary goal of coaching is to work with clients to establish specific goals that are important to them and then create a practical plan to achieve those goals. Coaches do not try to find inner meaning or to uncover the subconscious motivation of behavior. Instead, they seek to provide practical ways to harness energy and guide good intentions (Young & Giwerc, 2003).

Primary Principles Underlying Coaching

Coaching is different from traditional psychotherapy primarily because coaches concentrate on minimizing deleterious ADHD behavior. The emphasis is not on *why* the individual with ADHD has lost items, procrastinated, or exhibited other signs of ADHD behaviors, and identifying thought distortions is not considered pivotally important. Rather, the coach helps the individual determine practical ways to resolve problems, either through prevention or through dealing with the aftermath. Coaches also help with organization and time management.

Coaching is also collaborative: Rather than vaguely recommending that a patient take action, the coach suggests specific ways of incorporating structure into patients' lives by developing good habits. For example, many people with ADHD have a great deal of trouble using "to do" lists. The coach may recommend writing short lists on colored sticky notes that can be attached to a wallet or inside a purse or another place where they will see the note and be reminded of what needs to be done. Electronic organizers or calendars are effective for other individuals.

When Coaching Begins

The first meeting with a coach may occur in person or by phone. It usually lasts at least an hour, and during that time the client and coach establish what goals the client has and how the coach can facilitate the achievement of those goals. Creating a written agreement outlining the goals is helpful. After the first few sessions, the client and the coach should have established a good working rapport, and dedicated work toward achieving goals can begin.

Problems That Coaches Can Address

Coaches can provide assistance with several key issues relevant for nearly all clients with ADHD. These include: motivation, organization, task prioritization, hyperfocusing (concentrating intently on a subject to the exclusion of whatever else is going on), developing routines, and establishing exercise habits.

MOTIVATION

Coaches can motivate ambivalent clients. Some successful coaches emerge from a background of competitive athletics and have adopted the belief that individuals striving to improve will respond well to support and encouragement. Unlike some reserved therapists and doctors, coaches can be unashamed cheerleaders.

ORGANIZATION

Many individuals with ADHD have problems discarding anything. They may accumulate boxes of papers, books, and other items that they take with them with every move. They know that they have too much "stuff," but they cannot figure out what is important and what is not. They operate with the belief that one day they will catch up on their old newspapers and that old rusty bucket may prove helpful somehow.

An ADHD coach, aware of how indecision and hoarding can paralyze a person, can provide valuable guidance and figurative hand-holding as clients rid themselves of old unused materials. ADHD coaches instruct their clients to break down large tasks, like organizing their basement, into smaller doable tasks. Not all four rooms in the basement should be undertaken at once; organize them in sequence. Do not go from one room to the other, lest the client be distracted before the primary task is complete.

Instruct the client to start three different heaps. "Keepable" items belong in the first pile, discardable items belong in the second pile, and the third should be reserved for items to be given away. With the coach's organizational help, the client can emerge from the mire of a messy house. Cleaning one's house or desk can be like cleansing one's soul.

TASK PRIORITIZATION

Coaches can also help clients prioritize tasks. Individuals with ADHD often become overwhelmed if they need to perform several discrete tasks. They have difficulty processing what should be done first, second, and so on, and they become so confused that they do not do anything. The coach can help the client break down large tasks into smaller steps and determine which steps to take in what order. Once the client has a plan to achieve the goal, it seems much less daunting and is usually achievable.

HYPERFOCUSING

Some clients with ADHD have a tendency to endlessly ruminate about minor problems, which can consume a great deal of time. An ADHD coach can help the client put what is important in perspective. Some coaches recommend that clients who are heavy ruminators set aside a time when they dedicate 20–30 minutes to think about or worry about the problem du jour. When that time is up, they must move to another topic.

DEVELOPING ROUTINES

Coaching can help clients create simple routines that may have major payoffs. A client with ADHD may start eating breakfast and become engrossed in a newspaper article, losing all track of time. A coach may suggest a watch that beeps periodically (and might actually set the alarm for his client). ADHD clients also often have problems with punctuality. A pre-planned call from the coach can get the client back on track during a part of the day known to be one with treacherous disruptions (e.g., when kids come home from school). The coach can work with the client on strategies such as writing daily predetermined checklists. This ensures that routines for consistent awakening times, bathing, eating, and exercise take hold.

EXERCISE AND HEALTHY LIVING

Some coaches strongly recommend exercise as a means to help the mind and body focus and concentrate better and to disrupt constant ruminating. When the body is in motion, the brain must dedicate at least part of its function on the exercising and thus the individual is less likely to engage in endless ruminating. Exercise is also extremely useful in helping clients improve their concentration, focus, and attentiveness. The coach can help clients devise an exercise program that works for them, whether it is using the local gym or taking long walks at a rapid pace.

Some coaches analyze the client's diet and lifestyle and offer advice. For example, a diet of junk food and caffeinated soft drinks is not conducive to good health and sustained focus. Similarly, many clients with ADHD mistakenly regard sleep as an unimportant or annoying part of their lives rather than as a chance for the body to rejuvenate itself after the stress of the day. A good coach can make clients aware of the importance of sufficient sleep and a healthier diet, without resorting to guilt tactics.

Coaching Training

ADHD coaches come from a variety of backgrounds — including business, teaching, athletics, and homemaking. Some therapists also work as coaches, and sometimes, other family members serve as coaches to the adolescent or adult with ADHD. In all cases, coaches should have received extensive training and graduated from an established program. The ADD Coach Academy (ADDCA) trains the bulk of ADHD coaches. In addition to the training program, the ADDCA (www.addca.com) provides a large referral service for those wanting to obtain the services of a coach.

Finding the Right Coach

ADHD clients who decide to hire coaches should keep the following points in mind:

- Interview several coaches before deciding on one.
- Check references.
- Make sure the coach has ADHD experience.
- Give the coaching experience a trial of at least 3 months.

INTERVIEW SEVERAL COACHES

Clients should interview several coaches before hiring one. Often the individual with ADHD will act impulsively and hire the first coach interviewed, but physicians should advise their patients to resist this temptation. Candidate #2 or #3 may be much better suited to their needs.

Before contracting a particular coach, the client should contact references and inquire whether the coach was effective for them. With their permission, names of previous clients can be freely exchanged. However, for various reasons many clients do not bother with references. They may be reticent about asking for names of past clients, or they may decide that the coach seems competent and it would be a waste of time to contact past clients. This practice is not advisable, because, unlike with therapists, state governing boards do not regulate coaches. Some individuals portray themselves as better qualified than they truly are. Coaching does not have the deep ethos of confidentiality, as is evident with traditional psychotherapy.

MAKE SURE THE COACH HAS ADHD EXPERIENCE

Coaches serve many purposes—some specialize in athletes whereas others help business people perform better. The client with ADHD should only engage a coach experienced with ADHD issues and a proven record of accomplishment.

GIVE THE PROCESS SOME TIME

Clients with ADHD should also be advised that it takes time to create new goals and overcome old problems such as poor organization and procrastination. The client should give the coach a period of at least 3 months before stopping or switching to another coach. At the same time, clients should avoid coaches who demand a long-term contractual commitment.

Pros and Cons of Coaching

Ideally, ADHD coaches are nonjudgmental figures who focus on practical advice for common problems such as disorganization, punctuality, and developing routines. Although other therapists employ these techniques, coaches specifically take the time to delve into the details of daily functioning.

Coaches often have great zeal and tremendous empathy for their clients. Many began ADHD coaching later in life and chose the field because the condition directly affected their own life or the lives of their family. Unlike professional therapists, who are trained not to be self-revealing, coaches are usually comfortable sharing their personal stories. This connection can be highly valued, particularly by clients uneasy with the formal boundaries of traditional therapy.

Coaching can have a downside, however. At times, coaches get in over their heads and do not make appropriate referrals. They are not schooled in diagnosis and they may not recognize conditions, like anxiety and depression, that would respond to psychiatric medications. They also may not fully appreciate intrapsychic conflicts, the fodder of traditional psychotherapy.

There is always the chance that the person with ADHD may inadvertently hire a "bad fit"—a coach who is too lax, too authoritarian, or not substantive enough. After an unhappy experience, the client may dismiss the entire concept of coaching rather than concluding that the particular collaboration was not effective. Impatient ADHD individuals are averse to give second chances, but they should be reminded that, just as the first medication prescribed is not always effective, sometimes they might not mesh with their first coach.

Healthcare insurances do not cover coaching, but rates are usually less than for psychotherapy. In addition, sometimes coaching sessions can be as brief as 15 or 20 minutes and this also lowers the cost.

A final drawback to coaching is that some clients expect far too much from their coaches. Although coaches may be helpful with many issues of time management or planning and organization, they should not be

TABLE 10.1
Comparing Traditional Therapy with Coaching

	Therapy	Coaching
Seeks to find causes in the past for current problems	Yes	No
Seeks to find maladaptive thinking patterns so they can be changed	Yes	Sometimes
Helps patient/client with current goals	Yes, with a focus on general goals	Yes, with a focus on specific goals
Helps with time management and organizational issues	No	Yes
Offers advice on health issues, such as getting enough sleep or exercising	Sometimes	Yes
Recommends helpful devices, such as timers, calendars, and special watches	Sometimes	Yes
Sees patient/client in the office	Yes	No. Other than one in-person meeting, usually communicates with client by phone or e-mail.
Offers 45- to 50-minute sessions	Yes, usually weekly	Often not. May recommend shorter, more frequent contacts.
What patient/client says is confidential	Yes	Yes, but the process is less formal and not governed by strict confidentiality standards.
Covered by health insurance	Usually	Rarely
Therapist has advanced degree, such as a Ph.D. or a master's degree	Yes	Sometimes
Replaces the need for medications	No	No

called upon for matters such as marital discord, problems with children (whether they are young children or adult children) and other areas that fall in the realm of the psychotherapist. Clients should also note that coaches cannot transform the client's life without the client's active assistance—there is nothing magical about coaching.

THERAPY VERSUS COACHING

Many patients need both therapy and coaching because of the distinctively different goals that each type of assistance provides. Therapy helps patients resolve painful issues from the past that intrude into the present, whereas coaching generally concentrates on the present and near future. Table 10.1 describes other differences.

Sometimes there is overlap between the help provided by therapists and that provided by coaches. If a patient tells a therapist about a problem and the therapist sees an obvious solution (which has somehow eluded the patient), the therapist will usually share that information. If a coach notes that a client is very depressed or anxious, she may ask him what has gone wrong. If it is a problem that obviously needs therapy, the coach should recommend that the patient see the therapist. However, if the patient is upset by a current practical problem that stymies him, the coach may offer possible solutions.

Chapter 11

ADHD, Fibromyalgia, Chronic Pain, and Associated Syndromes

ADHD SYMPTOMOLOGY HAS BEEN DESCRIBED in the medical literature for decades, yet surprisingly little research has examined the natural history of the disorder—specifically, what happens to people who have had ADHD for decades. Medical decisions should be based on evidence-supported research as much as possible, but in newer fields of inquiry, such as adult ADHD, all is not known, many questions remain unanswered, and many questions have not yet even been formulated. The lack of hard data, however, should not dampen speculation; before controlled trials are undertaken, clinicians need to report observations. The observations in this chapter reflect early findings and are supported by the available basic science, some formal research, and much anecdotal information. The theory of a relationship between ADHD and chronic pain syndromes is included to spur discussion and debate.

Over the years that I have treated adult ADHD, many patients have reported chronic pain and fatigue. Most of these patients were referred for ADHD, but in the process of obtaining medical histories, I realized that a large number had been diagnosed with fibromyalgia (FM; chronic diffuse muscle pain) and chronic fatigue syndrome (CFS; chronic, excessive, debilitating fatigue). Frequent but less common complaints included irritable bowel syndrome (IBS), tinnitus (ear ringing), restless legs syndrome (RLS), and vulvodynia (gynecological pain). The goal of treatment for these patients was to improve their ADHD symptoms, but it soon became clear that on stimulants, many of these patients noticed improvement in their pain symptoms as well.

We set out to understand this phenomenon. Over the course of 18 months, our clinic received patients who identified themselves as having FM. The patients were evaluated by a team of mental health professionals and a board-certified rheumatologist. We found that about 70% of the patients met criteria for ADHD and most had a predominance of inattentive symptoms. Many of these patients reported pain reduction when they were prescribed stimulant medications. We concluded that a lifelong history of ADHD predisposed these patients to chronic pain syndromes. ADHD medications do not act as direct analgesics, but by improving focus and concentration, they allow patients to cope more effectively with their pain and fatigue (Young, 2006).

Pain syndromes such as FM, CFS, IBS, tinnitus, chronic headaches, vulvadynia, and RLS all share common clinical characteristics. All the conditions are widespread yet poorly understood. They affect women more than men. No consistently good treatment exists. Most importantly, the evidence is sparse that abnormalities in the tissues exist. Biopsies of the intestines of patients with IBS usually do not reveal pathology. Several studies have found no defects in muscle energy metabolism in patients with FM compared to control subjects (Simms, Roy, Hrovat, Anderson, Skrinar, LePoole, et al., 1994).

If the problems are not in the peripheral organs (muscle, joints, intestines, etc.), then where are they? Increasingly, researchers have proposed that pain syndromes result from a central process, essentially the central nervous system's inability to produce or break down pain-mediating neurochemicals such as serotonin, norepinephrine, and substance P. Staud (2002) reported that some FM patients have three times the level of substance P in their spinal fluid as those without FM. Fibromyalgia patients also have abnormally low levels of serotonin. Staud concluded that patients with FM suffer from pain more quickly and that the pain lasts longer than it does for those without the condition (Staud & Adamec, 2002).

WHO HAS CHRONIC PAIN AND FATIGUE?

Patients with somatic symptoms have typical presentations. They often present in their thirties and forties, although earlier and later presentations are also seen. The condition appears to occur more frequently in women than men. Many are unable to work, and they spend a good part of their time pursuing medical treatment. Many reject the idea that their underlying disability could be psychiatric in nature. Physicians specializing in physical medicine or rheumatology are often consulted. Common treatments include physical therapy, diet changes, and exercise regimens. When these prove unsatisfying, alternative treatments from chiropractic (spinal manipulation) or naturopathic (homeopathic) physicians are pursued. Not uncommonly, opiate-derived pain medications are prescribed and sometimes abused.

IMPACT ON THE INDIVIDUAL AND SOCIETY

Economic systems bear profound burdens as a result of the CFS/FM symptom complex, as well as other chronic pain conditions such as IBS and RLS. Fibromyalgia is the second most common of all rheumatologic conditions in the country, affecting approximately 4 to 6 million Americans. The Centers for Disease Control and Prevention (CDC) estimates that between 75 and 265 people per 100,000 are affected by CFS. Approximately half a million people in the United States have CFS or a condition that is similar to it.

These conditions drive worker absenteeism, lost productivity, and decreased income. Nearly a fourth of Social Security disability payments are related to psychiatric disorders, and nearly a fourth are due to rheumatological disorders. I speculate that of these rheumatologic cases, at least some are for CFS or FM. These conditions impact society, which at least in part has to pay the bill in terms of decreased worker productivity.

AFFECTIVE SPECTRUM DISORDER: A RELATED CONCEPT

Other researchers have grouped ADHD and other psychiatric problems with chronic pain conditions. James I. Hudson and his colleagues have described affective spectrum disorder, which precisely defines the patients described in this chapter. Affective spectrum disorder encompasses the common psychiatric conditions of major depression, panic disorder, social and generalized anxiety disorder, and ADHD with the medical conditions of FM, IBS, and chronic migraines (Hudson, Mangweth, Pope, De Col, Hausmann, Gutweniger, et al., 2003). Hudson's basic theory is that these disparate conditions commonly present together and he argued that many of the symptoms were responsive to antidepressant medications of the serotonin reuptake inhibitor (SSRI) class.

This finding has gained traction in the treatment community. SNRIs, antidepressants that inhibit both the reuptake of serotonin (primarily in the brain) and norepinephrine (downward through spinal cord projections), have overtaken the SSRIs. Duloxetine (Cymbalta) joins an older agent, venlafaxine (Effexor XR), as an effective treatment for painful symptoms associated with depression. Even in nondepressed patients with painful diabetic neuropathy, duloxetine has proven a rapid and effective treatment (Anttila & Leinonen, 2002). The use of dual reuptake inhibitors is becoming routine as more doctors pay attention to the relationship between physical and psychiatric symptoms.

ADHD AND PAIN/FATIGUE SYNDROMES: A WORKING THEORY

At a fundamental level, ADHD represents the brain's inability to efficiently filter incoming stimuli. Children with ADHD have obvious difficulties in this regard. Sitting in a classroom, they know that they should be listening to the teacher but are distracted instead by the falling leaves outside the window. The adult with inattentive ADHD tries to listen to the person speaking to him at a loud party but quickly realizes that he cannot distinguish the conversation from the background noise. Formal neuropsychological testing, through the use of continuous performance tests, can often identify these filtering problems in ADHD patients.

Consider a normal individual who is injured or develops a relatively minor musculoskeletal complaint. The normal brain recognizes the discom-

fort and responds with a rational soothing strategy. This might include rub-
bing or massaging the area of injury or finding other methods of calming the
irritation. The injury is resolved with time and with the natural healing
mechanisms of the body. Usually the patient is able to endure the injury,
compartmentalize it, and concurrently manage other parts of her life.

In contrast, the ADHD inattentive patient subjected to the same type of
injury may be less able to filter out unpleasant, low-level painful stimuli.
Unable to distinguish the intensity of the many stimuli that the brain is
receiving, the patient becomes overwhelmed by the discomfort. She becomes one with her pain. Although objectively the sensation may be relatively minor, it besieges the inattentive patient to the point that she cannot distinguish variations of painful stimuli. This deficiency comes to
define the individual as a "chronic pain patient."

Other authors have hypothesized that a basic pain-processing problem
is at the foundation of pain syndromes. They speculate that this is explained by the combination of environmental triggers superimposed on
a particular genetic predisposition. According to Aaron and Buchwald
(2003, p. 567), "A common finding among patients with FM, CFS, irritable bowel syndrome, temporomandibular disorders, chronic headache
and interstitial cystitis [irritable/spastic bladder] is a reduction in pain
threshold and tolerance. Alternations in pain perception are probably me-
diated by central factors because they occur in systemic conditions (e.g.,
CFS) as well as organ-specific conditions (e.g., interstitial cystitis)."

These findings and theories are consistent with my own. The "central
factors" may indeed be ADHD. For these purposes, ADHD may be better defined as a central (brain-based) inability to efficiently filter multiple
incoming stimuli. Although pain and fatigue often occur together, I propose that patients with ADHD inattentive type can develop both CFS and
FM, whereas patients with ADHD hyperactive type may be more likely
to develop RLS.

MEDICATION

Stimulant medications may be effective in treating some pain syndromes.
Although the use of dual reuptake inhibitors is in ascendancy throughout the psychiatric community in treating what Hudson termed affective

spectrum disorder, my clinical experience suggests that stimulant medications that increase brain dopamine levels can be even more helpful.

Yee and Bere (2004) reported that stimulants added to opiates can be helpful in treating cancer pain. Like the stimulants, pramipexole (Mirapex) is a highly dopaminergic medication. It is indicated for the treatment of Parkinson's disease and is widely used for RLS. Holman and Myers (2005) studied this pure dopamine receptor agonist in patients currently treated for FM. Compared to a control group, pramipexole-treated patients had significant improvements in pain, fatigue, and overall functioning.

The case studies presented in this chapter demonstrate the effect of ADHD medications have on the manner in which these patients perceive their pain and fatigue.

THE DOCTOR-PATIENT RELATIONSHIP

Faced with the daunting task of diagnosing and treating a condition for which there is neither a definitive test nor a universally accepted treatment, physicians are understandably reluctant to treat patients with chronic pain syndromes. Some physicians may convey initial optimism, but when multiple treatments fail to sustain improvement, hopefulness is succeeded by frustration. In the face of therapeutic failure, doctors become defensive and overtly skeptical of their patient's credibility. They resent their patients' requests for narcotics. Nevertheless, beneath this "psychological distancing," the physician may acknowledge a familiar constellation of symptoms so characteristic of accepted medical syndromes.

The deteriorating doctor-patient relationship mirrors the erosion of the patient's primary relationships. As a result of the unpredictable effects of CFS/FM, the patient's identity shifts from that of a productive worker and a contributing full-time family member to that of a chronic patient. Attempts at achieving a definitive remedy narrow down to a singular effort to find relief. Having exhausted the armamentarium of conventional practitioners, the patient may pursue more novel, and potentially exploitative, treatment alternatives. Ultimately, the patient may feel abandoned by loved ones and marginalized by the medical system. Many become profoundly depressed or suicidal. It is at this juncture that a psychiatric consultation is typically sought.

FIBROMYALGIA

Fibromyalgia is a chronic condition of muscle pain throughout the body. People with FM have specific tender points of the body. The American College of Rheumatology criteria for classification of fibromyalgia is detailed in Table 11.1.

Many patients with FM complain of poor memory or otherwise being cognitively dulled in addition to the musculoskeletal pain. Most report being depressed or anergic. This has been referred to, sometimes facetiously, as the "fibro fog." Notably, many inattentive ADHD patients voice the same complaints.

TABLE 11.1
Criteria for Classification of Fibromyalgia

Widespread pain for at least three months, defined as the presence of all of the following:

Pain on the right and left sides of the body

Pain above and below the waist (including shoulder and buttock pain)

Pain in the axial skeleton (cervical, thoracic or lumbar spine, or anterior chest)

Pain on palpation with a 4-kg force in 11 of the following 18 sites (nine bilateral sites, for a total of 18 sites):

- Occiput: at the intersections of one or more of the following muscles: trapezius, sternocleidomastoid, splenious capsemispinalis capitus
- Low cervical: at the anterior aspect of the interspaces between the transverse processes of C5-C7
- Trapezius: at the midpoint of the upper border
- Supraspinatus: above the scapular spine near the medial border
- Second rib: just lateral to the second costochondral junctions
- Lateral epicondyle: 2 cm distal to the lateral epicondyle
- Gluteal: at the upper outer quadrant of the buttocks at the anterior edge of the gluteus maximus muscle
- Greater trochanter: posterior to the greater trochanteric prominence
- Knee: at the medial fat pad proximal to the joint line

Adapted, with permission of John Wiley & Sons © 1990, from Wolfe, F., Smythe, H. A., Yunas, M. B., Bennett, R. M., Bombardier, C., Goldenberg, D. L. The American College of Rheumatology. 1990 criteria for the classification of fibromyalgia. Report of the Multi Center Criteria Committee. *Arthritis Rheumatology*, 33, 160–72.

Mary: A Case Example

Mary, a well-groomed and articulate 46-year-old married homemaker and mother of three adult children, typified the FM patient. She consulted her doctor seeking relief for widespread neuromuscular pain involving her arms and neck.

Mary's internist evaluated her sore elbow and concluded that she had localized tendonitis. In the succeeding several months, Mary complained more intensely about her muscle pain. She saw a rheumatologist who treated her with various nonsteroidal anti-inflammatory agents, including ibuprofen (Motrin). When this intervention proved unhelpful, Cox-2 inhibitors were introduced (Bextra). This worked for some time, but Mary's complaints continued, and acetaminophen with codeine was added. Mary's increasing reliance on these medications made her physician uncomfortable. After the third consecutive month that Mary called in for an early refill, he abruptly stopped writing for the medications, but offered her little explanation about his decision.

Soon thereafter, Mary developed episodes of breathlessness and chest pressure that brought her to the emergency room. This visit prompted a series of referrals to other specialists. Extensive and expensive workups for cardiac disease and gastrointestinal and neurological problems were all negative. Because her pain was persistent, Mary's internist referred her for psychiatric consultation, suspecting that she was either highly anxious, medication-seeking (for narcotics), or delusional.

MARY'S PSYCHIATRIC HISTORY

Upon presentation to the psychiatrist, Mary reported being very depressed over her medical condition. She said she felt overwhelmed, and commented that "her mind was betraying her." Mary's self-concept was notably low, and she exhibited long-standing memory problems, low energy, procrastination, and poor motivation: "I feel lazy; I cannot get myself to do things." Though Mary had been sober for 3 years, she believed that her previous episodes of alcohol abuse had soured her relationship with her husband and children.

Mary also related that she had been in counseling intermittently for the past 8 years and carried the diagnosis of dysthymia. Fluoxetine (Prozac), venlafaxine (Effexor XR), and olanzapine (Zyprexa) had been prescribed over the years to manage her anxiety and depression. The medications, along with psychotherapy, had initially helped her anxiety, but Mary felt that the benefits had plateaued. She now felt that the medications compounded her lethargy and failed to attenuate her pain symptoms in a meaningful way.

The psychiatrist also learned that Mary's mother had alcohol dependency and her 17-year-old son had been diagnosed in grade school with dyslexia. Due to her various medical problems, Mary received disability and was now a homemaker, but she had previously worked as an account executive.

MARY'S PSYCHIATRIC DIAGNOSIS

Mary reported doing "fine" in school; she had graduated from high school with a B average. She conceded that she never had to try very hard in school, nor did she take the academic experience too seriously. After high school, she married and several years later started her family. Matt, her oldest son, required a great deal of her time. He was frequently in trouble and did poorly academically and socially throughout his school years. Mary was actively involved in Matt's schooling, frequently having to extricate him from trouble. In eighth grade, Matt was diagnosed with dyslexia and ADHD. His refusal to take medications was typical of his oppositional behavior.

Ratings scales were given to assess depression, anxiety, and ADHD. Mary completed forms that evaluated her pain, sleep patterns, and quality of life experience. Many scales were elevated, although the psychiatrist took particular note of the high score on the inattentive part of the ADHD screen. ADHD was added to her diagnosis of major depression.

CLINICAL OUTCOME

Mary was placed on stimulant and antidepressant medications, combined with short-term psychotherapy. Within several doses, Mary reported an improvement in her energy level, mood, and motivational level. Her ability to concentrate had increased, as had her productivity in completing tasks. Her memory was sharper. At follow-up, Mary reported that she felt more spontaneous and better focused. As Mary felt better, the tension in her marriage lessened. Notably, Mary's pain complaints also diminished. Over the months of stimulant treatment, she made fewer trips to see doctors and physical therapists. She became convinced of the palliative role that the stimulants played when she forgot to obtain a refill for her medication: her physical symptoms returned within just a few days.

CHRONIC FATIGUE SYNDROME

As patients with ADHD inattentive type age, they develop fatigue and a lack of motivation. They may gain weight, feel lethargic, and complain of feeling slowed down or somehow held back from normal activity. They sense that they cannot keep up with the fast-moving world around them. Clinically, these patients appear underaroused, as if they have just awoken. They seem to be a second delayed in processing conversation and may miss subtle but important social cues. In the late afternoon, they can feel slowed down to the point of immobilization. As these complaints are persistent, a number are eventually diagnosed with CFS. (*Chronic fatigue syndrome* is the term that the CDC uses and is currently the most widely accepted. Others believe that the word *fatigue* should be removed from the name of the syndrome, as it may be misleading.)

I propose that CFS is the other half of the ADHD inattentive walnut, and treatment with conventional ADHD medications is the most effective way of addressing the nebulous syndrome. This theory is far from dogma. In the current diagnostic criteria, CFS is characterized by extreme lethargy and severe exhaustion. Absolutely no mention is made of preexisting ADHD.

According to the CDC, patients with CFS experience fatigue that has lasted 6 months or longer. In addition, the patient must have four or more of the following signs or symptoms:

- Substantial impairment with short-term memory or concentration
- Sore throat
- Tender lymph nodes

- Muscle pain
- Multijoint pain with no redness or swelling
- Headaches of a new type or severity
- Unrefreshed sleep
- Postexertional malaise that continues unabated for 24 hours or more

The CDC (2006) guidelines on CFS are outlined as follows:

A thorough medical history, physical examination, mental status examination, and laboratory tests must be conducted to identify underlying or contributing conditions that require treatment. Diagnosis or classification cannot be made without such an evaluation. Clinically evaluated, unexplained chronic fatigue cases can be classified as chronic fatigue syndrome if the patient meets both the following criteria:

1. *Clinically evaluated, unexplained persistent or relapsing chronic fatigue that is of new or definite onset (i.e., not lifelong), is not the result of ongoing exertion, is not substantially alleviated by rest, and results in substantial reduction in previous levels of occupational, educational, social, or personal activities.*
2. *The concurrent occurrence of four or more of the following symptoms: substantial impairment in short term memory or concentration; sore throat; tender lymph nodes; muscle pain; multi-joint pain without swelling or redness; headaches of a new type, pattern or severity; unrefreshing sleep; and post-exertional malaise lasting more than 24 hours. These symptoms must have persisted or recurred during 6 or more consecutive months of illness and must not have predated the fatigue.*

As with FM, the CDC instructs that before the diagnosis is given other medical causes must be ruled out. Patients who have these symptoms should be screened with routine blood and urine laboratory tests for anemia, hypothyroidism, hypotension, and kidney disease. Assuming that all the laboratory tests are normal, the diagnosis can be made solely on the basis of the patient's history, signs, and symptoms. There is no specific biological marker that can identify the presence of CFS.

Current Thought About the Causes and Treatment
of Chronic Fatigue Syndrome

Thus far, researchers have found no underlying cause for CFS. Clinicians do realize that anxiety and depression are commonly seen and many CFS patients benefit from antidepressants. Most popular theories compete as to the underlying cause of CFS, particularly with regard to whether the condition is caused by a viral or bacterial infection or an autoimmune process. As the cause is unclear, there is no consensus on how to best treat CFS. The use of antibiotic or antiviral agents has strong proponents, but in my experience, absent a known infectious process, this approach makes little sense scientifically and is unhelpful clinically.

Some clinicians contend that CFS is caused by nonspecific abnormal inflammation and prescribe hydrocortisone therapy to combat the fatigue and related symptoms. Goldberg (2004) and others have extended the argument that CFS may be an autoimmune process in which the body slowly rejects it own tissue. He advocated the use of low doses of alpha interferon to relieve pain in the muscles and joints and to interrupt the negative feedback loop that propels pain syndromes.

Goldberg (2004) asserted that ADHD is commonly seen with CFS patients but it is often overlooked. He cautioned that the patient's cognitive and academic problems occur before the pain and fatigue complaints and asserted that these symptoms reflect the undiagnosed ADHD condition. They should not be explained as a consequence of CFS but rather as the core issue. By underestimating the role of ADHD, the search for a cause of CFS has been limited to traditional physical causes.

Jackie: A Case Example

Jackie, 47, had recently returned to school to obtain a master's degree in social work. Jackie was specifically concerned about falling asleep during reading assignments. Despite being highly motivated and academically capable, she found that her attention inevitably drifted in class. She frequently missed simple instructions and often needed to ask fellow students about assignment due dates and other important information. Jackie complained of "feeling tired all my life" and reported that she often felt that she was in a "cave, unable to crawl out."

At home, Jackie routinely misplaced important documents and household bills. Her friends felt that she looked vacuous and they complained that she did not return phone calls. Her three younger sisters had long contended that Jackie was simply rude; they all felt that she was preoccupied with loftier thoughts and disinterested in their comments.

Jackie's psychiatrist found her to be cooperative and sincere. She appeared more frustrated than depressed, and she had a gentle, self-deprecating sense of humor. The doctor observed that Jackie appeared distressed and frustrated by her inability to perform at a level consistent with her ability and motivational level.

Jackie had been married for 18 years to a physician. She was frequently ill with colds and coughs, and although it was never proven, her husband felt she had a low-level immunological deficiency. Eighteen months after her father's death from Alzheimer's disease, Jackie continued to grieve and slept more than 12 hours a day. She had also had a recent automobile accident that was probably caused by her tendency to fall asleep during short driving trips. Her many ongoing complaints taxed her otherwise strong marital relationship.

In the last few years, Jackie had become caffeine-dependent. It was not unusual for her to drink four diet colas a day. Psychotherapy and antidepressant medications stabilized her depressive symptoms but did not meaningfully improve her chronic fatigue. Jackie was seen by a number of specialists, including the regional academic medical center. She did not have elevated Epstein Barr titers. Normal sleep studies ruled out narcolepsy and obstructive sleep apnea. Her rheumatologic workup was unremarkable, but she did demonstrate the trigger points seen in FM.

Jackie reported a family history of ADHD and depression. Her mother and grandmother were both diagnosed with atypical forms of depression, and both received antidepressant medications over the years. Jackie's brother never graduated from high school despite excellent aptitude. Her oldest child and two nephews had been on psychostimulant medications since grade school.

Jackie had supportive counseling following her father's death. In the past 2 years she was prescribed sertraline (Zoloft), fluoxetine (Prozac), escitalopram (Lexapro), and duloxetine (Cymbalta). The medications were moderately helpful, but they did not improve her daily functioning. Her sleep doctor had prescribed modafinil (Provigil), which did improve her wakefulness, but she had recently discontinued the medication because of its high cost.

Based on the comprehensive psychiatric clinical interview and ADHD rating scale, Jackie was given the diagnosis of ADHD predominately inattentive type. Surprisingly, her depression scale was not markedly elevated.

CLINICAL OUTCOME

Jackie was started on Adderall XR 10 mg and titrated up to 20 mg every morning. She returned for a medication check a month later, reporting increased wakefulness and a greater ability to focus on her classwork. Jackie noticed that she could concentrate on her assignments, submit them on time, and stay awake while reading her textbooks. Her friends and family complained less frequently about her inattention. At her next visit, now on Adderall XR 30 mg/day, Jackie reported far more energy, less depression, and a significantly enhanced sense of confidence. When the medication was changed to two times daily, her sleep-wake cycle normalized. School was going well and Jackie appeared happy and hopeful.

IRRITABLE BOWEL SYNDROME

Irritable bowel syndrome, also known as spastic colon, is a digestive disorder that leads to either diarrhea or constipation in affected individuals, and it is usually accompanied by abdominal pain. Some individuals alternate between diarrhea and constipation. This disorder can be very painful and embarrassing, and some patients must leave their jobs because they are so severely affected. The condition is aggravated by stress (Minocha & Adamec, 2004).

It is believed that up to 20% of the population may experience IBS symptoms. The age of onset is in the early twenties, and women are more likely than men to have symptoms. The symptoms do not alter the anatomy of the intestines; on colonoscopic examination it is difficult to distinguish IBS patients from patients with normal colons.

Patients with IBS are at risk for other medical problems such as FM and depression, and they may also have an increased risk for ADHD. Many patients with IBS also suffer from depression, and consequently, patients may be treated with antidepressants.

Much has been written about IBS, yet there is little consensus as to the underlying dysfunctional mechanism. Some of the individual symptoms, such as colonic spasms, are often treated with medications such as dicyclomine (Bentyl) or hyoscyamine sulfate (Levsin). If the patient suffers from chronic constipation, tegaserod maleate (Zelnorm) may be given. If the patient primarily suffers from diarrhea, drugs such as loperamide (Imodium), alosetron (Lotronex), or other antidiarrheals may be given. Antianxiety medications can be very helpful, but the most effective agents are highly controlled and doctors are wary of their long-term use. It is not surprising that the treatment doctors most often recommend is diet and exercise programs along with "stress reduction."

Irritable Bowel Syndrome patients seem to have a high rate of ADHD. We speculate that many patients with ADHD have high levels of free-floating generalized anxiety. The chronic anxiety ultimately "boils over" and manifests itself as colonic spasms. Treating the underlying anxiety (in these cases with ADHD medications) often reduces the irritable bowel symptoms.

CHRONIC MIGRAINES AND TENSION HEADACHES

Millions of people suffer from chronic severe migraines and tension-type headaches, and often it is difficult (and sometimes impossible) to pinpoint the cause. However, there is a wide variety of headache triggers, stress being one of the most common. Sometimes headaches are a part of another chronic pain syndrome, such as CFS or FM. In addition, many patients with IBS also suffer from frequent headaches. Many medications are useful; acetaminophen with caffeine (a weak stimulant) is perhaps the most common. Dependency on opiate medications is a distinct risk with this population.

Obviously, the severe pain of a migraine or tension headache causes patients to be inattentive and unable to concentrate, and thus it is easy to ascribe all cognitive symptoms to the headache. But the reverse can be also true. Chronic unremitting symptoms of ADHD can overwhelm the patient. Inattention and distractibility can cause underperformance. The patient reports high levels of stress or anxiety, and this can be manifest as head pain. I speculate that there is a high rate of cooccurrence between ADHD and chronic headaches. In this situation, it is my experience that medically addressing the underlying ADHD favorably affects both conditions. This approach also allows for less reliance on controlled substances.

RESTLESS LEGS SYNDROME: HYPERACTIVITY GROWN UP?

Restless legs syndrome is a neurological disorder characterized by a uniquely unpleasant sensation in the lower extremities. Patients with RLS describe their symptoms as burning, creeping, or like having insects crawling under their skin, similar to the formication symptom experienced by some psychotic patients or individuals undergoing withdrawal from scheduled drugs. To combat the uncomfortable sensations, patients have the urge to move their legs or immerse them in hot or cold water. The symptoms can be painful throughout the day, but they are often much worse in the quiet of the night. They can cause insomnia and nonrestorative sleep, which drives the cycle of daytime sleepiness.

Restless legs syndrome may affect up to 12 million Americans, women slightly more often than men. The incidence increases with age, with peak prevalence in the middle age. Most of the time, the underlying cause of RLS is unknown, although a minority of cases can be traced to medication side effects, anemia, or pregnancy. Chronic diseases like kidney failure, Parkinson's disease, and complications from long-standing diabetes have also been associated with RLS.

Conventional Treatments

Over the years, many RLS treatments have been employed, including low-dose benzodiazepines (for anxiety and muscle relaxation), anticonvulsants, and opiates for pain. More recently, dopaminergic agents associated with the treatment of Parkinson's disease have been studied for RLS. In 2005 the FDA approved ropinorole (Requip), a dopamine receptor agonist, for the treatment of RLS. Similar medications in this class are under review. The fact that this class of medication is helpful supports the theory that RLS and ADHD need to be thought of in a similar way.

The Link Between ADHD and Restless Legs Syndrome

As with FMS, CFS, IBS, chronic headaches, and tinnitus I have noticed high rates of ADHD predominately hyperactive type in patients who develop RLS. Should RLS be viewed as nighttime hyperactivity? Is RLS simply hyperactive ADHD grown up? There are many similarities clinically between the two conditions. All RLS and some ADHD patients complain of being unable to settle in bed and fall asleep. Both conditions result from dopamine deficiency and both respond to medications that modulate dopamine transmission. Furthermore, both ADHD and RLS patients paradoxically settle down when taking activating dopaminergic medications. The similarities, clinically and in treatment response, suggest a common pathological mechanism.

TINNITUS

Tinnitus is a neurological condition connected to the ear. It is characterized by a perception of a ringing or beating sound with no evident external source. The sounds are reported to be variable, sometimes quiet and sometimes loud enough to drown out all outside noise. Sometimes the tinnitus is measurable, but more often it is a subjective complaint. Tinnitus causes a great deal of suffering. Frequent visits to ear doctors are typical.

Like the other nebulous medical conditions described earlier in this chapter, no single entity has been linked to the cause of tinnitus. Sudden hearing loss, head injury, and some medications, notably aspirin, have been correlated. The mechanisms underlying subjective tinnitus are obscure. Most theories propose trauma to the inner ear or the innervating acoustic nerve, but it is difficult to prove this. For types of tinnitus caused by disorders outside the anatomy of the ear, the condition may be due to "central crosstalk," a diffuse miswiring of neurological input into the brain's hearing centers.

Also, like the other conditions discussed, tinnitus is worsened by an individual's stress perception. That said, although clinical recommendations to reduce stress are easy to prescribe, they are difficult to implement. Tinnitus remains a huge burden to those afflicted. In my limited experience in these patients who also have ADHD, conventional treatment of the ADHD improves this processing problem. Success has been more limited in these patients than in IBS or RLS, but when it has been helpful, it is too dramatic not to report.

ASK PATIENTS ABOUT CHRONIC PAIN SYNDROMES

Although the clinical interview is paramount, rating scales used to assess chronic conditions are also instructive. ADHD and mood scales, including the Hawthorne Self-Report Version Rating Scale and the Zung Depression Scale, should be administered to all patients with complaints of muscle pain or fatigue. In addition, the Fibromyalgia Impact Questionnaire and the Minnesota Pain Inventory can demonstrate baseline levels of pain and impairment. The Eppworth Sleepiness Scale helps to identify levels of daytime fatigue.

WE NEED TO KNOW MORE

It is important to note that the hypotheses asserted in this chapter—that the poorly understood conditions of FM, CFS, IBS, RLS, and headache are associated with ADHD and that chronic pain and fatigue conditions are central (brain) processes rather than peripheral (end organ) processes— are only preliminary in nature. It cannot be overemphasized that much more research needs to be done on both the epidemiological and cellular level before anything conclusive can be stated. There is currently insufficient proof that ADHD plays a central role in pain syndromes or chronic fatigue, despite the case studies, clinical studies, and theoretical framework presented in this chapter. The intention of this chapter is to illuminate interesting observations, pose an evidence of linkage, and generally raise questions—but by no means to suggest anything beyond this.

A long process separates a working theory from clinical practice. If ADHD is proven to be a common factor in any of these chronic conditions, primary-care physicians, rheumatologists, otolaryngologists, and other specialists will need to adopt psychotropic medications. This seems unlikely, but there is precedence for this type of shift. Two decades ago, most doctors did not treat clinical depression. Now more than half of all prescriptions of antidepressants are written by nonpsychiatrists.

Physicians need to be advocates for their patients. The special populations described in this chapter often are overlooked. They suffer for long periods and often feel desperate and marginalized by their caregivers. I believe that the prospective relationship of ADHD to these nebulous conditions deserves greater scrutiny.

APPENDICES

Self-Evaluation for ADHD

Answer "yes" or "no" to the following questions and then review what your answers may mean. Remember, however, that only a mental health professional or a physician can diagnose you with ADHD, and if you do have ADHD, only treatment will help you improve your symptoms. If the test suggests that you may have ADHD, you should consult a trained mental health professional for further evaluation.

1. Do you lose important items (like your car keys or wallet) once a week or more?
2. Have you forgotten one or more appointments or meetings in the past month?
3. In the past month, have you said something without thinking, causing embarrassment to you or to others, more than once?
4. Do people sometimes ask you what you are staring at when you are merely lost in thought and are not really staring at anything?
5. If someone in a group is most likely to decide to do something on the spur of the moment, is that person you?
6. Do you have a problem with credit card bills because you bought items that you felt you just had to have at the time?
7. Have you been fired from one or more jobs in the past 2 years when the company was not having a general layoff? (And you were the only person or one of the few who was fired?)

8. Has your spouse or partner complained to you sometimes that you are not really listening?
9. Have you ever forgotten to pick up your children or drop them off, as scheduled?
10. Do you start many projects but finish few of them (or none)?

If you answered "yes" to two or more questions, you may have ADHD and should consult with a trained mental health professional.

Adult ADHD Self-Report Scale-V1.1 (ASRS-V1.1) Screener*

*This screener is intended for people ages 18 years or older.

Date					
Check the box that best describes how you have felt and conducted yourself over the past 6 months. Please give the complete questionnaire to your healthcare professional during your next appointment to discuss the results.	Never	Rarely	Sometimes	Often	Very Often
1. How often do you have trouble wrapping up the final details of a project, once the challenging parts have been done?					
2. How often do you have difficulty getting things in order when you have to do a task that requires organization?					
3. How often do you have problems remembering appointments or obligations?					
4. When you have a task that requires a lot of thought, how often do you avoid or delay getting started?					
5. How often do you fidget or squirm with your hands or feet when you have to sit down for a long time?					
6. How often do you feel overly active and compelled to do things, like you were driven by a motor?					

Kessler, R. C., Adler, L., Ames, M., Demler, O., Faraone, S., Hiripi, E., Howes, M. J., Jin, R., Secnik, K., Spencer, T., Ustun, T. B., Walters, E. E. (2005). The World Health Organization Adult ADHD Self-Report Scale (ASRS). *Psychological Medicine, 35*(2), 245–256.

Add the number of checkmarks that appear in the darkly shaded area. Four (4) or more checkmarks indicate that your symptoms may be consistent with Adult ADHD. It may be beneficial for you to talk with your healthcare provider about an evaluation.

Appendix C

Adult ADHD Self-Report Scale (ASRS) Symptom Checklist and Instructions

The Symptom Checklist is an instrument consisting of the 18 *DSM-IV-TR* criteria for ADHD.

The questions below are designed to stimulate dialogue between you and your patients and to help confirm if they may be suffering from the symptoms of attention-deficit/hyperactivity disorder (ADHD). Physicians should consider using Symptom Checklist for patients whom they have reason to believe might have ADHD. This could be based on results of a screening instrument or if the patient presents with symptoms that may be consistent with ADHD.

1. **Provide the symptom checklist to the patient** [without the scoring algorithm]

   Ask the patient to complete it prior to the exam.

2. **Assess the patient's symptoms, impairments, and history**

   Assess symptoms

   - Add the patient's score for Part A (Inattentive)
   - Add the patient's score for Part B (Hyperactive/Impulsive)
   - If the score is in the likely or highly likely category for either Part A or Part B, the patient has symptoms consistent with ADHD and a more thorough clinical evaluation to understand impairments and history is warranted.
   - If the score is in the unlikely category for either Part A or Part B, but you still suspect ADHD, consider evaluating them for impairments based on the symptoms present. Sometimes adults with ADHD suffer significant impairment due to only a few symptoms.
   - An adult with ADHD may have symptoms that manifest quite differently when compared with a child. The ASRS checklist reflects the adult manifestation of ADHD symptoms.

   Assess Impairments

   Review the checklist with your patients and evaluate any impairments in the work/school, social, and family settings.

   Symptom frequency is often associated with symptom severity, and, therefore, the ASRS checklist may also aid in the assessment of impairments. If your patients have frequent symptoms, you may want to ask them to describe how this problem has affected the ability to work, take care of things at home, or get along with other people such as their spouse/significant other. This discussion will provide details about the extent of the impairments.

Assess History

Consider assessing the presence of these symptoms or similar symptoms in childhood. Adults who have ADHD need not have been formally diagnosed in childhood. In evaluating a patient's history, look for evidence of early-appearing and long-standing problems with attention or self-control. Some significant symptoms should have been present in childhood, but full symptomology is not necessary.

Request to see school report cards. But remember, many adults attended school at a time when ADHD and its symptoms were not commonly identified. Consider more than grades alone; often, written comments on the report card are of the most value. If report cards are not available, you might ask questions such as, "If I were a teacher, how would I describe you in class?" and "If I looked at your grade school report card, what would I read?"

3. **Keep the symptom checklist in the patient's file for future reference.**

Score	Evaluation
0–16	Unlikely to have ADHD
17–23	Likely to have ADHD
24 or greater	Highly likely to have ADHD

Adult Self-Report Scale (ASRS) Symptom Checklist

Patient Name	Today's Date					

Please answer the questions below, rating yourself on each of the criteria shown using the scale on the right side of the page. As you answer each question, circle the correct number that best describes how you have felt and conducted yourself over the past 6 months. Please give this completed checklist to your healthcare professional to discuss during today's appointment.	Never	Rarely	Sometimes	Often	Very Often	Score
1. How often do you make careless mistakes when you have to work on a boring or difficult project?	0	1	2	3	4	
2. How often do you have difficulty keeping your attention when you are doing boring or repetitive work?	0	1	2	3	4	
3. How often do you have difficulty concentrating on what people say to you, even when they are speaking to you directly?	0	1	2	3	4	
4. How often do you have trouble wrapping up the final details of a project, once the challenging parts have been done?	0	1	2	3	4	
5. How often do you have difficulty getting things in order when you have to do a task that requires organization?	0	1	2	3	4	
6. When you have a task that requires a lot of thought, how often do you avoid or delay getting started?	0	1	2	3	4	
7. How often do you misplace or have difficulty finding things at work or at home?	0	1	2	3	4	
8. How often are you distracted by activity or noise around you?	0	1	2	3	4	
9. How often do you have problems remembering appointments or obligations?	0	1	2	3	4	
				Part A—Total		
10. How often do you fidget or squirm with your hands or feet when you have to sit down for a long time?	0	1	2	3	4	
11. How often do you leave your seat in meetings or other situations in which you are expected to remain seated?	0	1	2	3	4	
12. How often do you feel restless or fidgety?	0	1	2	3	4	
13. How often do you have difficulty unwinding and relaxing when you have time to yourself?	0	1	2	3	4	
14. How often do you feel overly active and compelled to do things, like you were driven by a motor?	0	1	2	3	4	
15. How often do you find yourself talking too much when you are in social situations?	0	1	2	3	4	
16. When you're in a conversation, how often do you find yourself finishing the sentences of the people you are talking to, before they can finish them themselves?	0	1	2	3	4	
17. How often do you have difficulty waiting your turn in situations when turn taking is required?	0	1	2	3	4	
18. How often do you interrupt others when they are busy?	0	1	2	3	4	
				Part B—Total		

References

Aaron, L. A., & Buchwald, D. (2003). Chronic diffuse musculoskeletal pain, fibromyalgia and co-morbid unexplained conditions. *Best Practice & Research Clinical Rheumatology, 17*(4), 563–574.

Alpert, J. E., Maddocks, A., Nierenberg, A. A., O'Sullivan, R., Pava, J. A., Worthington, J. J., Biederman, J., Rosenbaum, J. F., & Fava, M. (1996, June). Attention deficit hyperactivity disorder in childhood among adults with major depression. *Psychiatry Research, 62*(3), 213–219.

Altfas, J. R. (2002). Prevalence of attention deficit/hyperactivity disorder among adults in obesity treatment [On-line]. *BMC Psychiatry, 2*:1–7. Retrieved May 15, 2005 from http://www.biomedcentral.com/content/pdf/1471-244X-2-9.pdf

Amann, B. (2005, October 15). Hyperactive boys, inattentive girls, tired women, angry men. Lecture at Oakland Community College, Farmington Hills, Michigan.

Amen, D. G. (2001). *Healing ADD: The breakthrough program that allows you to see and heal the 6 types of ADD.* New York: Putnam.

American Psychiatric Association. (2000). *Diagnostic and statistical manual of mental disorders* (text revision 4th ed.). Washington, DC: Author.

Anders, T., & Shaftstein, S. (2006). To the editor. *New England Journal of Medicine, 352*(21), 2296.

Anttila, S., & Leinonen, E. (2002, August). Duloxetine Eli Lilly. *Current Opinion in Investigational Drugs, 3*(8), 1217–1221.

Applegate, B., Lahey, B. B., Hart, E. L., Biederman, J., Hynd, G. W., Barkley, R. A., Ollendick, T., Frick, P. J., Greenhill, L., McBurnett, K., Newcom, J. H., Kerdyk, L., Garfinkel, B., Waldman, I., & Shaffer, D. (1997). Validity of the age-of-onset criterion for AD/HD: A report from the DSM-IV field trials. *Journal of the American Academy of Child and Adolescent Psychiatry, 36*, 1211–1221.

Arnold, L. E. (1996). Sex differences in AD/HD: Conference summary. *Journal of Abnormal Child Psychology, 24*, 555–569.

Arnold, P. D., Ickowitz, A., Chen, S., & Schachar, R. (2005). Attention-deficit hyperactivity disorder with and without obsessive-compulsive behaviours: Clinical characteristics, cognitive assessment, and risk factors. *Canadian Journal of Psychiatry, 50*(1), 59–66.

Ashtin J. B. Group. (2004, July 23). *Question and answer forum based on the roundtable meeting on a closer look at substance use disorders in individuals with ADHD.* Ann Arbor: Office of Continuing Medical Education, University of Michigan Medical School.

Ashtin J. B. Group. (2005). *A closer look at substance use disorders in individuals with ADHD*. Ann Arbor: Office of Continuing Medical Education, University of Michigan Medical School.

Barkley, R. A. (2002). Major life activity and health outcomes associated with attention-deficit/hyperactivity disorder. *Journal of Clinical Psychiatry, 63*(Suppl. 12), 10–15.

Barkley, R. A. (2004). Driving impairments in teens and adults with attention-deficit/hyperactivity disorder. *Psychiatric Clinics of North America, 27*, 233–260.

Barkley, R. A., DuPaul, G. J., & McMurray, M. B. (1990). Comprehensive evaluation of attention deficit disorder with and without hyperactivity as defined by research criteria. *Journal of Consulting and Clinical Psychology, 58*, 775–789.

Barkley, R. A., Fischer, M., Smallish, L., & Fletcher, K. (2003). Does the treatment of attention-deficit/hyperactivity disorder with stimulants contribute to drug use/abuse? A 13-year prospective study. *Pediatrics, 111*, 97–109.

Barkley, R. A., Guevremont, D. C., Anastopoulos, A. D., DuPaul, G. J., & Shelton, T. L. (1993). Driving-related risks and outcomes of attention deficit hyperactivity disorder in adolescents and young adults: A 3–5 year followup survey. *Pediatrics, 92*, 212–218.

Barkley, R. A., Murphy, K. R., & Kwasnik, D. (1996, December). Motor vehicle driving competences and risks in teens and young adults with attention deficit hyperactivity disorder. *Pediatrics, 98*(6), 1089–1098.

Bellak, L. (Ed.). (1979). *Psychiatric aspects of minimal brain dysfunction in adults*. New York: Grune & Stratton.

Biederman, J. (2003a). Pharmacotherapy for attention-deficit/hyperactivity disorder (ADHD) decreases the risk for substance abuse: Findings from a longitudinal follow-up of youths with and without ADHD. *Journal of Clinical Psychiatry, 64*(Suppl. 11), 3–8.

Biederman, J. (2003b). New generation long-acting stimulants for the treatment of attention-deficit/hyperactivity disorder [On-line]. Retrieved July 17, 2005 from http://www.medscape.com/viewarticle/464377

Biederman, J. (2004). Impact of comorbidity in adults with attention deficit/hyperactivity disorder. *Journal of Clinical Psychiatry, 65*(Suppl. 3), 3–7.

Biederman, J., & Faraone, S. V. (2004). The Massachusetts General Hospital Study of gender influences on attention-deficit/hyperactivity disorder on youth and relatives, (2004). *Psychiatric Clinics of North America, 217*, 225–232.

Biederman, J., Faraone, S. V., & Chen, W. J. (1993). Social adjustment inventory for children and adolescents: Concurrent validity in ADHD children. *Journal American Academy of Child and Adolescent Psychiatry, 32*(5), 1059–1064.

Biederman, J., Faraone, S. V., Spencer, T., Wilens, R., Norman, D., Lapey, K. A., Mick, E., Lehman, B. K., & Doyle, A. (1993). Patterns of psychiatric comorbidity, cognition and psychosocial functioning in adults with attention deficit hyperactivity disorder. *American Journal of Psychiatry, 150*, 1792–1798.

Biederman, J., Lopez, F. A., Boellner, S. W., & Chandler, M. C. (2002). A randomized, double-blind, placebo-controlled group study of SLI 381 (Adderall XL) in children with attention-deficit/hyperactivity disorder. *Pediatrics, 110*, 258–265.

Biederman, J., Wilens, T., Mick, E., Faraone, S. V., Weber, W., Curtis S., Thornell, A., Pfister, K., Jetton, J. G., & Soriano, J. (1997). Is ADHD a risk factor for psychoactive substance use disorders? Findings from a four-year prospective follow-up study. *Journal of the American Academy of Child & Adolescent Psychiatry, 36*(1), 21–29.

Biederman, J., Wilens, T., Mick, E., Milberger, S., Spencer, T. J., & Faraone, S. V. (1995). Psychoactive substance use disorder in adults with attention deficit hyperactivity disorder (ADHD): Effects of ADHD and psychiatric comorbidity. *American Journal of Psychiatry, 52*(11), 1652–1658.

Biederman, J., Wilens, T., Mick, E., Spencer, T., & Faraone, S. V. (1999). Pharmacotherapy of attention-deficit/hyperactivity disorder reduces risk for substance use disorder [On-line]. Retrieved January 31, 2005 from http://www.pediatrics.org/cgi/content/full/104/2/e20

Braun, D. L., Dulit, R. A., Adler, D. A., Berlant, J., Dixon, L., Fornari, V., Goldman, B., Hermann, R., Siris, S. G., Sonis, W. A., & Richter, D. (2004). Attention-deficit/hyperactivity disorder in adults: Clinical information for primary care physicians. *Primary Psychiatry, 11*(9), 56–65.

Brown, L. K., Houck, C. D., Hadley, W. S., & Lescano, C. M. (February 2005). Self-cutting and sexual risks among adolescents in intensive psychiatric treatment. *Psychiatric Services, 56,* 216–218.

Brown, T. E. (Ed.). (2000). *Attention-deficit disorders and comorbidities in children, adolescents, and adults.* Washington, DC: American Psychiatric Press.

Bush, G. (2002). Functioning and structural neuroimaging. In Veritas Institute for Medical Education (Ed.), *Adult Attention-Deficit Hyperactivity Disorder from Research to Clinical Practice* (pp. 25–31). Hasbrouck Heights, NJ: MedLearning, Inc.

Bussing, R., Halfon, N., Benjamin, B., & Wells, K. B. (1995). Prevalence of behavior problems in U.S. children with asthma. *Archives of Pediatric and Adolescent Medicine, 149*(5), 565–552.

Canaris, G. J., Manowitz, N. R., Mayor, G., & Ridgway, E. C. (2000). The Colorado Thyroid Disease Prevalence Study. *Archives of Internal Medicine, 160,* 526–534.

Carey, B. (2006, February 21). Heart risks with stimulant use? Maybe. Worry? For some. *New York Times,* p. D1.

Centers for Disease Control and Prevention (n. d.). Chronic fatigue syndrome [On-line]. Retrieved on March 1, 2006 from http://www.cdc.gov/ncidod/diseases/cfs

Connor, D. F., Barkley, R. A., & Davis, H. T. (2000). A pilot study of methylphenidate, clonidine, or the combination in ADHD comorbid with aggressive oppositional defiant or conduct disorder. *Clinical Pediatrics, 39*(1), 15–25.

Cox, D. J., Merkel, R. L., Kovatchev, B., & Seward, R. (2000). Effect of stimulant medication on driving performance of young adults with attention-deficit/hyperactivity disorder: A preliminary double-blind, placebo-controlled trial. *Journal of Nervous and Mental Disorder, 188,* 230–234.

Cuffe, S., Moore, C., & McKeown, R. (2003, October 20). ADHD symptoms in the National Health Interview Survey: prevalence, correlates, and use of services and medication. Poster presented to the Fiftieth Anniversary Meeting of the American Academy of Child and Adolescent Psychiatry, Miami, FL.

Dey, A. N., & Bloom, B. (2005). *Summary health statistics for U.S. children: National Health Interview Survey, 2003.* Hyattsville, MD: National Center for Health Statistics.

Dodson, W. W. (2005). Pharmacotherapy of adult AD/HD. *Journal of Clinical Psychology, 61,* 589–606.

Dukarm, C. P. (2005). Bulimia nervosa and attention deficit disorder: A possible role for stimulant medication. (2005). *Journal of Women's Health (Larchmont), 14*(4), 345–350.

Edwards, G., Barkley, R. A., Laneri, M., Fletcher, K., & Melevia, L. (2001). Parent-adolescent conflict in teenagers with ADHD and ODD. *Journal of Abnormal Child Psychology, 29*(6), 557–572.

Eli Lilly, Lilly Research Laboratories. (2006). Effect of atomoxetine on social, school, emotions, problem solving and self-regulation in ADHD and comorbid anxiety. STR20060116B, release.

Eli Lilly & Company. (2005). Questions and answers about the Strattera label change [On-line]. Retrieved October 15, 2005 from http://www.strattera.com/pdf/qa_strattera_label_update.pdf

Evans, S. W., Pelham, W. E., Smith, B. H., Bukstein, O., Gnagy, E. M., Greiner, A. R., Altenderfer, L., & Baron-Myak, C. (2001). Dose-response effects of methylphenidate on ecologically valid measures of academic performance and classroom behavior in adolescents with ADHD. *Experimental and Clinical Psychopharmacology, 9*(2), 163–175.

Faraone, S. V. (2002). A genetic perspective on the validity of adult AD/HD. In Veritas Institute for Medical Education (Ed.), *Adult Attention-Deficit/Hyperactivity Disorder from Research to Clinical Practice,* 21–25. Hasbrouck Heights, NJ: MedLearning, Inc.

Faraone, S. V. (2003). Understanding the effect size of ADHD medications: Implications for clinical care [On-line]. Retrieved November 1, 2005 from http://www.medscape.com/viewarticle/461543

Faraone, S. V., Biederman, J. (2004, May 5). A controlled study of functional impairment in adults. Presented at the 157th Annual Meeting of the American Psychiatric Association, New York, NY.

Faraone, S. V., Spencer, T. J., Montano, C. B., & Biederman, J. (2004, June). Attention-deficit/hyperactivity disorder in adults: A survey of current practice in psychiatry and primary care. *Archives of Internal Medicine, 164,* 1221–1226.

Faraone, S. V., & Wilens, T. (2003). Does stimulant treatment lead to substance use disorders? *Journal of Clinical Psychiatry, 64*(Suppl. 11), 9–13.

Feinstein, C., & Aldershof, A. (1991). Developmental disorders of language and learning. In *Child and Adolescent Psychiatry.* Washington, DC: American Psychiatric Press.

Fischer, M., & Barkley, R. A. (2003). Childhood stimulant treatment and risk for later substance abuse. *Journal of Clinical Psychiatry, 64*(Suppl. 11), 19–23.

Fischer, M., Barkley, R. A., Edelbrock, C. S., & Smallish, L. (1990). The adolescent outcome of hyperactive children diagnosed by research criteria: Academic, attentional, and neuropsychological status. *Journal of Counseling and Clinical Psychology, 58,* 580–588.

Fones, C. S., Pollack, M. H., Susswein, L., & Otto, M. (May 2000). History of childhood attention deficit hyperactivity disorder (ADHD) features among adults with panic disorder. *Journal Affective Disorders, 58*(2), 99–106.

Fong, T. (2003). Self-mutilation [On-line]. *Current Psychiatry, 2*(2). Retrieved May 1, 2005 from http://www.currentpsychiatry.com/article_pages.asp?AID=599&UID=926

Food and Drug Administration (2004). Suicidality labeling language for antidepressants. Retrieved May 10, 2005, from http://www.fda.gov/cder/drug/antidepressants/label Template.pdf

Giwerc, David. (Producer), & Camoin, David & Camoin, Michael (Directors).(1999). *Me, My ADD Coach and I* [Motion picture]. United States: Videos for Change Productions. available at ADDCa.com

Goldberg, M. (n. d.). Chronic fatigue syndrome and its connection to ADD/ADHD [On-line unpublished paper]. Retrieved March 1, 2005 from http://www.neuroimmunedr/cp,/Articles/CFS_-_CFIDS/chronic.pdf

Grant, J. E., Kushner, M. G., & Kim, S. W. (2002). Pathological gambling and alcohol use disorder. *Alcohol Research & Health, 26*(2), 143–150.

Hollander, E., DeCaria, C. M., Mari, E., Wong, C. M., Mosovich, S., Grossman, R., & Begaz, T. (December 1998). Short-term single-blind fluvoxamine treatment of pathological gambling. *American Journal of Psychiatry, 155*(12), 1781–1783.

Holman, A. J., & Myers, R. R. (2005, August). A randomized, double blind, placebo-controlled trial of pramipexole, a dopamine agonist, in patients with fibromyalgia receiving concomitant medications. *Arthritis and Rheumatism, 52*(8), 2495–2505.

Hudson, J. I., Mangweth, B., Pope, H. G., Jr., De Col, C., Hausmann, A., Gutweniger, S., Laird, N. M., Biebl, W., & Tsuang, M. T. (2003). Family study of affective spectrum disorder. *Archives of General Psychiatry, 60,* 170–177.

Kaplan, B., & Sadock, V. A. (2003). *Synopsis of psychiatry: Behavior science/clinical psychiatry* (9th ed.). Philadelphia: Lippincott, Williams & Wilkins.

Kelly, K., & Ramundo, P. (1996). *You mean I'm not lazy, stupid or crazy?! A self-help book for adults with attention deficit disorder.* New York: Scribner.

Kelly, S., & Raymond, K. B. (1997). *The effect of race and gender on the identification of children with attention deficit hyperactivity disorder.* Ann Arbor, MI: UMI Company.

Kelly, T. M., Cornelius, J. R., & Clark, D. B. (2004). Psychiatric disorders and attempted suicide among adolescents with substance use disorders. *Drug and Alcohol Dependence, 73,* 87–97.

Kessler, R. C., Adler, L., Ames, M., Demler, O., Faraone, S., Hiripi, E., Howes, M. J., Jin, R., Secnik, K., Spencer, T., Ustun, T. B., & Walters, E. E. (2005). The World Health Organization adult ADHD self-report scale (ASRS). *Psychological Medicine, 35*(2), 245–256.

Konofal, E., Lecendreux, M., Arnulf, J., & Mouren, M. C. (2004). Iron deficiency in children with attention-deficit/hyperactivity disorder. *Archives of Pediatrics & Adolescent Medicine, 158*(12), 1112–1115.

Korn, M. (2004). Treatment for adult ADHD: A newsmaker interview with Timothy Wilens, M.D. [On-line]. Retrieved January 31, 2005 from http://www.medscape.com/viewarticle/477487

Levin, F. R., & Evans, S. M. (2001). Diagnostic and treatment issues in comorbid substance abuse and adult attention-deficit hyperactivity disorder. *Psychiatric Annals, 31*(5), 303–312.

Levin, F. R., Evans, S. M., McDowell, D. M., Brooks, D. J., & Nunes, E. (2002). Bupropion treatment for cocaine abuse and adult attention-deficit/hyperactivity disorder. *Journal of Addictive Diseases, 21*(2), 1–16.

Lilly Research Laboratories. (2006). A study of Strattera, a selective norepinephrine reuptake inhibitor, for the treatment of patients 8–17 years of age, with ADHD and a comorbid anxiety disorder.

Linehan, M. M. (1993). *Training manual for treating borderline personality disorder.* New York: Guilford.

Lippman, S., Mazour, I., & Shahab, H. (2001). Insomnia: Therapeutic approach. *Southern Medical Journal, 94,* 866–873.

Malcolm, R., Book, S., Moak, D., DeVane, L., & Czepowicz, V. (2002). Clinical applications of modafinil in stimulant abusers: Low abuse potential. *American Journal on Addictions, 11*(3), 247–249.

McCabe, S. E., Teter, C. J., & Boyd, C. J. (2004). The use, misuse and diversion of prescription stimulants among middle and high school students. *Substance Use and Misuse, 39*(7), 1095–1116.

McElroy, S. L. (2003). Citalopram in the treatment of binge-eating disorder: A placebo-controlled trial. *Journal of Clinical Psychiatry, 64,* 807–813.

Milberger, S., Biederman, J., Faraone, S. V., Chen, L., & Jones, J. (1997). ADHD is associated with early initiation of cigarette smoking in children and adolescents. *Journal of the American Academy of Child and Adolescent Psychiatry, 36*(1), 37–44.

Millstein, R., Wilens, T. E., Biederman, J., & Spencer, T. J. (1997). Presenting ADHD symptoms and subtypes in clinically referred adults. *Journal of Attention Disorders, 2,* 159–166.

Minocha, A., & Adamec, C. (2004). *The encyclopedia of the digestive system and digestive disorders.* New York: Facts On File.

Molina, B. S. G., & Pelham, W. E., Jr. (2003). Childhood predictors of adolescent substance use in a longitudinal study of children with ADHD. *Journal of Abnormal Psychology, 112*(2), 497–507.

Moline, S., & Frankenberger, W. (2001). Use of stimulant medication for treatment of attention deficit/hyperactivity disorder: A survey of middle and high school students' attitudes. *Psychology in the Schools, 38*(6), 569–584.

Morton, A. A., & Stockton, G. G. (2000). Methylphenidate abuse and psychiatric side effects. *Journal of Clinical Psychiatry, 2*(5), 159–164.

Murphy, K., & Barkley, R. A. (1996). Attention deficit hyperactivity disorder in adults: Comorbidities and adaptive impairments. *Comprehensive Psychiatry, 37*(6), 393–401.

Murphy, K. R., & Adler, L. A. (2004). Assessing attention-deficit/hyperactivity disorder in adults: Focus on rating scales. *Journal of Clinical Psychiatry, 65*(Suppl. 3), 12–17.

Musser, C. J., Ahmann, P. A., Theye, F. W., Mundt, P., Broste, S. K., & Mueller-Rizner, N. (1998). Stimulant use and the potential for abuse in Wisconsin as reported by school administrators and longitudinally followed children. *Journal of Developmental & Behavioral Pediatrics, 9*(3), 187–192.

Nadeau, K. G., & Quinn, P. O. (Eds.). (2002). *Understanding women with AD/HD.* Silver Spring, MD: Advantage Books.

National Women's Health Resource Center. (2003, February). ADHD & women's health. *National Women's Health Report, 25*(1), 1–8.

New York University School of Medicine. (2003, June 25). *Survey reveals adult ADHD often undiagnosed by primary care physicians.* Press release.

Nissen, S. E. (2006). ADHD drugs and cardiovascular risk. *New England Journal of Medicine, 351*(14), 1445–1448.

Othmer, E., & Othmer, S. (2002). *The Clinical Interview Using DSM-IV-TR. Volume 1: Fundamentals.* Washington, DC: American Psychiatric Association.

Pallanti, S., Quercioli, L., Soud, E., & Hollander, E. (2002). Lithium and valproate treatment of pathological gambling: A randomized single-blind study. *Journal of Clinical Psychiatry, 63,* 559–564.

Patel, N. C., & Sallee, F. R. (2005). What's the best treatment for comorbid ADHD/bipolar mania? [On-line] *Current Psychiatry Online, 4*(4). Retrieved May 23, 2005 from http://www.currentpsychiatry.com/article_pages.asp?AID=954&UID

Perwien, A. R., Hall, J., Swenson, A., & Swindle, R. (2004). Stimulant treatment patterns and compliance in children and adults with newly treated attention-deficit/hyperactivity disorder. *Journal of Managed Care Pharmacy, 10*(2), 122–129.

PhamaDeals Shire and New River: Buying up the Competition. (2006, March 5). Retrieved October 8, 2006, from http://www.pharmaventures.com/ag_demo/57_article1.pdf #search=%22non%20abusable%20Adderall%22.

Potenza, M. N., Kosten, T. R., & Rounsaville, B. J. (2001, July 11). Pathological gambling. *Journal of the American Medical Association, 286*(2), 141–144.

Poulin, C. (2001). Medical and nonmedical stimulant use among adolescents: From sanctioned to unsanctioned use. *Canadian Medical Association Journal, 165*(8), 1039–1044.

Poulton, A. (August 2005). Growth on stimulant medication: Clarifying the confusion, a review. *Archives of Disease in Childhood, 90*, 801–806.

Quinn, P. (2002). Hormonal influences on women with AD/HD. In Nadeau, K. G. & Quinn, P. O. (Ed.), *Understanding Women with AD/HD* (pp. 86–102). Silver Spring, MD: Advantage Books.

Quinn, P. (2005). Treating adolescent girls and women with ADHD: Gender-specific issues. *Journal of Clinical Psychology/In Session, 61*(5), 579–587.

Quinn, P., & Wigal, S. (2004, May 4). Perceptions of girls and ADHD: Results from a national survey [On-line]. Retrieved June 22, 2005 from http://www.medscape.com/viewarticle/472415

Quinn, P. O., & Nadeau, K. G. (2002). *Gender issues and AD/HD: Research, diagnosis, and treatment.* Altamonte Springs, FL: Advantage Books.

Ratey, N. A. (2002). Life coaching for adult ADHD. In S. Goldstein & A. Teeter Ellison (Eds.), *Clinician's guide to adult ADHD: assessment and intervention* (pp. 261–277). San Diego, CA: Academic Press.

Reiff, M. I., &Tippins, S. (Eds.). (2004). *ADHD: A complete and authoritative guide.* Elk Grove Village, IL: American Academy of Pediatrics.

Rief, Sandra F. (Director). (1996). *ADHD: Inclusive Instruction and Collaborative Practices* [Motion picture]. United States: National Professional Resources.

Ringdahl, E. N., Pereira, S. L., & Delzell, J. R., Jr. (2004). Treatment of primary insomnia. *Journal of the American Board of Family Practice, 17*, 212–219.

Robin, A. L. (1998). *ADHD in adolescents: Diagnosis and treatment.* New York: Guilford.

Rosack, J. (2006, January 6). Methylphenidate skin patch approved for ADHD. *Psychiatric News, 41*, 37.

Rucklidge, J. J., & Tannock, R. (2001). Psychiatric, psychosocial, and cognitive functioning of female adolescents with ADHD. *Journal of the American Academy of Child and Adolescent Psychiatry, 40*(5), 530–540.

Safren, S. A., Sprich, S., Chulvick, S., & Otto, M. W. (2004). Psychosocial treatments for adults with attention-deficit/hyperactivity disorder. *Psychiatric Clinics of North America, 27*, 349–360.

Scheffer, R. E., & Niskala Apps, J. (2005). ADHD or bipolar disorder? Age-specific manic symptoms are the key. *Current Psychiatry, 4*(5), 42–52.

Schubiner, H. (2005). Substance abuse in patients with attention-deficit hyperactivity disorder: Therapeutic implications. *CNS Drugs, 19*(8): 643–655.

Schubiner, H., Robin, A. L., & Young, J. (2003). Attention-deficit/hyperactivity disorder in adolescent males. *Adolescent Medicine, 14*(3), 663–676.

Shaywitz, B. A., & Shaywitz, S. E. (1989). *Learning disabilities and attention disorders.* In K. F. Swaimar (Ed.), *Pediatric Neurology: Principles and Practice* (pp. 857–890). St. Louis, MO: C.V. Mosby.

Sheehan, D. V., Lecrubier, Y., Harnett-Sheehan, K., Janaus, J., Weiller, E., Bonora, L. I., Keskiner, A., Schinka, J., Knapp, E., Sheehan, M. F., & Dunbar, G. C. (1997). The reliability and validity of the Mini International Neuropsychiatric Interview (MINI) according to SCIP-P. *European Psychiatry, 12*, 232–241.

Simms, R. W., Roy, S. H., Hrovat, M., Anderson, J. J., Skrinar, G., LePoole, S. K., Zerbini, C. A., de Luca, C., & Jolesz, F. (1994, June). Lack of association between fibromyalgia syndrome and abnormality in muscle energy metabolism. *Arthritis and Rheumatism, 37*(6), 790–794.

Smith, B. H., Molina, B. S. G., & Pelham, W. E., Jr. (2002). The clinically meaningful link between alcohol use and attention deficit hyperactivity disorder. *Alcohol Research & Health, 26*(2), 122–129.

Solden, S. (1995). *Women with attention deficit disorder: Embracing disorganization at home and in the workplace.* Grass Valley, CA: Underwood Books.

Spencer, T. J., Biederman, J., Ciccone, P. E., Madras, B. K., Dougherty, D. D., Bonab, A. A., Livni, E., Parasrampuria, D. A., & Fischman, A. T. (2006, March). PET study examining pharmacokinetics, detection and likeability, and dopamine transporter receptor occupancy of short- and long-acting oral methylphenidate. *American Journal of Psychiatry, 163*(3), 387–395.

Stahl, S. M. (2002). The psychopharmacology of energy and fatigue. *The Journal of Clinical Psychiatry, 63*(1), 7–8.

Stahl, S. M. (2005). *Essential psychopharmacology: The prescriber's guide.* Cambridge, U.K.: Cambridge University Press.

Staud, R., & Adamec, C. (2002). *Fibromyalgia for dummies.* New York: Wiley.

Stein, M. A. (2004). Innovations in attention-deficit/hyperactivity disorder pharmacotherapy: Long-acting stimulant and nonstimulant treatments. *The American Journal of Managed Care, 10*(4), Suppl. S89–S98.

Stoner, S. C., Dubisar, B. M., & Strong, S. (2003, September). Management of attention-deficit hyperactivity disorder in children and adults [On-line]. Retrieved November 23, 2004 from http://www.uspharmacist.com/print.asp?page=ce/2912/default.htm

Triolo, S. J. (1999). *Attention deficit hyperactivity disorder in adulthood: A practitioner's handbook.* New York: Brunner/Mazel.

Turner, D. C., Clark, L., Dawson, J., Robbins, T., & Sahakian, B. (2004). Modafinil improves cognition and response inhibition in adult attention-deficit/hyperactivity disorder. *Biological Psychiatry, 55,* 1031–1041.

Verispan Research, prepared for Shire, Inc. (2003, October). *A quantitative phone survey of 250 physicians who treat ADHD in adults in the U.S.*

Visser, S. N., & Lesesne, C. A. (September 2, 2005). Mental health in the United States: Prevalence of diagnosis and medication treatment for attention deficit/hyperactivity disorder—United States. *Mortality and Morbidity Weekly Review, 54*(34), 842–847.

Volkow, N. D., Wang, G. J., Fowler, J. S., Ding, Y. S. (2005). Imaging the effects of methylphenidate on brain dopamine: New model on its therapeutic actions for attention-deficit/hyperactivity disorder. *Biological Psychiatry, 7*(11), 1410–1415.

Weiss, G., & Trokenberg Hechtman, L. (1993). *Hyperactive children grown up: ADHD in children, adolescents, and adults* (2nd ed.). New York: Guilford.

Weiss, M., Trokenberg Hechtman, L., & Weiss, G. (1999). *ADHD in adulthood: A guide to current theory, diagnosis, and treatment.* Baltimore: Johns Hopkins University Press.

Weiss, M. D., & Weiss, J. R. (2004). A guide to the treatment of adults with ADHD. *Journal of Clinical Psychiatry, 65*(Suppl. 3), 27–37.

Wilens, T. E. (2004a). Attention-deficit/hyperactivity disorder and the substance use disorders: The nature of the relationship, who is at risk, and treatment issues. *Primary Psychiatry, 11*(7), 63–70.

Wilens, T. E. (2004b). Attention-deficit/hyperactivity disorder and the substance use disorders: The nature of the relationship, subtypes at risk, and treatment issues. *Psychiatric Clinics of North America, 27,* 283–301.

Wilens, T. E. (2004c). Impact of ADHD and its treatment on substance abuse in adults. *Journal of Clinical Psychiatry, 65*(Suppl. 3), 38–45.

Wilens, T. E., Faraone, S. V., & Biederman, J. (2004, August 4). Attention-deficit/hyperactivity disorder in adults. *Journal of the American Medical Association, 292*(6), 619–623.

Wilens, T. E., Gignac, M., Swezey, A., Monuteaux, M. C., & Biederman, J. (2006). Characteristics of adolescents and young adults with ADHD who divert or misuse their prescribed medications. *Journal of the American Academy of Child & Adolescent Psychiatry, 45*(4), 408–414.

Wilens, T. E., Faraone, S. V., Biederman, J., & Gunawardene, S. (2003). Does stimulant therapy of attention-deficit/hyperactivity disorder beget later substance abuse? A meta-analytic review of the literature. *Pediatrics, 111,* 179–185.

Yee, J. D., & Bere, C. B. (2004, February). Dextroamphetamine or methylphenidate as adjuvants to opioid analgesia for adolescents with cancer. *Journal of Pain Symptom Management, 9*(2), 122–125.

Young, J. (2002). Depression and anxiety in women with AD/HD. In Quinn, P. O., & Nadeau, K. G. (Eds.), *Gender issues and AD/HD: Research, diagnosis and treatment* (pp. 270–291). Silver Spring, MD: Advantage Books.

Young, J. (2006, October). ADHD/fibromyalgia and chronic pain issues. Michael Gold Memorial Conference Paper presented at Oakland Community College, Farmington, Hills, Michigan.

Young, J. L. (2003). Nonstimulant treatment options for ADHD. In J. Biederman (Ed.), *ADHD: New ADHD treatment options for optimizing outcomes (Pt. 3)* (pp. 29–36). Boston: Veritas Institute for Medical Education.

Young, J., Amann, B., & Lenhardt, K. (2006, October). *Use of methylphenidate in treatment resistant depression.* Poster presented at the Institute on Psychiatric Services conference, New York.

Young, J. L. (2005). AD/HD: *Not just a child's disorder* [Educational video]. (Available from ADD Coach Academy at addca.com)

Young, J. L., & Giwerc, D. (2003, December). Just what is coaching? *Attention Magazine, 10*(2), 36–45.

Young, Joel (Producer) Cicurel, Sari. (Director). (2005). *ADHD: Not Just a Child's Disorder* [Motion picture]. United States: available at ADDCa.com

Index

Aaron, L., 278
access to care, 153–154
adaptation, 252
Adderall, 223, 225–226
Adderall XR, 194, 212, 224
addiction
    clinical features, 183
    gambling, 192
    patient concerns, 249
    stimulant use and, 183, 185–186
    see also substance use/abuse
adolescents
    acting-out behaviors, 137–139
    aptitudes and interests, 121
    assessment instruments, 119–121
    attitudes toward treatment, 75
    compliance issues, 130–131, 149–150
    confidentiality issues, 121
    course of ADHD, 139
    depression in, 114
    diagnostic challenges, 113–114, 115–117
    diversion and misuse of prescribed drugs,
        106–107, 183–185, 197–199
    fear of therapy, 132–135, 249–251
    female patients, 144–145
    hyperactive-impulsive type ADHD in, 70–75
    inattentive type ADHD in, 92–95
    initial interview, 121
    interviewing strategies, 121–125
    learning disabilities in, 120–121
    medical assessment, 119
    medication non-compliance, 204
    motor vehicle operations, 72–73, 140
    offensive language, 129–130
    parental involvement in therapy, 135–136,
        144, 151–152
    parental understanding of ADHD, 141–144
    peer relationships, 139–140
    prescribing trends, 211
    presentation, 114–115
    resistance to therapy, 125–131, 150–151
    self-injurious behaviors, 194–195

sexual behavior, 125, 140–141
smoking behavior, 123
substance use, 73–74
therapeutic relationship, 115, 118–119, 121
treatment, 145–154
adult ADHD
    with children without ADHD, 89
    help-seeking motivation, 75–80
    inattentive or combined type, 89–92
    misuse of prescribed drugs, 200–203
    prevalence, 3
    problem behaviors, 180
    public knowledge and understanding,
        109–110
    risk of progression from childhood ADHD,
        102
    therapist attitudes and beliefs, 82, 100, 101,
        102
    undiagnosed population, 3
Adult ADHD Self-Report Scale Symptom
        Checklist, 41, 299–302
Adult ADHD Self-Report Scale V1.1 Screener,
        41, 297–298
affective spectrum disorder, 277
aggressive behavior, 61
    adolescent acting-out, 137–139
alpha 2 agonists, 213, 228–229, 236–237
Amann, B., 82
Amen, Daniel, 25
amitriptyline, 235
amphetamines
    abuse potential, 228
    dosing, 239–240, 247–248
    formulations, 217, 223–224
    mechanism of action, 222–223
    new forms, 228
    screening for, 24
    see also stimulants
anger
    adolescent acting-out behaviors, 137
    overreaction to criticism, 60
    symptoms of ADHD, 20–21

antidepressant medications, 228–229
    suicide risk, 236
    see also specific class of drugs; specific drug
antisocial personality disorder
    ADHD and, 72
    comorbid ADHD, 45, 61
anxiety and anxiety disorders
    in affective spectrum disorder, 277
    assessment, 42–43
    atomoxetine effects, 231
    comorbid ADHD, 45, 54–55, 88
    in females with ADHD, 171
    prevalence in ADHD, 46, 54
argumentativeness, 124
    adolescent patient, 130
assessment
    adolescent interviewing strategies, 121–125
    adolescent presentation, 114–115
    anxiety, 42–43
    behavioral, 9–10, 15–21
    body language, 13–14
    childhood history, 30
    chronic pain conditions, 291
    closing initial session, 15
    comorbid disorders, 48–51
    depression, 42
    disorganization, 17, 33–34
    displays of anger, 20–21
    distractibility, 17, 34–35
    drug-seeking patient, 201–202
    family history, 29
    female patient, 174–176
    forgetfulness, 37
    functional outcomes of treatment, 95–96
    gender considerations, 159
    hyperactivity, 6–9, 16, 35–37, 85
    impulsivity, 20, 31–33
    individual differences in ADHD manifesta-
tions, 31
    instruments, 37–43, 119–121, 166
    laboratory tests, 24–25
    learning disabilities, 120–121
    listening strategies for, 11–15
    marital problems, 28
    medical history, 22–27, 123–124
    mental focus, 17
    monitoring, 243
    mood lability, 60–61
    normal adolescent behavior vs. ADHD,
115–117
    onset of symptoms, 21
    patient attributions for blame, 19
    patient educational videos, 43
    patient timeliness, 17–18
    potential for misuse of prescribed drugs,
199–200
    problem formulation, 10–11, 14
    psychosocial functioning, 26–29
    school and social life, 117–118, 122–123
    school performance, 27–28, 136–137
    self-evaluation for ADHD, 295–296
    self-referring patient, 80
    significance of stimulant effects, 4–5
    for stimulant therapy, 225
    substance use, 23–24, 26–27, 184–185
    symptoms, 5
    targeted questions, 21–22
    tendency to lose or misplace things, 17
    work and professional behaviors, 27
    see also diagnosis
atomoxetine (Strattera), 55, 59–60, 213, 228
    abuse potential, 106, 186, 187
    advantages, 106, 231
    allergic reactions, 232
    cognitive distortions associated with, 232–233
    dosing, 229–231, 248
    mechanism of action, 215, 229
    precautions, 232
    side effects, 231
attention problems
    disorganized life, 17, 33–34
    distractibility, 17, 34–35
    hyperactivity assessment, 6–8
    hyperfocusing, 36–37, 172, 268

Barkley, R., 72, 255
basal ganglia, 214–215
benzodiazepines, 55, 238, 289–290
Biederman, J., 73
binge eating disorder
    prevalence, 45, 61
    symptoms, 61
    treatment, 66
    see also eating disorders
bipolar disorder
    ADHD vs., 20, 56–58
    comorbid ADHD, 45, 55
    diagnosis, 29
    forms, 56
    symptoms, 55–56
    treatment, 58–60
blame attribution, 19, 98, 126
blood pressure, 24
    atomoxetine cautions, 232
    stimulant therapy and, 225–226
body language, 13–14

borderline personality disorder, 60–61
broken bones, 123–124
Brown Attention-Deficit Disorder Rating Scale
    for Adults, 40
Brown Attention-Deficit Disorder Scales for
    Adolescents, 42, 119
bulimia nervosa, 45, 63. *see also* eating disorders
bupropion (Wellbutrin), 63, 187, 213, 215, 229,
    233–234

Campbell Interest and Skill Survey, 121
carbamazepine, 58
cardiac conditions, 232
Catapres. *see* clonidine
Celexa. *see* citalopram
cerebral hyperactivity, 9
child abuse, 188
Childhood Depression Inventory, 119
children
    hyperactive-impulsive type ADHD presenta-
tion, 70
    parents with ADHD, 89
    transdermal stimulant delivery, 222
chronic fatigue syndrome
    ADHD and, 45, 88, 274–275
    assessment, 284
    causes, 285
    clinical features, 283–284
    patient characteristics, 276
    research needs, 291–292
    social and personal costs, 276
    treatment, 283, 285–287
chronic pain conditions
    ADHD and, 45, 88, 274, 277–278
    assessment, 291
    neurophysiology, 275–276
    patient characteristics, 276
    research needs, 291–292
    social and personal costs, 276
    stimulant therapy, 278–279
    therapeutic relationship and, 279
    see also fibromyalgia
citalopram, 55, 63, 235
client perspective
    laboratory tests for ADHD assessment, 24–25
    perception of medication effects, 205–206
    problem formulation, 10–11
    treatment expectations, 212–213
clonidine, 61, 236–237
clonidine (Catapres), 215
coaching
    goals, 266
    good qualities, 271

initial interview, 267
limitations, 271–273
psychotherapy and, 273
role of, in ADHD treatment, 266, 267–269
selection of coach, 270
techniques, 266–267
training for, 269
trial period, 270–271
cocaine, 24
cognitive-behavioral therapy
    applications in ADHD, 187, 255–263
    goals, 254–255
    selecting a therapist, 264
    techniques, 263–264
cognitive functioning
    ADHD thought patterns, 86
    assessment, 17
    fibromyalgia manifestations, 280
    filtering of stimuli, 277–278
    medical disorders resembling ADHD, 23
    model of pain and fatigue syndromes,
277–278
    patient fears of medications, 249–250
    see also psychosocial functioning
combined type ADHD
    case examples, 89–92
    clinical features, 84
    comorbidities, 88
    diagnosis, 5–6, 86–89
    gender differences, 84
    manifestations, 83–84
    obstacles to diagnosis, 86–89
    treatment rationale, 96–98
comorbid disorders, 28–29, 37–38
    ADHD-associated disorders, 45
    assessment and diagnosis, 44, 45–51
    gender differences, 115, 157–158
    with inattentive type ADHD, 88
    multiple comorbidities, 65–66
    pain and fatigue syndromes linkage with
ADHD, 277–278
    prevalence, 46
    therapeutic significance, 44
    treatment plan, 29, 44, 50, 66, 239
    see also specific diagnosis
compliance
    adolescent patient, 130–131, 149–150
    lost prescriptions, 204–205
    patient perception of medication effects and,
205–206
    reasons for noncompliance, 203–208
    risk in ADHD, 203
    strategies for improving, 245–246

Concerta, 185–186, 193, 200–201, 219–221
conduct disorder
    in adolescent hyperactive-impulsive type
ADHD, 71–72
        comorbid ADHD, 45, 61
confidentiality, adolescent interview, 121
Connors' Adult ADHD Rating Scales, 38–40
Connors-Wells Adolescent Self-Report Scale,
        42, 119
continuum of severity, 97, 100
Copeland Symptom Checklist for Adult
        ADHD, 42
course of ADHD
    in adolescence, 139
    into adulthood, 102
    chronic fatigue in, 283
    comorbid mood disorders, 46
    onset, 21, 56, 163
    oppositional behavior, 71–72
    research needs, 274
    symptom progression, 45–46
Cox, D. J., 72–73
Cruise, Tom, 207
Current Symptoms Scale, 42

daydreaming, 86, 174
Daytrana, 222
Depakote. see divalproex sodium
depression
    in adolescence, 114
    affective spectrum disorder, 277
    assessment, 42
    in bipolar disorder, 56
    comorbid ADHD, 29, 45, 51–53, 80–82, 88,
157–158
    in females with ADHD, 171
    prevalence in ADHD, 53
    treatment-resistant, ADHD and, 53–54, 88
desipramine, 235
development, individual
    childhood history assessment, 30
    hyperactivity and aging, 6
    life stage considerations in women with
ADHD, 167–169
    risk of ADHD progression into adulthood,
102
    stimulant effects on growth, 225
    undiagnosed inattentive type ADHD, 85
Dexedrine. see dextroamphetamine
dextroamphetamine (Dexedrine), 217, 223
dextromethylphenidate, 219
diagnosis
    ADHD variants, 5–6

    in adolescence, 113–114, 115–117
    bipolar disorder vs. ADHD, 56–58
    challenges in, 67
    chronic fatigue syndrome, 284
    combined type ADHD, 5–6, 86–89
    comorbid disorders, 44, 45–47
    criteria, 5, 6, 163
    differential, 4, 20
    gender considerations, 166–167
    goal, 9
    hyperactive-impulsive type ADHD, 74–75
    inattentive type ADHD, 85–89
    irritable bowel syndrome, 287–288
    in primary care, 105
    psychological benefits, 97–98
    therapeutic significance, 4
    therapist attitudes as obstacles to, 82, 99–103
    therapist stance, 9
    undiagnosed ADHD among adults, 3
    see also assessment
Diagnostic and Statistical Manual of Mental
        Disorders, 4, 5
dialectical behavior therapy, 196
diazepam, 238
diet and nutrition, 269
differential diagnosis, 4
    bipolar disorder, 20
    medical conditions, 23
disorganization
    adolescent, 124
    assessment, 17, 33–34, 124
    coaching interventions, 267–268
    gender differences in symptoms, 162
distractibility
    assessment, 17, 34–35
    definition, 34
divalproex sodium, 58
Dodson, W., 237
dopaminergic system, 164, 214
    atomoxetine action, 229
    stimulant effects, 214–215, 216, 217, 219,
222–223
dorsal anterior cingulate, 213–214
duloxetine, 235, 277
dyslexia, 63

eating disorders, 45, 61–63, 66, 88
economic status, 153
educational videos, 43
education and training of health providers,
        104–105, 109
    ADHD coaches, 269
    mental health professions, 265–266

electrocardiogram, 24
epidemiology, 3, 153
  anxiety in ADHD, 46, 54
  combined type ADHD, 84
  comorbidities, 46
  depression in ADHD, 53
  eating disorders, 62
  fibromyalgia, 276
  inattentive type ADHD, 84
  irritable bowel syndrome, 287
  learning disorders, 63, 120
  substance abuse disorders, 180–181
Eppworth Sleepiness Scale, 291
Equatrol. *see* carbamazepine
escitalopram, 235
estrogen, 164–165
eszoplicone, 238
exercise, 269

family history assessment, 29
females with ADHD
  assessment instrument, 166
  behavioral manifestations, 157
  biased perceptions, 156–158
  comorbidities, 115, 157–158
  crisis presentation, 172
  diagnostic considerations, 70, 103–104,
166–167
  hormonal factors in, 163–166
  interview questions, 174–176
  life stage considerations, 167–169
  onset of symptoms, 163
  pregnancy and, 169–170
  selecting treatment goals, 170–171
  self perception, 157
  sexual behavior, 163
  shyness in, 171
  sociocultural attitudes and, 176–178
  symptoms, 70, 103–104, 156–157, 158–162,
171
  therapist attitudes and beliefs, 101, 103, 156
  treatment case example, 173–174
  treatment considerations, 157
  underdiagnosis, 103–104, 156
  see also gender differences
fibromyalgia
  ADHD linkage, 274–275, 277–278
  in affective spectrum disorder, 277
  clinical features, 280
  comorbid ADHD, 45, 88
  diagnosis and treatment, 281–283
  pharmacotherapy, 279
  prevalence, 276
  research needs, 291–292
  social and personal costs, 276
Fibromyalgia Impact Questionnaire, 291
fluoxetine, 53
fluvoxamine, 192, 235
Focalin, 55, 173–174, 197, 219–220, 221–222

gambling, 192
gender differences
  adolescent ADHD presentation, 115,
144–146
  combined type ADHD, 84
  comorbidity risk, 115
  drug diversion, 198
  inattentive type ADHD, 84, 103–104
  pain syndrome prevalence, 275
  prevalence of ADHD, 156
  suicidality and substance use, 74, 144, 145
  symptoms, 159
  therapist bias as obstacle to diagnosis, 101, 103
  see also females with ADHD
generic drugs, 240
genetic risk of ADHD, 78, 89, 103
glaucoma, 226
guanfacine (Tenex), 215, 229, 236, 237

Hamilton Depression Scale, 42
Hawthorne Self-Report Version Rating Scale,
291
headaches, 45, 277, 288–289, 291–292
head injury, 25
hearing problems, 5
help-seeking behaviors
  drug-seeking strategies, 106, 201–202
  hyperactive-impulsive type ADHD, 75–80
  self-referrals, 68, 77–80
hippocampus, 214
hoarding, 193, 267–268
Hudson, J., 277, 278–279
hydrocortisone, 285
hyperactive-impulsive type ADHD
  adolescent presentations, 70–74
  behavioral manifestations, 68–69
  childhood presentation, 70
  comorbid depression, 80–82
  delayed diagnosis, 74–75
  diagnosis, 5–6
  gender differences, 70
  help-seeking behaviors, 68, 75–80
  oppositional behavior in, 71–72
  restless leg syndrome and, 278, 290
  symptoms, 67
  see also combined type ADHD

hyperactivity
  assessment, 16, 35–37
  diagnostic significance, 6–9, 85
  neurophysiology, 214–215
  sexual behavior and, 188–189
hyperfocusing, 172, 268
hypothalamus, 215, 233

imipramine, 235
impulsive behavior
  adolescent assessment, 116, 123
  angry outbursts, 21
  assessment, 20, 31–33
  neurophysiology, 214
  non-ADHD conditions, 179–180
  sexual behavior and, 188, 189–191
  in women with ADHD, 177–178
inattentive type ADHD, 5–6
  age at onset, 163
  associated pain and fatigue syndromes, 278
  clinical features, 84, 86
  comorbidities, 88
  development, 85
  diagnosis, 85–86
  gender differences, 84, 103–104, 158
  obstacles to diagnosis, 86–89
  school performance and, 92–95
  treatment outcome assessment, 95–96
  treatment rationale, 96–98
  undiagnosed, 85
  see also combined type ADHD
insurance, 243
  obstacles to care, 105–106
intelligence, ADHD and, 87, 260–261
intermittent explosive disorder, 60–61
Internet pharmacies, 202–203
interpersonal relationships
  adolescent assessment, 118
  adolescent peer relationships, 139–140
  impulsivity and, 20
  medication compliance factors, 208
  overreaction to criticism, 60
  psychotherapy intervention, 253–254
  societal expectations for women, 178
  see also psychosocial functioning
iron deficiency anemia, 23
irritable bowel syndrome, 88, 275, 287–288,
    291–292

Lamictal. see lamotrigine
lamotrigine, 58, 66
lateness, 17–18
learning disabilities

ADHD and, 45
  assessment, 120–121
  clinical features, 63–64
  definition, 63
  nonverbal, 63–64
  treatment, 64–65
legal issues, drug diversion, 198–199
listening problems, client's, 5
listening skills, therapist's, 11–15
lithium carbonate, 58, 192
losing items, 18
  adolescent assessment, 123

magnesium, 24
mania
  in bipolar disorder, 20, 56, 66
  insomnia and, 9
marijuana, 24, 68
marital problems, 28
medical assessment, 22–27
  adolescent patient, 119, 123–124
melatonin, 238
memory problems
  assessment, 37
  medication compliance and, 204
  medication effects, 251
Metadate CD, 217, 219–220, 221
Metadate ER, 219, 220
methylphenidate
  abuse potential, 185–187, 200–201
  abuse rate, 198
  chemical structure, 221
  comorbid oppositional or aggressive
disorders, 61
  dosing, 239–240, 247–248
  eating disorder treatment, 63
  efficacy, 211–212
  formulations, 217, 219
  long-acting, 55, 219–221
  mechanism of action, 217, 219
  personality effects, 219
  short-acting, 219
  transdermal delivery, 222
migraine headaches, 45, 277, 288–289
MINI Patient Health Survey, 42–43
Minnesota Pain Inventory, 291
Mirapex. see pramipexole
mirtazapine, 235, 238
modafinil (Provigil; Sparlon), 66, 213, 215, 228,
    233
monoamine oxidase inhibitors, 226–227
motor vehicle operations
  as ADHD symptom in adolescence, 140

adolescent assessment, 122
adolescent hyperactive-impulsive type
ADHD manifestations, 72–73
  indications for ADHD assessment, 28, 68
myADHD.com, 42

Nadeau, K., 166
naltrexone, 192
Nardil, 226–227
neurophysiology
  abnormalities in ADHD, 213–214
  ADHD imaging, 25, 103
  atomoxetine action, 229
  chronic pain conditions, 275–276
  stimulant effects, 214–215, 216
  tinnitus, 290–291
nonverbal learning disabilities, 63–64
norepinephrine, 214, 275, 277
  antidepressant action, 235
  atomoxetine action, 229
  medication effects, 214–215, 217, 219,
222–223
nortriptyline, 235
not otherwise specified, ADHD, 6
NRP104, 228
nucleaus accumbens, 229
nurse practitioners, 265–266

obesity, 45, 62–63
obsessive-compulsive disorder, 54, 90, 192
  self-harm behaviors and, 196
opiates, 24, 183
oppositional defiant disorder, 137–139
  in adolescent hyperactive-impulsive type
ADHD, 71–72
  comorbid ADHD, 45, 61
Oros technology, 220–221
overdose risk, 247
oxcarbazapine, 58

pain. *see* chronic pain conditions; fibromyalgia
panic disorder, 54, 231
  in affective spectrum disorder, 277
Parnate, 226–227
paroxetine, 235
Pemoline (Cylert), 217
pharmacotherapy
  abuse potential, 185–186, 200–201
  addiction risk, 101, 108
  adolescent experimentation with
medications, 35
  with adult client with history of substance
abuse, 107

assessment of patient's current use, 22–23
  benefits of, 211
  brand name drugs *vs.* generics, 240
  chronic pain conditions, 276, 277
  client expectations, 212–213
  client resistance to, 110
  combination therapy, 237
  common errors, 243
  comorbid bipolar disorder, 58–60
  comorbid depression, 52–53
  concerns about client motivation for ADHD
treatment, 106, 201–202
  current utilization, 211
  diagnostic significance of stimulant effects,
4–5
  drug holidays, 241–242
  drug schedules, 216–217
  eating disorder with ADHD, 62
  effectiveness, 211–212
  effects on personality, 110, 133–134, 219,
249–250
  effects on sexuality, 189
  forged prescriptions, 202
  gambling compulsion and, 192
  increased self-awareness in, 251
  for insomnia, 238–239
  Internet pharmacies, 202–203
  limitations, 212, 252–253
  long-acting time release formulations, 185–
186, 200–201
  long-term stimulant use, 186–187
  lost prescriptions, 204–205
  misuse by family members, 199
  misuse of prescribed drugs, 106–107, 197–
199, 205
  monitoring, 243
  motor vehicle operations and, 72–73
  multiple comorbidities, 66
  neurophysiological action, 214–215
  non-stimulants, 228–229
  obesity in ADHD, 62–63
  opposition to, 207–208
  organization of medications, 246
  overdose risk, 247
  parental attitudes and beliefs, 143–144
  patient attribution of effects, 206–207
  patient expectations, 205
  patient fears, 248–251
  patient perception of effects, 205–206
  patient understanding of, 244–245
  in patient with bipolar disorder, 58–59
  pregnant patient, 169–170
  prescribing trends, 211

pharmacotherapy (*continued*)
    restless leg syndrome, 289–290
    routine administration schedule, 245–246
    side effects, 250–251
    substance use risk and, 73–74, 101, 108,
    181–183
    therapist attitudes as obstacles to ADHD
treatment, 101, 106–108
    trial regimen, 213, 248
    underdosing risk, 247–248
    see also compliance; stimulants; treatment;
specific drug
positron emission tomography, 103
pramipexole (Mirapex), 279
prefrontal cortex, 214–215, 229
pregnancy, 169–170
premenstrual dysphoric syndrome, 165
primary care providers
    education and training for ADHD treatment,
104–105
    obstacles to ADHD treatment, 104–106
    recognition of adult ADHD, 78
    see also therapist factors
Provigil. *see* modafinil
psychiatric disorder
    ADHD comorbidity, 28–29
    family history, 29
    see also specific disorder
psychiatrists, 265
psychologists, 265
psychosocial functioning
    assessment, 26–29
    gender differences in adolescent ADHD
presentation, 144–145
    see also interpersonal relationships
psychotherapy
    client understanding of mental health
profession, 265–266
    coaching and, 273
    goals, 253
    rationale, 252–253
    see also cognitive-behavioral therapy
psychotic disorders, 194
public perception and understanding, 99–100,
101
    ADHD in females, 156–158
    expectations for women with ADHD, 176–
178
    obstacles to ADHD treatment, 108–110
    resistance to psychiatric referral, 106

Quinn, P., 103, 164–165, 166

race/ethnicity, 153–154
ramelton, 238–239
reading disorder, 63
referrals, 76–78
    for learning disability, 120–121
    obstacles to care, 105–106
    patient resistance to psychiatric referral, 106
    patterns in primary care, 104–105
reflective listening, 12–13
Requip, 290
resistance to therapy
    in adolescent, 125–131, 150–151
    fear as basis of, 132–135, 249–251
    pharmacotherapy beliefs, 110
    stigma of psychotherapy, 106
restless leg syndrome, 275, 278, 279, 289–290,
    291–292
restlessness assessment, 5
Ritalin, 73, 217, 219
Ritalin LA, 217, 219–220, 221
Ritalin SR, 217, 219, 220
Robin, A. L., 116
ropinorole, 290

schizophrenia, 194
school performance and behavior
    adolescent patterns, 122–123
    assessment, 27–28, 117–118, 124, 136–137
    girls with ADHD, 171–172
    hyperactive-impulsive type ADHD manifesta-
tions, 70, 74–75
    inattentive type ADHD manifestations, 87–
88, 92–95
selective serotonin reupdate inhibitors, 55, 196,
    229, 234, 235, 277
selegiline, 227
self-blame
    ADHD features, 19, 98, 109–110, 253
    adolescent patient, 135
    cognitive-behavioral interventions, 258–260
    gender differences, 159
    parents of child with ADHD, 142
    treatment, 98, 253
self-concept
    bipolar disorder *vs.* ADHD, 58
    cognitive-behavioral interventions to
improve, 255–263
    failure beliefs, 261–263
    laziness, 261
    psychotherapy goals, 253, 254
    stupidity, 260–261
    see also self-blame

self-harm behaviors
  ADHD and, 88
  clinical conceptualization, 196
  continuum of behaviors, 194
  crisis response, 196
  cutting, 88, 194
  risk factors, 194–195
  sexual behavior and, 195
  suicidal behavior and, 195–196
  treatment, 196–197
serotonergic system, 164, 191, 275, 277
sertraline, 235
severity of ADHD, 97, 100
sexual abuse risk, 188
sexual behavior
  adolescent ADHD and, 125, 140–141
  assessment, 125
  clinical significance, 187
  gender differences in ADHD manifestations, 163
  impulsivity and, 188
  medication effects, 189
  poor decision-making in, 189–191
  self-harm behaviors and, 195
  to sublimate excessive energy, 188–189
  therapeutic intervention, 191–192
shoplifting, 193
shopping compulsion, 192–193
single photon emission computerized tomography, 25, 103
sleep problems
  antidepressant therapy and, 238
  bipolar disorder *vs.* ADHD, 58
  cerebral hyperactivity and, 9
  pharmacotherapy for, 238–239
  stimulant therapy and, 237
smoking in adolescence, 123
social workers, 265
Solden, S., 103, 158
Sparlon. *see* modafinil
Spencer, T., 200
Stahl, S., 214
Staud, R., 275–276
stimulants
  abuse potential, 216, 217, 228
  action, 216
  addiction risk, 249
  black box warnings, 225, 226
  combination therapy, 237
  developmental effects, 225
  dosage creep, 240
  dosing, 239–240

  drug–drug interactions, 226–227
  effectiveness, 215–216
  future prospects, 228
  for pain and fatigue syndromes, 278–279
  physician opposition to, 226, 227
  precautions, 225–226
  prescribing practices, 242–243
  rebound effects, 224, 241
  regulation, 216–217
  side effects, 224–225
  sleep effects, 237
  trial regimen, 226
  see also amphetamines; methylphenidate;
specific drug
Strattera. *see* atomoxetine
striatum, 229
substance P, 275
substance use/abuse
  as ADHD symptom, 139
  adolescent hyperactive-impulsive type
ADHD manifestations, 73–74
  in adult ADHD patient, 200–201
  adult client with history of, 107
  assessment of ADHD patient, 23–24, 26–27,
184–185
  assessment of patient risk for, 199–200
  clinical relationship to ADHD, 179–180
  concerns about client motivation for ADHD
treatment, 106, 201–202
  misuse of prescribed drugs, 106–107, 183–
185, 197–199, 200–203
  relapse risk in ADHD pharmacotherapy, 182
  risk in ADHD, 73, 180–181
  as self-medication, 180
  stimulant therapy and risk of, 73–74, 101,
106, 108, 181–183, 249
  suicidality and, 74
  withdrawal symptoms, 183
suicidal behavior/ideation
  antidepressant therapy and, 236
  atomoxetine precautions, 232–233
  gender differences, 145
  self-harm behaviors and, 195–196
  substance use and, 74
symptoms
  ADHD criteria, 5, 6
  comorbidity assessment, 48–50
  diagnostic assessment, 5
  heightened self-awareness as medication
effect, 251
  hyperactive-impulsive type ADHD, 67, 70
  indications for ADHD assessment, 68

symptoms (*continued*)
    individual differences, 31
    medical disorders resembling ADHD, 23
    normal adolescent behavior *vs.*, 115–117
    onset, 21, 56
    pain and fatigue, 274–275
    patient punctuality, 17–18
    progression, 45–46
    see also assessment; attention problems; disorganization; hyperactivity; impulsive behavior

task prioritization, 268
temazepam, 238
Tenex. *see* guanfacine
therapeutic relationship
    with adolescent patient, 115, 118–119, 121
    resistant adolescent, 128–129
    in treatment of chronic pain and fatigue syndromes, 279
therapist factors
    ADHD knowledge and understanding, 104–105, 109
    causes of misdiagnosis, 99–103
    listening skills, 11–15
    perceptions of gender differences in ADHD, 101, 103, 156
    see also therapeutic relationship
thyroid disorder, 23, 24
tinnitus, 275, 290–291
Topamax. *see* topiramate
topiramate (Topamax), 63
Tourettes syndrome, 226
transdermal drug delivery, 222
trazadone, 238
treatment
    adolescent patients, 145–154
    challenging patients, 179, 180
    chronic fatigue syndrome, 285–287
    comorbid depression, 80–82
    comorbid disorders, 29, 44, 50, 239
    depression with ADHD, 51–53, 80–82
    functional outcomes, 95–96
    inattentive and combined ADHD, 96–98
    learning disabilities with ADHD, 64–65
    multiple comorbidities, 66
    obstacles to, 104–110
    parental involvement, 135–136, 144
    patient education, 43

    in primary care settings, 104–105
    problem formulation, 10–11, 14
    race/ethnicity and, 153–154
    self-harm behaviors, 196–197
    sexual issues, 191–192
    therapist attitudes and beliefs, 82
    see also compliance; pharmacotherapy; resistance to therapy
tricyclic antidepressants, 213, 215, 229, 235
Trileptal. *see* oxcarbazepine
Triolo, S., 264–265

uncensored speech, 20, 178
untreated ADHD, 3–4, 97
urine drug screen, 23–24

valproate acid, 192
Vanderbilt ADHD Diagnostic Teaching Rating Scale, 42, 119
variants, ADHD, 5–6. *see also specific type*
venlafaxine, 187, 235, 277
verbosity, 58
vitamin B12 deficiency, 24
vulvodynia, 275

webMD, 42
Weiss, G., 102
Wellbutrin. *see* bupropion
Wender, P., 102
Wender Utah Rating Scale, 40–41
Wide Range Aptitude Test, 120
Wilens, T. E., 73, 183–184
withdrawal symptoms, 183
Women's AD/HD Self-Assessment Symptom Inventory, 166
work and professional behaviors
    assessment, 27
    frequent job changes, 27
    medication use, 208

Yee, J., 279
You Mean I'm Not Crazy, Stupid, or Lazy?, 109–110, 260

zaleplon, 238
zolpidem, 238
Zung Depression Scale, 42, 291